Nigel Havers has played many starring roles in theatre, film and TV – from *Chariots of Fire* and *Empire of the Sun* to TV dramas such as *Upstairs, Downstairs* and *Murder in Mind*. More recently he returned to comedy with *Manchild*. Nigel's father was Lord Havers QC, a Conservative MP, who was also Attorney General and Lord Chancellor. Nigel lives in London.

'This is a devil-may-care, extremely endearing book with not a luvvie line in it. "Absolute bollocks. Total Fun."'
Sunday Times

"*Playing With Fire* is a highly amusing read, self-deprecating suprisingly well written and it zips along at a rate of knots as he reduces his life as a thirtysomething into one jolly jape after another" *Scotsman Magazine*

"Frank and witty . . . one of Britain's most engaging actors gives a gloriously entertaining account' *Mail on Sunday*

'A thoroughly entertaining autobiography, packing his pages with a wealth of hilarious, often self-deprecating, stories about the highs and lows of his glittering life and career' *Daily Mail*

'A book that makes it sick-makingly evident that the smoothy actor has lived one hell of a fun life' *Sunday Times*

"His amusing autobiograph. . . . . strates a keen eye for life's many absurdities and i . . . . anticipate, the highs and l . . . . much fodder for enterta . . . .

D1280167

Playing With Fire

Nigel Havers

headline
review

First published in 2006
by HEADLINE REVIEW
An imprint of Headline Publishing Group

First published in paperback 2007
by HEADLINE REVIEW

2

Cataloguing in Publication Data is available from the British Library

978 0 7553 1461 4

Typeset in Goudy Old Style by Palimpsest Book Production Limited,
Grangemouth, Stirlingshire
Printed and bound in Great Britain by
Clays Ltd, St Ives plc

Headline's policy is to use papers that are natural, renewable and recyclable
products and made from wood grown in sustainable forests. The logging and
manufacturing processes are expected to conform to the environmental
regulations of the country of origin.

HEADLINE PUBLISHING GROUP
A division of Hachette Livre UK Ltd
338 Euston Road
London NW1 3BH

www.reviewbooks.co.uk
www.hodderheadline.com

For Mum

Acknowledgements

I blame Mark Lucas. The guy stalked me for a year. Finally it was either have him arrested, have him eliminated or write the damn book. And Oh! those Headline blondes – Jo, Georgina and, of course, the fabulous Val. Nobody does it better.

My thanks must go to Terry O'Neill – friend and genius – for kindly agreeing to do the cover photo, to Peter Mayle, his inspiring paradise making me believe, just for a moment, that I could pull this off. To Al Cluer for some great advice and support and a lot of bad jokes. To Jules who did a bit, and a bit more, and more . . .

To Bruce Dundas, good friend that he is, for offering to launch the effort at Asprey's – and forcing at least some people to buy it, and finally my daughter Kate who continues to delight me and to George who lived through the "me, me, me" months with grace and good humour.

Oh yes – and I still blame that pushy bugger Lucas – I told him it was all bollocks.

Contents

Prologue

By the time we came to shoot what would be the opening scene in *Chariots of Fire*, I had been inhabiting the skin of Lord Alfred Lindsay for several months, so when Hugh Hudson, the director, asked if I felt able to 'age up' in order to play my character as a man well into his eighties, I had little hesitation.

The scene was a memorial service for the sprinter Harold Abrahams and took place in a London church. I had to spend six hours in make-up. As the face in the mirror got steadily older, I started remembering my grandfather – the way he walked, the way he talked and held his head – and as the finishing touches were at last applied I suddenly remembered that Dad's chambers were just round the corner, so rang and invited him to come to the set and watch some of the morning's filming.

When he arrived, he walked straight past me, and professed

not to recognise me at all until he heard my voice. I'm not sure if his reaction was genuine, or whether he was doing it to give me pleasure. Either way, it was rather charming.

My father was quite a guy; he had two passions, the law and living, the first providing the second. Law runs through the Havers family like blood through veins. My grandfather was Sir Cecil Havers, a notable high-court judge who was famous for, among other things, sentencing Ruth Ellis, the last woman to be executed in this country. My aunt is Dame Elizabeth Butler-Sloss, also a high-court judge and until recently head of the Family Justice System. My brother Philip is an eminent human rights barrister, and my niece Holly has recently joined one of London's largest firms of solicitors.

Then there's me.

Actually, I think every successful barrister has to have something of the actor in him, and Dad didn't just have a little something, he had it in spades. In 1981, as attorney-general, he was obliged to be chief prosecutor in the trial of Peter Sutcliffe, the notorious Yorkshire Ripper, who, back in the late seventies, went on a five-year rampage in the north of England and killed thirteen young women, claiming he was given a 'mission from God' to rid the streets of prostitutes.

On the day Dad started his case for the prosecution, I slipped into the viewing gallery. He had rung the week before to ask whether I wanted to come and see something special.

'Is it that new play at the National?' I asked.

'No,' he replied. 'I thought you might like to come and see me for a change.'

Peter Sutcliffe was surprisingly small, with wild, black, curly hair and very black eyes – the sort of eyes that have swallowed up the horror they have witnessed, and sacrificed all life and expression in the process, leaving dark holes the colour of deadly nightshade in their place.

When the judge gestured for proceedings to begin, my father got slowly to his feet. He stood, motionless, looking down at his notes. Silence. He stayed like that for several minutes, the tension building to breaking point. Just as the judge was about to intervene, he looked up, straight into Sutcliffe's eyes.

Another silence.

'Could you confirm how you spell your name?' he said. 'One T and two Fs – is that right?'

Sutcliffe just nodded.

Dad turned. There was a flurry of activity from the junior counsel huddled behind him. Everyone in the courtroom seemed to be holding their breath.

Another long silence. I think the judge thought Dad had lost the plot.

Eventually Dad turned and fixed Sutcliffe with a hawk-like stare. 'At least we've got that right,' he said. 'Tell me, did you enjoy killing those women?'

The air suddenly seemed to have been sucked out of the room. It became difficult to breathe and people started to lick their lips. I looked down and saw goosebumps on my arms – it felt as if the air-conditioning had suddenly been cranked up to maximum.

Chapter 1

Mum and Dad

Mum, I swear, came out of the womb clutching a champagne glass and asking, 'Where's the party?' She's one of life's enhancers, and lights up the room wherever she goes. Stunningly pretty, she has made a career of effortlessly enslaving all who meet her, men, women and, particularly, waiters, hotel staff and taxi drivers, thereby ensuring the sort of service the rest of us can only dream of.

She always exaggerates everything, good and bad, so mosquitoes are the size of jackrabbits and the rain is horizontal, but a party is always The Best and she focuses unfailingly on a person's good points rather than the bad. She tried and, surprisingly, failed to get into drama school. Instead, luckily for us, she met and married Dad at nineteen, producing my brother, Phil, a year later, and therefore placing all thoughts of stage and screen firmly on the back burner. With that gene pool swirling around, you can see why acting was not such a deviation after all. In fact, it was downright inevitable.

A lot of my parents' friends were actors. Dad was naturally gregarious and got on well with fellow storytellers. They appealed to his 'devil may care' philosophy of life and he found them fun. Of course, he was a member of the Garrick Club – as were many of the legal profession – so he spent many a long lunch there, swapping stories and gaining friends. Not that I realised any of this at the time. In fact, I remember being very confused when I was about five and found Robin Hood, alias Richard Greene, sitting at home with a glass of whisky in his hand, and certainly not wearing tights. Who the hell was looking after things back home in the forest?

By far the best and most influential of Dad's friends was Kenneth More, whom he had met when he was in the navy during the war. Kenny became one of the most famous actors of his day, making his name in films such as *Reach for the Sky* and *Genevieve*. He was not particularly tall, and had the stocky build of a boxer, but he managed to combine this less-than-screen-idol physique with a Jimmy Stewart-style vulnerability which made him extremely appealing to men and women alike.

He seemed impossibly glamorous and larger than life to us children, and became a lifelong pal. Thank God for Kenny. I have a feeling that persuading Dad that I wanted to become an actor would have been much more of an uphill struggle if it hadn't been for their friendship. Kenny proved that not all actors were poofs in tights shouting, 'Fly, fly, my liege!' I've done a fair bit of that myself, mind you – but that's another story.

The Garrick Club played an enormous part in sealing my father's approval. The club originated in 1751. David Garrick was an untouchable – an actor – so was barred from joining any decent gentlemen's club. He had no option but to open his own. A good few years and many a curtain call later, Kenneth More joined, and where Kenny went my father swiftly followed. And then my grandfather, and then me, and then my brother, and so on.

One night, three generations of the Havers family dined together at the long table. Halfway through dinner I noticed that every member of our family had managed to spill soup on their club tie. I pointed this out to my father. 'I know,' he said. 'This is ridiculous. There must be a soup magnet in my tie.'

Phil had the perfect answer (they always said he got the brains and I got the hair). 'Why don't we fling our ties over our shoulders?'

'What a perfectly brilliant idea,' my father said.

'So we can stain the shirt and cover it up with the tie?' I asked.

No one seemed much impressed by my logic, but it remains a Garrick tradition to this day.

By now I had already breathed in enough theatrical ether to make my future seem obvious, but it was reinforced by the fact that as children we were taken to see an enormous number of plays. Mum and Dad were both mad about the theatre, so by the time Phil and I were into double figures we had seen most of the important plays and actors and actresses of the day.

Although the Havers family originated from Norfolk, Dad completed his legal training articled to a firm of solicitors in Suffolk. The senior partner, Allan Goatlee, another friend from navy days, was to become my godfather and give me my middle name.

In the mid-fifties, Dad bought a tumbledown cottage in Suffolk for the princely sum of two hundred pounds. With no electricity or running water, and no facilities beyond an old tin bath, I expect Mum thought of it as less of a bargain than it now seems.

Dad was very ambitious and saw his chance to be a bigger fish in a rural Suffolk pond, so we used to weekend at White Shutters, and later we spent all our school holidays there. It was a wild and woolly place – it still is, a world away from the fleshpots of Newmarket, eight miles to the west.

The cottage gradually took shape. Mum was in charge of the interior and Dad became obsessed with the garden. He wasn't keen on flowers, but set out on a quest to fill the place with every variety of British tree and vegetable. Every so often a few bulbs and cuttings were smuggled into place by Mum, who longed for a bit of colour, but these anarchic uprisings were soon spotted and dealt with – apart from the roses, which were tended with loving care.

Dad took enormous pleasure in providing produce for the table and used to erect rather dodgy-looking plastic greenhouses which, come the slightest puff of wind, were blown into the next-door field.

'Mike,' we'd hear Mum shout, 'there's a greenhouse on the move.'

He was out of the house like a ferret down a hole, while the rest of us sat grinning with relief that we hadn't been dragged off to help. Bearing in mind the fact that there is barely a hillock in between East Anglia and Siberia, you can imagine that this happened all the time.

Knowing how keen he was on fresh eggs, I decided to give Dad some hens as a birthday present, and proceeded to research my mission thoroughly. I finally settled on a Marron/Rhode Island Red cross as this, I discovered, combined rich, dark yolks with prolific laying capability. I advertised in *Country Life* for ten hens and within a week got a reply, complete with telephone number.

'Hello, I gather you have Marron/Rhode Island Reds. Er, I was wondering if I could have ten? Yes . . . Oh, that's great . . . Whereabouts are you? . . . I don't believe it! Really? Wickhambrook? That's great. I'll be there this afternoon.'

My advertisement had been answered by someone living in the next-door village, less than half a mile away. The deal was done, and Dad was thrilled. Those hens were spoiled rotten. I took hours preparing their hot mash and made sure they had very superior accommodation. They became champion layers and we breakfasted on the most beautiful, rich, dark-yolked eggs imaginable.

We had a chap from the village helping in the garden. Jim was a man of few words, and would appear in the kitchen every morning with a bowl, say, 'Eggs', plonk them on the table and disappear. Of course, he soon became known as 'Eggs', not only by us, but by all our friends as well.

I often called home from London to speak to Mum or Dad and Eggs occasionally answered the phone.

'Hello,' I'd say. 'It's Nigel here.'

'No, Nigel's not 'ere,' he'd say, and put the phone down.

I discovered he was in cahoots with Dad for years, weeding not only the weeds but also the flowers out of the garden. 'I don't 'old with flowers,' he said. 'Only vegetables. You can't eat a daffodil, can you?'

Every so often we were taken to Newmarket; Dad liked a flutter and had a lot of friends in the racing game. In fact, one of his bigger wins provided our first family holiday abroad. Harry Carr, the Queen's jockey, lived in the next-door village. 'I'm riding Parthia in the Derby this year,' he told Dad at their New Year's Eve party. 'I rather fancy his chances – worth a few bob.' By Easter, over at our place, it had become, 'I really fancy this horse – put a bit more on.'

Phil, eighteen months older but a lifetime smarter than I was, picked up on this and decided to have his own flutter.

A week before the race, Harry rang again to say, 'Mortgage the house.'

Dad went for it.

What a win! There was a new car in the drive and I remember learning to swim in northern Italy, where Dad had rented a huge villa for the whole of August. Go on, my son!

The racing crowd have always been tremendous fun and we used to love the craic. Phil once spotted an unclaimed winning betting slip lying on the ground and after that we both used to hang around long after the last race – presumably the parents were living the high life in the bar – and scour the stands for slips, which we packed into an old rubbish bag brought along for the purpose. We would lug it home and painstakingly examine every one. It took for ever, but we used to clear between five and ten pounds per bag. Bearing in mind that the average weekly wage was about five pounds in 1963, that wasn't bad going at all.

Nowton Court, my prep school, was a wonderfully romantic, mock-Gothic building set in glorious parkland outside Bury St Edmunds. It was run by the Blackburn family, an eccentric, whisky-quaffing trio: two brothers and a sister who insisted the boys call them by their Christian names. Charles, Neville and

Betty were tremendous snobs. I heard later that they always thought of Dad as someone who was going places so were all over me like a rash – rather worrying for my parents, considering their rather obviously dodgy sexuality.

I was sent there at the age of six and felt a little sorry for myself as my parents drove away. Actually, 'suicidal' would cover it.

'You're not to cry,' my father had said. 'And never sneak on your mates.' During the first week I found myself staring at a notice board somewhere near the dining room. The two boys to my left suddenly scarpered. I had no idea why, but I scarpered too.

At the end of lunch, the headmaster rang the bell. 'There were three boys in hall before lunch; I want them to stand up now.'

Nobody moved. Phew! It can't have been me, then.

'I want Playle, Collins and Havers to come to my study immediately after lunch.'

Bollocks, it *was* me.

I got three of the best. What for, I have no idea. I didn't know the rule, I didn't know where I was, but I got beaten for it – that's just how things were. I learned pretty quickly that if you respected them . . . You know the rest.

The Blackburns had some pretty high-profile friends in the artistic community – such as the author Angus Wilson, the composer Geoffrey Wright and the broadcaster Nancy Spain. They were an eccentric bunch of inverted snobs who would discuss the merits of *Coronation Street* for hours, knowing that most of their ilk would rather stick pins in their eyes than watch one episode of the gritty soap opera. They appeared from time to time and mingled with us boys during lunch, as if it were completely normal.

Drama was of prime importance at Nowton and an enormously sophisticated production of a Shakespeare play was staged in the grounds each summer. I got lucky, because Charles was looking for a junior to play Mamillius, the son of the King of Sicilia in *The Winter's Tale*. I only had a couple of lines, but once you were in a play, you were part of the troupe for life.

Leontes: 'How now you wanton calf, art thou my calf?'

Mamillius (in a high-pitched voice): 'Yes, if you will, my lord.'

That was about the size of it. Thrilling for me – not sure there was huge audience appreciation.

The Blackburns were also on the restoration committee of the Theatre Royal, Bury St Edmunds, a beautiful Regency edifice which had fallen into disrepair and been dark for many years. Charles decided to mount a grown-up production of *A Midsummer Night's Dream* during the summer holidays in order to raise money for the appeal. He wanted to charge a pound a seat – a lot of money in those days – so the production had to be as professional as possible.

My parents were away for the entire summer holidays (Dad was doing some high-profile legal case in Pakistan), so I spent the whole time at Nowton rehearsing. I was Puck. Charles had decided, rather brilliantly, that the fairies in the play should be played by children. This gave it a tremendous charm and if I ever get asked to direct a production of the *Dream*, I shall steal his idea.

It was one of those summers that linger in the memory – always sunny, always fun; so much so that I couldn't be bothered to finish learning my lines. Charles put me in Coventry for a day or two to speed up the process. It worked like a charm; on the first night I was word perfect.

At the end of the play, Oberon's penultimate speech ends: 'Trip away, make no stay, meet me all by break of day,' and at that moment the entire cast came to take their bow, as if the play had ended. My job was to sneak in and sit cross-legged at the back as the last of the players left the stage. It was perfectly set up. All I had to do was deliver the final speech – 'If we shadows have offended, /Think but this, and all is mended . . .' – as simply and as sweetly as possible.

I suddenly realised I had the audience in the palm of my hand. I could change the speed, the tone, the pitch. The audience went with me whichever way I did it. It was a magic moment. I knew this was what I wanted to do for the rest of my life.

What I didn't know was that my parents had returned from Pakistan early and were in the audience for the final performance. They were in tears afterwards. Maybe they were relieved that I hadn't screwed up, or maybe it was just the jetlag.

Some time later, Charles told me that I should seriously consider becoming an actor.

'Are you sure?' I said.

'Without question,' he replied. 'And I'll tell you why. You only think in the present.'

I'm not entirely sure that that was a compliment, but I know exactly what he meant.

I ended up being head boy. Phil had been a particularly good one, and I suppose they were hoping it ran in the family. As far as the boys themselves were concerned, I think I was right up there in the top ten; I let everyone get away with murder and even introduced cigar smoking onto the curriculum. Phil had gone on to Eton and absolutely hated it, so I decided pretty smartly that I wasn't going to suffer the same fate.

Chapter 2

An Education in the Arts

Picture this: a perfect day, the sky as blue as a Chelsea supporter's strip, the beginning of the summer holidays at White Shutters, our thatched cottage in the middle of the Suffolk countryside. It had started so well. I'd made myself a spot of scrambled eggs and a cup of coffee, then strutted out into the garden like a lollipop just waiting to be licked.

Let's take the dog for a walk, I thought. Now this was quite unusual for me, because we didn't rub along together too well, Barley and me. Barley was a Welsh Corgi, and they're grumpy little buggers at the best of times – I can never understand why the Queen should have such an affection for them, always snapping at your heels and liable to take a finger off at the drop of a hat.

But today was different. Today was a perfect day. So it was off to the back of the garden, over the fence and into the fields of corn, stretching out like a Constable painting. As usual,

Barley disappeared. I'm buggered if I'm going after him, I thought, and legged it home after half an hour or so.

As I swung round by the garage, I passed the main greenhouse. Wait a minute, I thought, I spy a tomato. I popped the little red beast into my mouth. The flavour burst around my tongue. The first tomato of the season – taste sensation.

I circled round the house, through the French windows, into the drawing room, savouring every sweet tang. What's next? I thought. I know, I'll put on the latest Beatles album, *With the Beatles*.

I was about to lower the needle onto the vinyl when I heard what sounded like my father, swearing like a trooper. I popped my head out of the window, only to have it practically taken off by Dad as he marched past muttering, 'Some little shit's eaten my tomato.' He was obviously on his way to harangue the gardener.

'What's up, Dad?' I asked, suddenly apprehensive.

'Some little bastard's eaten my tomato – my *first* tomato.'

I obviously failed to disguise my panic.

'It wasn't you, was it?'

I'd learned over the years that it was always best to be honest with Dad. He could spot a lie at fifty paces; that's his job – he's a lawyer for Christ's sake. I took it like a man. I listened to the encyclopaedic account of the painstaking process of growing the perfect tomato; how every gardener thinks of them as their babies; and so on, and so on. Bored the pants off me, but I kept saying, 'Oh, Dad, I'm so sorry,' and 'I really am sorry, and I'll never do it again.'

When we got onto the third tomato thing, pricking out, or something like that, I had a madly daring idea: in for a penny, in for a pound. 'Dad, just one more thing, while you're here . . . I've decided that I'm not going to Eton.'

Silence.

Maybe he hadn't heard me. I waited. His face turned slowly purple. This perfect day was going rapidly downhill.

I'd done my research, and worked out where I was going to send myself: the Arts Educational Trust, 144 Piccadilly, London SW1. It was the smartest address I could find.

Mum was on my side; she had, after all, wanted to be an actress herself. Later that evening, after a couple of large Scotches, Dad also started to warm to the idea. I have a shrewd suspicion that he'd been doing some mental arithmetic. The Arts Ed was a quarter of the price of Eton. So that was how a certain fourteenth-century establishment came to escape the attendance of one NH.

144 Piccadilly was bang next door to the birthplace of the Queen Mother. It had belonged to Alexander Korda before the war and had fallen into disrepair before the Arts Ed had picked it up for a nominal sum in the early sixties. It was an incredibly imposing, Robert Adam-designed building, with a magnificent staircase sweeping round and round up to a pale blue dome which seemed higher than heaven to a thirteen-year-old. It was mostly falling to pieces, and largely held together by scaffolding, but hell, I never really noticed.

I had to do a series of auditions in front of a whole bunch of very scary people. There was the famous ballerina Beryl Grey, for starters, and then row upon row of rather odd-looking theatricals. Thinking about it now, it seems terrifying, but back then I appeared to breeze through without too much of a problem.

I think I must have been slightly ahead of the game because Charles Blackburn had focused so much attention on drama;

I was already well used to delivering Shakespeare and even vaguely understanding what the hell he was on about. I chose Puck's final speech from A Midsummer Night's Dream because I could do it in my sleep. I gave it the full Monty, sitting cross-legged on the floor, just like I had done at Nowton Court, then standing up and finishing with a flourish.

There was total silence.

Oh dear! The last time I'd delivered the speech, I'd been greeted with rapturous applause, if not a standing ovation.

I spluttered on to the 'modern' piece. Journey's End is set in the trenches during the First World War, something I didn't know a great deal about (why should I?), but I thought it might produce a tear from the assembled luminaries. As it turned out, I got a little tongue-tied. I forgot a whole section of it, and had no choice but to improvise in what I thought was an appropriate style.

At the end I looked up to find a row of shell-shocked faces.

Bugger, I thought. I've blown it.

'Thank you, Mr Havers. We'll let you know.'

It was the first time I heard that line; I knew it wasn't going to be the last.

That afternoon I had to do a bit of singing and dancing for them – quite a different matter. We hadn't done much of either at prep school – cricket and football don't sit that comfortably with tights and tutus. It was the worst afternoon of my life, and I realised that the only way to get through it was to copy everything the other applicants were doing.

I learned quite a good lesson that day: throwing myself in at the deep end. It's what actors have to do the whole time. I've been constantly embarrassed and not a little shy doing some of the things I've been asked to over the years, and I always think back to that afternoon.

'What are you going to sing for us, Mr Havers?'

'"God Save the Queen",' I replied, and I belted it out like I was Lulu doing 'Shout'. I went home that night convinced that I would have to crawl back to Dad and tell him how much I was dying to go to Eton and be a fag to some toerag and cater to his every whim. 'Havers, warm my lavatory seat,' shrieked the voice in my ear. 'I'm on it, you bullying piece of shit,' I heard myself mutter.

Dad got a call a couple of days later; they had accepted me.

They must be mad, I thought.

So there I was on the first day at a new school. I was living in my parents' flat in the Temple. I had to catch a number 9 bus from Fleet Street to Hyde Park Corner, and I was really excited about this. There was one major problem: I had real trouble making out the numbers on the buses. I often flagged down a number 14 at the request stop and found myself sailing off to Hampstead. Maybe I'm going blind, I thought. I could see the written word perfectly if it was close enough, but anything at any distance at all was suspiciously hazy.

Anyway, as I walked through the enormous front door of one of the most imposing houses in London on that first day, I remember thinking: What the hell have I done? This is bloody scary stuff. I was pretty paralysed with nerves for a couple of days, and hardly spoke to a soul, but then I made a really exciting discovery. There were forty-eight boys in this joint, and two hundred and twenty-five girls.

That's pretty good odds, I thought. I'm already one up on Phil.

Most of the first term was spent trying to fit in. It didn't take a rocket scientist to work out that I looked and sounded a bit different – a bit too bloody posh, not to put too fine a point on it.

The girls seemed to think I was OK – a little exotic, perhaps, almost foreign, and I managed to turn this to my advantage – but the boys decided I was a right tosser, and somewhat pleased with myself to boot. This was, of course, complete nonsense.

'What the hell are you talking about? I'm just like you.'

'Bollocks,' followed by a swift blow to my bollocks.

Now, the only way to deal with third-rate, below-the-belt behaviour is to thump the opposition back, where it hurts most, and pile in for a major scrap, after which, eventually, you emerge the best of mates.

I made a big effort to sound a bit more like everyone else and become one of the lads. The fact that I had my own pad didn't do me any harm on either front. Dad used the Temple flat when he was in London on a case, but most of the time my parents were in Suffolk. This suited me just fine.

'Darling, I hate to leave you on your own. Are you sure you'll be all right?' Mum would say.

'Don't you worry about a thing,' I'd reply, with a brave smile. 'I've got so much work, I can't possibly get up to any mischief.' I managed to look just the right amount of crestfallen as they drove away (too much and they'd never have left me alone), but the moment I heard the door shut and the echo of their retreat down the stone staircase, I set about planning my newly acquired freedom.

It was a pretty steep learning curve, going from spoilt prep-school brat to self-catering drama student. For one thing, I had to learn to cook. I used to raid the larder in Suffolk the weekends that I went home, and Mum used to cook things like shepherd's pie for me to take back, but I quickly learned the rudiments and really enjoyed pottering about in the kitchen, slipping on an apron, getting out the chopping board and hacking away at an onion. It made me cry buckets, of course (I wondered if I could turn this on to order if a scene required it). God, this was fun – it sure did beat being locked away in some fourteenth-century prison outside Windsor.

One day, out of the blue, I was asked to go and see the school's resident theatrical agent. I hadn't got a clue what an agent did – could have sold houses, as far as I was concerned. I later discovered that they find you work and take ten per cent.

She turned out to be a formidable woman, slightly cross-eyed and with what looked to me like a badly applied wig. I wasn't going to mess with her.

'The BBC wants to see you. There's a part in *Mrs Dale's Diary* – her grandson, Billy Owen. You'll probably get it; you're the only boy who speaks like her.'

She was right: nothing to do with talent, just the way I sounded. So I ended up playing Billy on and off for the next couple of years. It was nerve-racking and very hard work, but also fun, and my first professional experience. Best of all, I got paid; not a lot, but enough to take a pretty girl out to Bistro Vino once in a while.

Jessie Matthews had taken over the role of Mrs Dale some years before. She was an old battleaxe of a woman and took a big shine to me – all fifteen years of me! One afternoon, when everyone had gone off for lunch, she made a lunge at me and I ran round the back of the piano in the studio.

'You can't get away from me,' she cried.

I did; there was no choice. The age gap was a wee bit too much – about forty-eight years.

I ended up doing all sorts of radio and voiceover stuff, and it was a great learning curve for what was to come later. The BBC was a fantastic place to start a career in those days. The people were great to work with, intelligent, wise and, most of all, kind to anyone just starting out.

Outside the imposing Temple gates lies Fleet Street, then the heart of the legal and journalistic professions – strange bedfellows in some ways, but each does seem to feed the other. Appropriately, there was a newspaper stand just outside our entrance, spilling out into the street, and I got quite pally with the seller. One evening I asked if he wanted someone to help with the rush of commuters buying the *Evening Standard* and *Evening News* on their way home from work. To my amazement he said yes.

He used to start packing up while I sold the papers, and each evening he paid me my supper money and a smoke – a single, untipped Senior Service – pure unadulterated lung rot. I would sit on the loo with the window open, puffing away, in heaven. The taste was delicious and I understood why Dad went through three packets of these little blighters in a day.

I would sit all alone, watching *The Saint* or *The Man from UNCLE* on the television, dying for another stogie – king of all I surveyed. Occasionally, Dad appeared, which used to piss me off – how dare he want to use his own flat? Didn't he realise how inconvenient it was?

Anyway, there I was, doing something approaching normal school work in the mornings, and Theatre, Musical Appreciation and Ballet or Modern Dance in the afternoons. The dress code for Ballet was tights. White tights. I cannot think of a single man who looks good in white tights. OK, I lie. Nureyev and the rest of those woofters fill them pretty impressively, but apart from them, I swear to God, no one. So, I lasted one day. I just didn't do tights. For Modern Dance we wore trousers; I decided there and then that I was a trouser man to the core, and a trouser man I have remained.

A shared allergy to tights bonded me to Gavin Miller. Gav didn't do tights, either; in fact, he didn't do dancing, period. That put him automatically into 'best friend' category. His stocky build and sharply chiselled crew cut singled him out in those days of long hair and dripping scarves. He also smoked like a trooper – Piccadilly untipped; not as good as Senior Service, but they still hit the spot. I was wary of buying cigarettes, but Gav, who was sixteen, looked thirty-five; in other words, he scored.

We became inseparable, which turned out to be rather dangerous. At the beginning of the next summer term Gav produced a BB gun. I didn't have a clue what it was. 'It's a fantastic bit of kit,' he said. 'Watch this . . .' and he fired a pellet out of the common-room window, smashing a large pane of glass in the building opposite.

'Jesus!' I screeched. 'What the hell do you think you're doing?'

'Don't be such an arse,' he said. 'The place is derelict – fantastic for target practice.'

So for the rest of that summer, we'd be up in the common room during any sort of break, peppering the poor, unfortunate building.

One afternoon the common room door burst open to reveal half a dozen armed policemen. Christ, I thought, this is like *Starsky and Hutch*. We were in deep shit. Our target turned out to be owned by the Ministry of Defence. Nice one, Gav.

We were given a choice: either the matter would be taken

up by the Board of Governors, or we could take six of the best then and there and no more would be said.

We could hardly walk downstairs that evening, but as I glanced over my shoulder I noticed Gav grinning like an idiot.

'What a result!' he said.

'What happened to the gun?' I asked.

'I chucked it out of the window as they came through the door. I know exactly where it is; we'll go and collect it now.'

'Not on your life,' I said.

I have a suspicion he never really wanted a future in drama, but knew that he would have more fun trying than going down the conventional education route. But he must have straightened out at some point; I think he ended up as a bank manager.

At the end of every term we students had to put on a review to showcase our various talents. The play was no problem to Gav and me; we sailed through the drama bit, usually with me playing the juvenile lead and Gavin being brilliant as a seventy-year-old, preferably one who smoked a lot.

The dancing, however, always proved a bit of a stumbling block. One term, at the last moment, we threw together a skit about two blokes who couldn't dance to save their lives. We took the piss out of the whole thing something rotten. They hated it, and were furious that we weren't taking things seriously. Dad got a letter – heavy stuff – about me having to change my attitude and buckle down to some hard work, or my future at Arts Ed might be in doubt.

I was unrepentant, maintaining that dancing was for poofs. Stupid, I know, and something I've always regretted.

*   *   *

Time to get back to those two hundred and twenty-five girls. Actually, it was all a bit confusing. At a distance I couldn't tell one from another – they all looked absolutely knockout, but, rather alarmingly, exactly the same. I was also finding it harder than ever to flag down the right bus to get me to school. I mentioned this to Mum and before you could say 'spectacles' I was wearing a pair not dissimilar to Michael Caine's in *The Ipcress File* – quite a cool look, as it turned out.

After some exhaustive research, I finally landed my first ever girlfriend, Sonia Bingham. Sonia was stunning. She had long dark hair, a very pretty face with dark eyes and a gorgeous mouth, and, would you believe, one hell of a body. She was a dancer. She was also Jewish.

I knew things must be getting pretty serious when I was invited back to her parents' for Friday dinner. Jews go big on Fridays, and the joint was swarming with them. Her parents owned a very smart and extremely tidy apartment in a huge block in St John's Wood, round the corner from Lord's cricket ground.

These could be my sort of people, I thought, and as I was introduced to them I banged on about how convenient it must be for a Test match. No response – I felt like the proverbial pork sausage in a synagogue. To break the ice, I decided to tell a joke. 'Why was the elephant sitting on an orange outside the synagogue?'

I wasn't sure whether their expressions denoted politeness or anticipation, but I decided to go for it. 'Waiting for the Jews to come out!'

It seemed to do the trick; they laughed and laughed.

'Oh my God, that was so funny, my dear. Have you got any more of those? You're such a funny boy.'

Even at the time, I had the feeling their response was rather better than the gag deserved. Still, I became an immediate member of the circumcision club.

Later on that term I experienced my first French kiss. Gav and I had speculated about this endlessly. What would it be like? Would it be exciting? Would it be disgusting? Would we get a hard-on?

It was all those things and more, actually. It was also my cue to invite her 'back to my place' to crank things up to the next level. I made one of my killer shepherd's pies and spent the rest of the evening desperately trying to make progress.

I started by turning off a few lights. 'God, it's so bright in here!' A click here and there and we could hardly see each other. This was followed by me sliding over to the record player. I nonchalantly pulled out a couple of albums. I had no idea what they were; I couldn't read the labels. Suddenly Edmundo Ross burst into the room.

'Christ, what's that?' she said.

'Sorry, sorry . . .' I rammed on another. Acker Bilk and his fucking clarinet ricocheted off the walls. 'Oh my God, I'm really sorry.'

I needed to get a grip; she could leave at any minute.

Thank God for Astrid Gilberto. 'Tall and tanned and young and lovely, the girl from Ipanema came walking . . . aaaaaaaaaah . . .'

I sashayed towards her. 'So whadayathink?'

She thought it was good, but not that good. A tongue sandwich was fine. A fumble with a covered nipple was just about OK, but further south was way out of school. She was having none of it, sadly, and continued to resist me for weeks.

This wasn't doing my health any good at all – let's face it, it's never wise to bottle things up – so I decided I would have to find someone a bit more accommodating – and fast. Who says romance is dead?

The end of that summer term we had to produce our usual drama gem in front of the rest of the school. I was paired up with a very pretty girl called Susie Blake, who lived with her mum in Barnes. Her whole family were warm and friendly, and for the first time I felt completely at home with a girl. Susie was extremely sexy and good fun. Best of all, she wanted to have a proper relationship, not just sex. She wanted us to be together. It was rather grown-up, suddenly, but I thought: Why not? Let's give it a go.

By the time the summer term ended, Susie and I were inseparable, so the holidays were going to be a problem. She solved it, at least temporarily, by asking me to stay at her mother's little cottage in Broadstairs for a long weekend. I jumped at the chance, and caught a train to the seaside as soon as I could.

I was bang in the middle of my Rock God phase, so I was looking sharp: hair slightly too long, trousers far too tight. On the journey down I thought I was going to burst with excitement, and as soon as I clapped eyes on her I thought I might faint with the thought of what could happen.

My jubilation lasted all the way to the picture-book cottage near the beach. But oh no! Not only did we have separate rooms, but her mum's was in the middle, so there was absolutely no chance of corridor creeping. As we all know, parents develop hearing on a par with Superman's once the sun goes down. I was going to have to be Superman to do something about it.

Friday night was out, but by Saturday lunchtime I had

persuaded Susie that we should take in the promenade with an early evening stroll, followed by fish and chips and a bottle of Tizer, and then relax, just really, well, relax on the beach, way down on the beach, the bit where no one goes after sundown.

She immediately agreed. We were on.

I love it when a plan comes together. There we were, on the beach, locked in a passionate embrace. It turned out not to be quite as secluded as I had hoped, though; in fact, above us, way above us, there were about two thousand people enjoying a Saturday-night piss-up. But at least we were in the shadows beneath the promenade.

And then, as only God can explain, it happened. Oh boy, did it happen! It was everything I wanted it to be and more. To be honest, it didn't last as long as I'd have liked, but nonetheless it was . . . fantastic. But wait a minute – where's she off to?

Susie leapt up and disappeared into the darkness, heading out to sea. I sat up and stared after her. I waited, and waited, and then waited some more. Oh my God, what have I done? Oh God, she's gone off to drown herself. Oh Jesus, was I that bad? Was it that bad?

Then out of the darkness came the light. Her body, glistening with salty water.

'You're alive,' I cried. 'Thank God!' and I burst into tears.

'What's the matter with you?' she whispered in my ear.

'Well, I just . . . I don't know, I just thought that you . . . well, didn't . . .'

She put her hand across my mouth. 'I just wanted to have a moment to myself. Thank you.' And with that she lay back down beside me and squeezed me till I nearly burst. I felt like a million dollars. Was I in love? Big question for such a young fella. A tiny grin crept across my face – Casanova was unleashed.

Suddenly 'I' became 'we', and I slowly got used to the idea of being a couple. Actually, it was rather cool, sharing that lover and friend stuff and having a pretty girl in tow. We became part of a gang which met after school in the Wimpy Bar next door to the Hilton Hotel. A far cry from the ultra-cool Met Bar that has taken its place, but in those days we thought we were very much part of the 'it' crowd.

Life was good for a couple of months until the inevitable bombshell.

'Er, I think I may be pregnant.'

I stopped stone dead and stood looking at her in the long, green-lino-floored corridor that connected Modern Drama and Classical Ballet. 'Right,' I said, taking control of the situation. 'So, on a scale of one to ten, how pregnant do you think you are?'

I'm surprised she didn't smack me in the face. Looking back, it seems unbelievable that I could have been so naive, but I'd somehow missed out on the 'sex talk' with Dad, Phil was incarcerated at Eton, so not much help, and anyway I was probably ahead of him at that point in the experience stakes.

The scare turned out to be just that, but the realisation of what could have happened a few weeks short of my sixteenth birthday was a timely reality check, so I had a word with my mate the newspaper seller to see if he could slip me a few condoms along with the fags.

'Be a bloke, for Christ's sake' was his reply. 'If you need rubbers you gotta get them yourself.'

I found the nearest chemist, a rather old-fashioned affair in Fleet Street, and did a few dummy runs to check out the staff. There were two: a ratty-looking old guy and a pretty young girl. I pretended to find the fluoride content of toothpaste completely consuming until the pretty girl disappeared out the back and I could approach the counter.

For my first two attempts the girl came back and I chickened out, but there is only so much cough mixture one can buy on a tight budget, so third time round I decided to go for it, no matter what, and came away the proud owner of a packet of three.

Suitably protected, there was only one thing on my mind – all the time. Sadly, I have to admit that my half of the relationship didn't remain faithful; in fact, it wasn't long before I discovered Big Hottie. The word was that she 'blew for Britain'. One afternoon, in the back passage between Modern Dance and Poetry, I discovered that the word was pretty much spot on. I could hardly walk into Poetry that day, or indeed any other day for weeks. Big Hottie left at the end of that term, but her memory lingered long. They should have a blue plaque in that passage.

On Christmas Eve that year I was asked to go pigeon shooting in the woods belonging to a neighbouring farmer. Sixpence a bird was his offer, and although we didn't think we'd shoot that many, it was a bloody good excuse for a spot of fun. It had been a raw day, and Phil, my oldest friend Rick Marsh and I set out just before dusk.

Rick lived in the next-door village. His father Marcus had been a famous Newmarket trainer, and he and his wife Wendy were great friends of my parents. Rick was extremely good-looking and always smiling – life was fun when he was around.

Our mission had hardly begun when he announced that he was desperate for a crap and disappeared into the woods in front of us. After a moment or two, I spied the first pigeon of the evening, whipped my gun up and, would you believe it, shot the thing. It nose-dived straight into the middle of the wood. I heard a scream ... The ex-pigeon had landed on top of the squatting Rick's head – double bull's-eye.

As the sun disappeared, the frost sparkled on the hard furrows of the fields, and the sky began to turn pink. We could hear the pigeons calling in the woods and our breath billowed out in huge clouds around our heads. I felt a burst of extreme happiness. I had a gorgeous girlfriend, I was doing what I loved to do, and here I was at home, looking forward to Christmas with my family and some time with my best mate. Could life get any better?

Phil turned to me and said, 'OK, tell us what it's like, then.'

'What are you on about?' I asked.

'You know, girls, sex, fucking – tell us what it feels like.'

Could life get any better? Yes, it could. Not only was I truly happy, but my elder brother was jealous. Now, that's what I call satisfaction.

Chapter 3

Butterfly on a Wheel

The Beatles arrived with a bang in the early sixties. We all loved them and our parents loved them, too. That really confused me. My parents weren't supposed to like my kinda music. Worse still, their friends clicked their fingers and tapped their heels to 'Please, Please Me' – a fucking disgrace, if you ask me. Even my grandfather got in on the act. He was a high-court judge at the time, and on circuit in Newcastle staying in judge's lodgings. The Beatles were in town and appearing at the Corn Exchange. This caused a frenzy of excitement and even Grandfather couldn't contain himself. He invited them over for tea and managed to extract their autographs. It caused quite a stir, I still have it.

Anyway, parents are supposed to hate our groovy sounds, thereby satisfying our rebellious inclinations.

'What do you mean, you like the Beatles, Dad? How can you possibly like these guys? They're from Liverpool.'

He smiled, tapping his fingers to the beat.

'I think they look really nice,' Mum would say.

Thank God for the Rolling Stones. That's more like it, Phil and I thought; much longer hair, far groovier clothes, and a half-way decent bad attitude. The music? It was fantastic; sort of out of tune and a bit off the beat, but it was *supposed* to be . . . raw, and thrillingly sexy. Best of all, our parents hated it! And the more they hated it, the more we loved it, and the bigger the Stones became. In fact, they became so big that we had to imitate them. We spent a lot of time and not a lot of money trying to look like a cross between Mick and Keith.

Growing your hair costs nothing, and looking like a filthy rock star not a lot more. So here I was, aged fifteen, spending the summer of 1966 holed up with my brother and the parents in White Shutters. One blazing hot afternoon Phil and I were picked out by a reporter at a local tennis tournament and the next day the *Bury Free Press* said: 'There were two young men to be seen wandering aimlessly around the public areas, wearing kaftans and flowers, with bells around their necks, interrupting the play. A couple of hooray hippies.'

That was about as near as I could get to bliss. My parents never said a word, good or bad, about our appearance. I swear my father never noticed that sort of stuff.

The following spring something strange happened. It had the whiff of a Cold War thriller about it, in so much as I didn't really know what was going on. There was only one television set on the ground floor of our cosy cottage, and if my father had a particular programme that he wanted to watch – and they were mostly political – it wouldn't interfere with dinner; we'd simply move it into the dining room.

One evening, probably in the middle of *Panorama*, the

programme was interrupted by a newsflash. 'Two leading members of the Rolling Stones have been arrested on a drugs charge and are being held in custody overnight.'

That was some breaking news.

'Good God, I hope they don't ask me to defend them,' my father spluttered.

Phil and I wondered if this was some sort of elaborate joke, maybe even one of *Panorama*'s famous April Fool spoofs.

An hour later the phone rang. My father took the call.

Some time afterwards, he came back into the room. 'I shall be defending the Rolling Stones.'

The following morning Dad drove to London to meet Mick and Keith, 'the boys', at his chambers. Number 5, King's Bench Walk is smack in the middle of the Inner Temple – an intimidating address, even if you're innocent. This part of London hasn't changed much in over three hundred years. The cobbled paths are still lit by gas lamps, and at dusk shadows dart about the gloom, sending a shiver up your spine. Jack the Ripper would feel right at home around there.

Dad's chambers consisted of a spartan little room, rather Dickensian in flavour, with bare boards and a small coal fire burning in the corner. Legal files, known as briefs, rose up like mountain ranges all over the floor.

I once asked him how he was ever going to get through them all.

'I don't have to,' he replied. 'It just makes me look like the busiest barrister in London.'

'But you are, Dad,' I said.

'I know,' he replied. 'But a little dramatic licence never goes amiss.'

* * *

The meeting must have gone well, because when he returned that night those uncouth, scruffy and worryingly rebellious youths had been replaced by two charming, intelligent and articulate young men who shared a wonderful sense of humour.

'Got any Scotch, Mike?' Mick kept asking him.

Improbably, Dad hadn't and had to steal some from a neighbouring chambers. That was the start of a well-stocked cocktail cabinet nestling between the briefs.

Back in Suffolk, Dad was well pleased with himself. With hindsight, I wonder if he realised what a can of worms had been opened. He suddenly became very serious, and a little scary. He made Phil and me promise that we would never talk about this case to anyone, especially at school. It was such a solemn moment that I never broke my promise. Actually, I never wanted to; sometimes, keeping a secret is one of the most exciting things you can do.

It's difficult to believe now, but back in those heady days Jagger and Richards were probably more famous than Posh and Becks. Celebrity for its own sake had yet to get a stranglehold on our popular culture, and rock singers were the only fodder available to the tabloids. There were only two television channels, for heaven's sake, so *Top of the Pops* was watched by virtually the whole country, even if most of the older, male viewers were just drooling over Pan's People.

The establishment was getting nervous; there was a whiff of change in the air, and the old guard was steadfastly refusing to admit that sex and drugs and rock 'n' roll were fast becoming the lifestyle of choice for Britain's youth. This was the perfect moment for a run-of-the-mill hack to spy Mick Jagger in a London nightclub, and, by eavesdropping, manage to get enough salacious gossip to wake his *News of the World* editor at two in the morning.

'This better be good.'

'Oh, it is, sir. It's Mick Jagger spilling the beans.'

They didn't even bother to do the usual checks, and ran with the story on the following Sunday. There was just one problem: it wasn't Mick Jagger, it was Brian Jones.

Can you imagine Mick Jagger waking up to the papers that Sunday morning? He wasn't cross, he was apoplectic. He responded by announcing on the Eamon Andrews show, broadcast live the following Thursday, that he intended to sue the paper, and he was going for the jugular – a million smackers.

That concentrated Fleet Street's attention. Panic stations. As with any cornered animal, it didn't take long for them to come out fighting. Before you could say 'Jumping Jack Flash', the police carried out a drugs raid at Keith Richard's home, Redlands, in Sussex, prompting the notorious reports of Marianne Faithfull dressed only in a fur rug, doing 'something unusual' with a Mars bar.

Ah, those were the days: miniskirts and Mars bars. What happy memories.

There was no drugs squad in England at the time, so the police didn't really know what they were looking for. Apparently, Keith kept saying, 'I don't know who you are. Why are you all wearing the same clothes?' It was chaos. Some people had left before the raid, including George Harrison. Odd, that; did the police wait before they swooped? We knew for a fact that the Beatles were untouchable, because our parents loved them. Mick and Keith were different, and were duly arrested and carted off to the clink. A few days later, despite Dad's best efforts at Chichester crown court, they received sentences of three and twelve months respectively.

Word soon got out that the *News of the World* had provided a tip-off to the police, and it wasn't long before legions of fans, about five thousand in all, whipped into action by stories of a set-up, stormed the paper's offices, armed with Molotov cocktails. The police didn't seem to be able to do much about it. It was the first time for hundreds of years that a newspaper building had been threatened by the public.

The Establishment shook their heads, muttering that they knew this would happen sooner or later, and let this be a lesson to us all. But then – shock, horror – a leader appeared in that bastion of respectability *The Times*, written by the editor, William Rees-Mogg, under the headline 'Who Breaks a Butterfly on a Wheel?'

The shock waves were enormous; the whole world looked on.

This was the cauldron into which my father was thrown, and I was to find that he had some surprising views on it all.

Dad was shocked and upset by the original ruling, and vowed to get the boys off on appeal. He managed to get Mick out of jail after only one night; Keith had to suffer for three. Bail hadn't proved quite as easy as he thought. When he eventually got them into chambers and tried to calm them down, Keith refused, and kept muttering that he wanted to 'prosecute the Queen'.

'What on earth are you talking about?' Dad said.

'What was I done for, then?'

'Well,' my father replied, 'you were sentenced for allowing people to smoke cannabis on your property.'

'Right,' said Keith. 'Last night I was offered half a dozen joints – they were fab. But who owns the prisons, then?'

'Ah, I see where you're going. But I think we'll just sit on that for the time being, thank you very much. Now, let's get on with this rather complicated little problem . . .' And with that he set to work.

One night – Mum was away somewhere, and Phil was at school – Dad and I sat up and I watched him nursing a bottle of Scotch. We talked until the early hours. He looked tired, but with his blond hair swept back and his pale-blue eyes full of fire, he looked more like a young Henry Higgins than a barrister. I suddenly realised that, far from being the right-wing, judgemental old fuddy-duddy I'd seen clicking his fingers to those catchy but safe Beatles sounds, he was still a passionate idealist who hated seeing wrong being done.

He admitted that he'd been the first to make assumptions about Mick and Keith, but once he had met them, and seen the gathering momentum of uninformed prejudice, he became determined to seek justice on their behalf. He could have written the *Times* leader himself, so keenly did he identify with its sentiments.

Even more crucial was his firm belief that the *News of the World* had used an agent provocateur in the form of a rather shadowy figure, the late David Schneiderman, otherwise known as 'the acid king'. He was a hanger-on who had only been part of the entourage for about two weeks, but was a known pusher, and mysteriously disappeared soon after the original trial. This, of course, was something that the *News of the World* furiously denied. However, they did agree that the tip-off had come from them in the first place, adding a certain amount of fuel to the flames.

My respect for my father increased enormously that night. It culminated with him saying he wanted to take 'the boys' for

lunch at the Garrick Club. This was his idea of cocking a snoop
at the old guard. It reminded me forcibly of Peter O'Toole in
Lawrence of Arabia, walking into the officers' mess in Cairo with
his young Arab companion after crossing the desert, both of
them dressed in filthy Arab robes. Conversation stops dead. 'A
glass of lemonade for my friend,' says Lawrence. 'And I want a
bed, with clean sheets. It's not for me, it's for him.' The Arab
boy drains the glass of lemonade as the silence continues.
Lawrence turns his penetrating gaze on the barman. 'He likes
your lemonade.'

'Champagne, Mick? Keith?'

'Perfick.'

Silence. The bar slowly emptied.

'Nice pub you've got here, Mike.'

'Quiet, too,' Dad replied.

And with that Dad, like Lawrence, struck a blow for fair
play.

During the run-up to the trial, Phil and I contrived to drop by
Dad's chambers quite by chance one afternoon when we knew
Mick and Keith were due to visit. By this time we were used
to meeting famous people, but nothing and no one compared
to this. Lawrence Olivier, Peter O'Toole, Kenneth More – they
were chickenfeed and relegated to the third division when up
against these perfect beings.

We weren't disappointed. They were *so* cool, and *so* well
dressed! Thin to the point of wasted, and wearing velvet frock
coats and frilly white shirts; I'd never seen trousers so tight. I
swear to God, if Mick had bent down the seams wouldn't have
held. They were smaller, somehow, and rather better-looking,
in the flesh. I envied their long hair; I hadn't been as bold as

they had. There were times when I couldn't see Mick's face at all, just a very large pair of lips.

Mick told me they'd written a new track called 'Havers Chambers'. It never made the album, but so what. How cool was that?

Dad managed to get the date of the appeal set during the last week of the legal term, thinking that he might catch the three appeal judges in a good mood. So confident was he of winning that getting ready that morning felt like preparing for a huge party. Every so often the bell would ring and people would deliver cases of booze, glasses, even food, for the celebrations later.

'What happens if you lose?' I asked.

'I suppose we'll just have to send it all back,' he replied, looking less confident.

Dad had insisted on 'the boys' wearing suitably sombre clothes for their 'gig' in court, and had arranged for them each to have a dark suit made at Gieves & Hawkes. A white shirt and proper tie were also part of the required uniform. It was agreed that they would come and get ready with us, and we would all walk across Fleet Street to the high court together.

The day arrived and so did Mick, dragging with him a sorrowful-looking creature covered in spots. Keith had chicken pox. Mum had by this stage become a surrogate mum to them too, and I have a wonderful memory of her saying to Keith, 'Now, take off your pants,' while brandishing a large bottle of calamine and a wad of cotton wool. All we could hear through the bedroom door were little cries for mercy as Mum sploshed freezing-cold liquid onto his itching arse.

'Don't be such a baby,' she squealed, having the time of her life.

A few frantic telephone calls later, Dad was informed that Keith's presence was not required in court. One of the trial judges hadn't had chicken pox, and was less than keen to catch it, so Dad secured a separate room for him during the trial. He could still take part, without appearing in public.

Crossing that road with Mick and Keith was terrifying and exciting all at the same time. Despite the sober suits, it took less than a heartbeat for them to be recognised. The place went ballistic and within a minute or two the boys were marched off by a police squad 'for their own security', and slipped into court via a back entrance.

As the rest of us braved the chaos, Dad took my hand to protect me from the legions of photographers and fans. He hadn't done that since I was six, and I suddenly felt so secure, and so full of love for this compassionate man. How I admired him and longed never to let him down.

As we approached the main entrance, I noticed something that really alarmed me – my father's hand was damp with sweat. I had a moment of panic as I realised something that had never previously crossed my mind: he was nervous.

I shut my eyes and prayed hard. Oh, God, if there is one, please let him win – please, please let him win. Then I remembered those briefs piled up in his chambers, and told myself to stop worrying. He's the best, I thought. He really is the best.

When Mick appeared, the public gallery went wild. It was as if they were at a rock concert, not the highest courtroom in the land. I was sitting some way back, on ground level, but could see Dad very clearly. He had the ghost of a smile on his face.

No one could make the fans quieten down; not the clerk of the court, not the police, no one. I watched Dad lean over and whisper something in Mick's ear. He nodded, stood up and turned to the gallery. He put his finger to his lips. Silence. Wow! I bet even the Dalai Lama would have a job doing that.

Dad had to prove that the original ruling by Judge Block was incorrect, by questioning who had tipped off the police, what had become of their informant, what was the News of the World's involvement in all of this, who had authorised the abuse of police power in the raid on Keith's home, why did the jury convict on such flimsy evidence, why were the sentences so harsh, given the trivial nature of the actual findings, and wasn't the decision influenced by a desire to make a public example of these two young men, in order to nip some perceived dangerous threat in the bud?

The three appeal judges deliberated for one and three-quarter hours. They finally returned to court just before lunch. We all stood up as we watched these wise old men take their seats. This was the moment of truth, and boy, did they make us wait. Bit by bit they revealed the extent of Dad's victory. There was a God. The previous sentence was overturned; Mick and Keith were given a conditional discharge for three months and were told they could leave without a stain on their character.

Both these things were very important to them. A prison sentence would have been a hideous experience for them both, and as they were about to take on the notoriously difficult American market with an imminent tour, there was something else at stake. Without that ruling, they would never have been allowed into the country. To be a hit in England is one thing, but to crack America is something else entirely.

Dad turned and gave me the thumbs-up. What a moment!

There was sweat on his forehead and, I swear to God, a tear in his eye. He was smiling from ear to ear.

Out in the street, hundreds of reporters were running down Fleet Street to file their copy, mobile phones being still some way in the future; it was quite a sight. We fought our way through the mêlée, and sped round the back to collect Mick and Keith. Chicken pox or no chicken pox, they were ready to rock and roll. The calamine lotion had obviously done the trick.

Our home in London at that time was number 2, Dr Johnson Buildings, in the Temple. The Inner Temple comprises row upon row of chambers. As Dad was a bit of a leading light, he had managed to secure one of the much-sought-after flats that perched at the top of each building.

There were seventy-eight stone steps up to our front door. It wasn't the most kicking venue for a party, but, oh boy, half of London seemed undeterred by the trek, and our fairly small flat was bursting at the seams. I was sitting on the floor getting happily hammered when I glanced up at Marianne Faithfull. Oh my God, I thought, she really is the prettiest girl in the world. I fancied her more than was legal. Her long, blond hair, pale-grey eyes and sexy mouth and . . .

Oh, fuck, she wasn't wearing any knickers.

Can this be possible? Please don't move, never ever move. Just stay there for the rest of my life. Kill me now.

To this day, that remains one of my most electrifying moments. Sharon Stone seemed pretty tame by comparison, and a lot further away. Let's just say I found my Holy Grail without bothering with da Vinci.

Liquid lunch soon turned into liquid tea, followed swiftly by liquid dinner. El Vino's, the wine suppliers to most of the Temple, had one of their busiest days in history.

Mick and Keith left soon after tea. Keith went home to nurse his spots and Mick was whisked by helicopter to a live TV debate, orchestrated by a young John Birt, with, among others, William Reese-Mogg and Malcolm Muggeridge.

Mick managed to seal his reputation as the rebellious voice of youth while at the same time coming across as incredibly intelligent and articulate. I thought he was breathtaking.

Soon after the last person had left, I staggered off to my bedroom to change into my pyjamas. There, on my bed, I found most of Mick's wardrobe. He'd used my room as his changing room. Pissed. I laughed out loud: the conservative green tie that he had worn with his dark suit in court had a naked picture of Marianne printed just below button level. He had also left the purple velvet suit he'd been wearing when he arrived that morning. Was it really only that morning? It seemed like days ago.

I stared open-mouthed at this sartorial feast. I touched it. I knew what I had to do.

It fitted like a glove. The suit took me over. I started to dance, to jive, jump, leap. I suddenly had a microphone in my hand. I am Mick Jagger! I burst out of the bedroom into the drawing room to find Dad with a cigar in his left hand and a large whisky in his right.

He looked up. 'Christ, I've already said goodbye to you.'

'How cool is this, Dad?'

'Well,' he said, taking a long pull on his stogie, 'it doesn't get cooler.'

With that I gave Dad 'Jumping Jack Flash'. The long version. My version.

Chapter 4

Knowledge and Confidence

The recorder is a funny old instrument; it's strange that such rich and varied musical knowledge can be absorbed through such a simple little pipe.

My music teacher at Nowton Court announced this fact as he handed me the little wooden blighter. 'This is going to teach you everything you will ever know about music,' he said, and he was right.

Once you'd got the fingering down and learned to read music, you could pretty well play a whole number of really interesting instruments: the trumpet, the clarinet, the flute, even the piano, all follow the same principles of finger movement.

There was one major drawback. It just didn't look cool. The only way to look cool was to play a guitar – any guitar – and yell into a microphone – any microphone. 'What band are you in?' people would ask me.

What did they mean, what band was I in? How could I

possibly be in a band? Hang on a minute. 'Phil? Isn't it about time we started a band?'

'Yeah, awright,' he said, giving it the full Etonian twang. 'Why the fuck not?'

So we had a band, and it was good. Well, what I mean is, it was fun. In fact, it was the best fun you could have at the time. Apart from learning drama in London surrounded by gorgeous girls, and having your own pad to stay in, the cream was going to be playing bass guitar in a band called Crinkle.

I couldn't play bass guitar – to be honest I couldn't play any guitar – so I had to learn from scratch. In those days you could buy a book called *Teach Yourself Bass Guitar* and that's what I did.

I wanted to look like Paul McCartney (the coolest-looking bass guitarist in the world, even though he wasn't a Rolling Stone) so I bought a violin bass guitar – it looked vaguely like a violin and sounded as sweet as a nut. At least, it did when Paul played it. It took me a little longer to master the touch.

So there we were, Crinkle, playing at debs' parties, birthday parties – you name it, we played it, and at sixty quid a crack we managed to make enough money to buy ourselves a slightly better amplifier one week or a slightly better PA system the next, always ploughing the profits back into the group.

We ended up being asked to play in a nightclub in Portugal for the summer holidays. It was incredible. I never saw the day; I went to work at dusk and went to bed at dawn – heaven when you're sixteen. Susie had moved on to pastures new, although we remained friends, so I was free to enjoy the perks, and a band tends to pull the prettiest girls. We weren't any good, but in those days it didn't seem to matter. Nothing seemed to matter that summer, until the time came to pack up the guitar and head home to the ghastly reality of A-levels.

It would have been easy enough to stay on at Arts Ed but, as tends to happen, I felt that I had outgrown it and was ready to move, and didn't quite trust their teaching skills at that level. For some reason, I had a moment – just a moment – of sensible, conservative thinking. I wanted to make sure of some reasonable exam results, so that university would be a viable option should I fall flat on my face in the acting arena.

I was hungry for knowledge, in that idealistic teenage fashion, and for the first time in my life I was keen to get my teeth into some serious study. I suppose nowadays I could have slotted into almost any public school in the country, but back in the dark ages it was unthinkable to join a school in the sixth form. It was for this reason – and the need to provide places where those misfits and oddballs who had either failed or been chucked out of public school could finish off their patchy education – that crammers came into being.

By some extraordinary fluke, I hadn't yet been chucked out of any establishment, a fact which immediately made me an oddity, and I therefore slotted in with no bother. Not only was I eager to learn, but I was also in a hurry, and determined to achieve two A-levels in one year.

One Sunday morning, the *Observer* boasted an education supplement, giving all sorts of details on the various options for people like me, and I leaped on them. The majority were in and around London, but I knew I couldn't cope with the distractions of London, and would be too easily led astray. There was one in the Hebrides; picturesque, undoubtedly, but too few other distractions. I kept looking.

I finally found one in a place called Market Harborough. Where the fuck was Market Harborough? As it turned out, it was in a perfect location, not too near London, but not too far away, either. I didn't want to burn my bridges completely; I wasn't turning into a monk, for God's sake.

Brook House was an eighteenth-century rectory on the outskirts of Market Harborough. It had obviously been empty for years, until one Charles Lister had the bright idea of turning it into a crammer for disparate teenagers. There were eleven of us for the first term, and we were split up into various dormitories.

I struck gold with my first roommate, Henry Jones-Davis. Not only was he good fun but, joy of joys, he had a car, a Morris Traveller, one of those little estate cars with wooden bits down the sides. I was still a couple of months short of my seventeenth birthday, but of course I used to drive it whenever I could.

Henry was a brilliant instructor.

'What do I do now?' I'd ask.

'Just drive the bloody car and for God's sake don't hit anything.'

I took my test two days after my birthday, and passed with flying colours.

After it was over, the examiner looked at my provisional licence. 'Hang on a minute,' he said. 'When was your seventeenth birthday?'

'Erm, well, let me think, er . . . a couple of days ago.'

'Where the hell did you learn to drive, then?'

'My father has . . . a huge estate,' I replied, hardly missing a beat.

Mr Lister was quite a creepy headmaster. His uniform was thick green cords, brothel creepers, check shirt, red cardigan, beard and a pipe. He was very firmly of the opinion that the key to passing all exams was to be found in 'knowledge and confidence'.

This became our catchphrase and the inspiration for all our activities – legal or not. The trick when taking exams in a year is to pick the easiest subjects, and for me they were English and History. I fell upon the set books. It was as if I'd never read a novel before. A *Passage to India*, *Romeo and Juliet* and *Julius Caesar*.

Initially, I wasn't sure about *Romeo and Juliet*; I'd always found it a bit soppy. But when I got down to studying the text, I realised it was much more menacing than I'd thought. *Julius Caesar*, on the other hand, does exactly what it says on the tin. I thought it was a great slice of historical drama – fantastically brought to life by the Royal Shakespeare Company's production at Stratford. I have never forgotten the spine-tingling thrill of seeing massed phalanxes of legionnaires march straight down the centre of the stage and stop just short of toppling into the stalls; awesome stuff.

Alexander Pope and the Metaphysical poets John Donne and Andrew Marvell were on the syllabus. Glorious! I was like a sheet of blotting paper, mopping it all up and eager for more.

> I wonder by my troth, what thou, and I
> Did, till we lov'd? were we not wean'd till then?
> But suck'd on country pleasures, childishly?'

Of course, good teachers helped. Most of ours came from Leicester University and were to a man inspiring. The English tutor was fabulous; he was called Farouk Dhondy, and is a very successful screenwriter today. The History teacher, who used to arrive each morning on a 50cc moped and looked like a cross between Mickey Rooney and a garden gnome, held us spellbound once he got onto his subject, the Tudors and Stuarts. He romped through the numerous beheadings and other assorted grisly ends with relish.

Fantastic. But at the end of the day, not quite as fantastic as barrelling down to London to see a girl in a miniskirt. Even the most dedicated swot has his limits, and I soon began to hear the siren call of London's finest.

It took all of three seconds to convince Henry – he was prepared to drive pretty well anywhere, at any time of the day or night. He was from Wales, completely mad of course, and not a little terrifying. He played rugby and was tough as old boots. If you laid one hand on his girl he'd punch your lights out, but he never turned down an invitation and made sure I didn't either – you never quite knew how things were going to pan out.

Each Friday evening, we were given a mock exam paper – more 'knowledge and confidence' – and were therefore not allowed out or away for the weekend until the Saturday morning. Henry and I decided that there were better ways to spend a Friday night.

The exam paper finished, everyone would be fast asleep by midnight. Not us. Around twelve thirty, we'd sneak out of our room, down the fire escape, and tiptoe across the drive. Hand brake off, we'd roll the motor silently down the drive, occasionally looking back to see if old 'knowledge and confidence' had been disturbed.

Once we hit the road, we did a running start – I felt as if I was part of a bobsleigh team – and we were out of prison and on our way to London. Henry had this theory that the car would go faster if we had all the windows up and the heating on full. It was like a Turkish bath in there, but boy did we go like the wind – all of seventy-three miles an hour.

Two and a half hours later, we would be at Dad's flat in the

Temple, the whole weekend ahead of us. It was always fun, principally because we managed to eat like kings. We needed to. The food at Brook House made a Japanese prison canteen look like the Ritz.

I discovered that Dad had accounts at a couple of nearby restaurants, one of which was a very classy Italian joint called Trattoria Est, just round the corner in Fetter Lane. It was one of the first trattorias in London, and the only place in town for a decent bowl of spaghetti. They got to know us pretty well and always made a great fuss of us, probably because we racked up some hefty bills.

'Give us the bill, Mario,' I'd say cheerily as we left, feeling no hint of a conscience. I'd sign it and give it back. 'Grazie.'

'Prego.'

Dad never seemed to cotton on. He was entertaining pretty lavishly himself in those days, so I thought I might have got away with it, but one day, out of the blue, I heard Dad complaining about a bill.

'Good God,' he said, 'those bloody Italians.'

A couple of my bills had snuck in while he was away in Hong Kong on a case. I spluttered something about having to take some very important person for an extremely important dinner, m'lud. 'Please forgive me.'

'Of course,' he said. 'Just give me a cheque for twenty-seven pounds and ten shillings, and you will receive a conditional discharge.'

Case closed.

I invited Henry to stay in Suffolk one holiday. As we approached our village, the Morris screeched to a halt on a small bridge. Before I knew what was happening, he had pulled a pot of paint and a brush out of the back of the car and was busy daubing 'Free Wales Army' on the side of the bridge in large white letters.

The following morning, Dad drove us both to Newmarket to do a bit of shopping. As we passed over the bridge I held my breath. The Bentley screeched to a halt. 'God,' he said, staring at Henry's graffiti. 'Who the hell did that?'

'It was me, sir,' Henry piped up from the back.

I didn't know if Dad would hit him or kiss him.

'I couldn't agree with you more.'

And that was it. We drove on to Newmarket and no more was said. It's still there.

Henry was rummaging in the garage for a tennis racquet one afternoon when he came across a Nazi flag – huge and red, complete with outsize swastika in the middle. He let out an enormous whoop of joy. Dad had retrieved it from a captured German submarine during the war, and Henry used it as a bedspread at Brook House from that moment on, much to the consternation of Mr Lister and his wife.

Henry was obsessed with all things military, especially dangerous and noisy things. He had a mate who was doing SAS training. Through him, Henry had managed to acquire a mark eight grenade. I'd never seen anything like it in my life. It looked bloody lethal and I asked Henry what the hell he was going to do with it.

'Lob it out of the window,' he said.

It was only a matter of time before Brook House was rocked by an almighty explosion and one hell of a hole appeared in the drive. The police questioned us collectively to see if we could shed any light on the matter. We all played dumb – until it came to Henry. 'I didn't see anything, Officer, but I can tell you one thing: it sounded suspiciously like a mark eight grenade.'

From their faces they clearly thought they were dealing with a lunatic, and they weren't far wrong.

Another of Henry's tricks was scaring old ladies. He kept a stash of bangers in each of the side pockets of his Morris – and we're not talking sausages here. Every so often, when he spied a suitable target, he would light one, fling it out of the window, and watch the pantomime in his rear-view mirror as he sped away.

For a while I thought this was fine sport, until one day, just as I was about to fling a couple out of my window, I suffered a moment of remorse, and in my confusion managed to drop the little blighters back into the pocket. The whole lot went up, making one hell of a racket and filling the car with smoke. I had set the car on fire, and yelled at Henry to stop.

'Bollocks' was his reply and we made steady progress through St John's Wood, unable to see anything in front of us. Henry drove beautifully, never hit anything, never hesitated.

I didn't feel too good for a week or two. I think I managed to breathe in the equivalent of three hundred cigars in thirty seconds. In fact, I was a walking firework – if you'd lit my blue touchpaper you wouldn't have seen me for dust. It was terrifying: God knows how we didn't kill ourselves or, worse still, someone else.

My birthday is the day after Guy Fawkes Day, and that year it fell on a Saturday. I decided to have a party in Dad's flat. Henry and I had built up a sizeable little black book, so it was just a question of getting in the booze. Strangely, things got a little out of hand. The flat was jam packed, the noise deafening. Every bed was used – more than once, probably – including Mum and Dad's. In fact, that's where I ended up with . . . I can't remember who, but I know there was more than one.

The next morning I was woken by my door nearly being taken off its hinges.

'What in God's name is going on here?'

Dad was en route back to Suffolk after some case down south, and had popped in to collect his mail. The scene that confronted him was something akin to Dante's Inferno. There were fourteen Turnbull & Asser shirts soaking in the bath – washing machines were still a luxury in those days. There were bodies everywhere (sometimes several to a bed) and overflowing ashtrays and half-filled glasses covered every surface.

I had never seen him so angry.

'I'm going out to have a civilised breakfast; you have got one hour precisely to get rid of everyone and get this place cleaned up, or you will face the music.' He turned on his heel and walked out, slamming the door.

I grabbed Henry and shook him. 'For God's sake, you've got to help me – Dad's given us an hour to get everything cleaned up or we'll have to face the music.'

Henry stretched and opened an eye. 'What sort of music are we talking about?'

'The full orchestra,' I yelled.

'What? You mean the Philharmonic?'

'Yes, the full fucking Philharmonic. Now for Christ's sake move your arse.'

An hour later we surveyed our handiwork and felt pretty pleased with ourselves. The girls had gone, the beds were made, the bottles and fags removed and the washing-up completed. The fourteen Turnbull & Asser shirts were in a soggy plastic bag under a bed. We sat down to face the music, confident that it wouldn't be too deafening.

Dad never returned. He knew the message had got through and had decided to carry straight on to Suffolk.

I decided it was time I owned some wheels of my own. A car was out of the question, but I managed to save up enough to buy a bike from a boy called Geoffrey Tilleard – a cool French guy who was also at Brook House. It was a 250cc Honda and quite the most gorgeous creature I had ever clapped eyes on.

As with all such clandestine relationships, I didn't tell Mum and Dad – the word 'bike' sends all parents into spasms of fear and horror, and understandably so. But there is nothing quite like the thrill of tearing along at full tilt, the wind in your hair (you didn't have to wear a crash helmet in those days), feeling like James Dean on one of his more successful outings.

After a few months I reckoned I was ready to ride it down to London – quite an undertaking. I made it with no problem and was riding up Piccadilly feeling pretty pleased with myself when there was an almighty *bang!* The clutch blew and I went from sixth gear down to first without passing Go. A taxi hurtled into the back of me and I flew over the handlebars, landing some distance away, seeing stars but miraculously unscathed.

The same could not be said for my poor bike. She was minus several vital organs and had a broken bone or two, not to mention severe internal injuries. I managed to wheel her over to the side door of Fortnum & Mason, and there I left her – for ever. Of course, she wasn't insured or taxed, so not traceable to me in any way. I did go back a few weeks later to check her out, but not surprisingly there was no sign. I never saw her again.

The point of being at Brook House finally became apparent: it was exam time. We couldn't sit them in Market Harborough – it wasn't licensed for that sort of thing – so we had to travel to Cambridge along with a couple of thousand other examinees. Henry and I took off in the burned-out wreck of the Morris and, as we were going to be there for at least ten days, moved into digs.

A couple of hours later, I noticed we were sharing with some really pretty girls. Jesus, I was going to have to be disciplined here. I vowed there and then not to speak to any of them, and, surprisingly, I managed to keep to it.

Sitting on my hard little wooden chair, waiting to turn the exam paper over, I prayed that Brook House was going to come up trumps. I flicked the white sheet over and held my breath. It was OK; a whole bunch of questions I had answered a thousand times before. Good old Mr Lister. The old sod was absolutely right. All it took was a little bit of knowledge and confidence.

Entr'acte

The Suit

The First Suit

When I was studying drama at the Arts Educational Trust in the mid-sixties, my father bought me my first suit. It came from Burtons, was a dark-blue, mohair three-piece and cost the princely sum of £19.96. That rite-of-passage moment made me feel rather like a Masai warrior at his circumcision: 'Go into Burtons a boy and come out a man.' It was a bit of a heavy-duty construction and was selected out of a catalogue, with no fittings. I felt like a god.

The suit gave its first performance at the Eton and Harrow cricket match, held every year at Lord's. Phil, my brother, although not in the Eton team, went along to watch, and I joined him. As we sat there in the stands, I remember thinking the suit was performing at the top of its game, when suddenly there was a thud on my back. Some little Harrovian squirt had thrown an ice-cream which had hit its target like a heat-seeking missile. I turned in a rage, preparing to beat the shit out of him, when a voice said, 'Don't even think about it.' Phil's housemaster was sitting a couple of rows back and wanted to watch the game, not a re-enactment of World War II. The oily impression of chocolate and vanilla wouldn't quite come out. I never wore the suit again.

The Suit That Wears You

For my part in *Upstairs, Downstairs* in the early seventies, a suit was made for me which somehow didn't touch any part of my body. On screen I looked as if I was drowning. I really fancied Lesley-Anne Down, the gorgeous actress who played Georgina, the daughter of the house, and tried to do some home alterations to make myself look a bit sharper. Needless to say, sewing proved not to be my most obvious talent and there were some hairy moments during filming when there would be an alarming ripping sound and suddenly there I'd be, re-engulfed by my suit tsunami. Miss Down somehow managed to remain untouched by the old Havers magnetism.

The Mess Kit

In 1982 I made a TV mini-drama called *Nancy Astor*. I played the part of her son, Bobby Shaw Jr. My screen father – Nancy's first husband, a serial womaniser who was the great love of her life – was played by Pierce Brosnan. It still gives me a kick to call James Bond 'Dad', which I do at every possible opportunity – the more public, the better. For this part, I had a regimental mess kit made for me by Mr Davis at Angels, the famous theatrical outfitters. Mr Davis was well known as the best cutter in London. He went on to make several suits for me, but none so flash as that mess kit. It was fabulous and so was I – the only fly in the ointment being that as I strutted my stuff in that skin-tight suit, brimming with machismo like a matador going in for the kill, I was, in fact, playing the part of someone who was gay.

The Hand-Me-Down Suit

Actually not a suit at all, but Dad's old plus-fours re-modelled for me by Gieves & Hawkes in Cambridge. I had become fond of shooting and was thrilled to look the part for the first time. Shooting is not just about murdering birds, oh no. You have to have the right kit, and some people take this very seriously. My much-missed friend Patrick Lichfield was one such. He never wore wellies, thinking they were far too unstylish and ugly. He always wore a pair of very natty studded boots. Now this was all very well, and stylish they may have been, but waterproof they certainly weren't. As a result, his feet were permanently soaking wet. One of my favourite photos is of me carrying Patrick on my back over a flooded field to his stand, both of us roaring with laughter. Happy times.

The Oriental Suit

While making *A Passage to India* in Bangalore, I discovered a neat little street which had a faint – very faint – whiff of Savile Row about it. Shop after shop promised a perfect suit within twenty-four hours. This was something I couldn't resist and I disappeared swiftly into Mr Patel's Suitings Emporium. The first question I was asked was: 'Are you hero?' 'Of course I am' was my immediate response, and before you could say 'Peggy Ashcroft' a photo of me had appeared on their wall, with a caption announcing that they were the tailor of choice to the 'hero' of David Lean's esteemed epic. The suit was made of pale-grey silk, and looked ravishing. As soon as I got home to London it was out of the box. 'Where did you get that beautiful suit?' everyone cried. 'My tailor in Bangalore.' 'Wow! How exotic is that?' The second time of wearing I hailed a taxi – and the sleeve fell off. By the end of the evening, I was practically naked.

The Rip-Off Suit

While my brother, Phil, was an undergraduate at Corpus Christi College, Cambridge, I wasn't doing much. Well, I was meant to be doing my A-levels, but I much preferred the role of undergraduate manqué and spent a lot of time in the spare room in Phil's lodgings. I would whirl round Cambridge on a bicycle, wearing the college scarf – quite indistinguishable from the real students. At night we ate 'in halls' and quite early on I discovered that Corpus had a spectacular wine cellar. It became my job to choose the wine for dinner and slap it on the bill – whose bill I never quite discovered.

Opposite the college was the tailor and Phil let slip that Dad had opened an account there for his university needs. Within a very short time I was the proud owner of a gorgeous dark-blue suit. 'Would sir like an overcoat to go with that – these November days can be chilly?' 'Yes, sir most certainly would.' 'Cashmere?' 'Definitely.'

Dad never found out. Or did he? Maybe Phil got one hell of a bollocking – I must remember to ask.

The Morning Suit

During the seventies and eighties, I invariably ended up playing the 'toff', and an indispensable part of a toff's wardrobe is, of course, the morning suit. I decided to have one made, instead of constantly hiring ones that didn't fit. This proved to be a wise decision, as I have worn it ever since.

Each year it gets its most glamorous walk-out at Royal Ascot. It's much easier for the men. All we have to do is find a pretty little waistcoat to brighten up the look. For girls it's another matter. I should know, I've paid for a few Chanel outfits in my time. In recent years, my great friend John Chalk has hosted his annual party in a marquee opposite the main entrance. Some years back the rental became prohibitively expensive. What did John do? He bought the site! Very showbiz, very Ascot, very Morning Suit.

The Perfect Suit

Eventually, my best mate Al Cluer suggested it was about time to get a really good suit. 'You look like a bag of nails. Go and see Doug.'

'Doug' was Douglas Hayward, the legendary London tailor who had been making suits for the great and the good for over twenty years, including Michael Caine's sharp suits in *Get Carter* – not my sartorial benchmark, I grant you, but pretty fuck-off glamorous. Al marched me through the door and introduced me.

Doug is always good with the patter. That day, apparently, a Chinese supplier of material had gone 'belly up' so he was prepared to make me a couple of suits, charging one thousand pounds and throwing the material in for free. Of course, I fell for it willingly and we agreed that I would open an account and pay in so much per month, an arrangement which continues to this day. On the day of my final fitting, Doug gave me the once-over and said, 'Don't go and see your bank manager in that.'

Some years later, at the Emmy Awards in Los Angeles, I was

introduced to the head honcho of HBO, the largest independent television production company in the world. As we shook hands he murmured, 'Doug Hayward?' 'Yes,' I replied. 'Yours, too?' He nodded and with that we became firm friends, fellow holders of a sartorial passport which those in the know never fail to acknowledge.

Talking of passports, I managed to mislay mine coming back from America not so long ago. (It turned out that I'd put it in my luggage, which of course doesn't join you until after Immigration.) I hunted around for an embarrassed ten minutes, holding up a queue of hundreds of frustrated and jet-lagged passengers. Then bingo! 'Will this do?' I said to the poker-faced Immigration official. Inside the inside pocket of my jacket was Doug's identification label: 'Nigel Havers' and, underneath, '6/11/95'. Oh yes, a birthday present to myself.

'That'll do,' he said, and I scarpered.

Chapter 5

A Brighter Prospect

As far as I was concerned, when I left the Arts Educational Trust that was the education done with. It was time to get to work. There was no way I was even going to pretend to go to university. Phil was already up at Corpus Christi, Cambridge, reading law, so Dad needn't worry what I was up to. You only need one son to carry on the family tradition I thought, the other one is free to slide under the radar and go forth to seek his fortune.

Luck is an essential part of being an actor and, as luck would have it, Charles Blackburn called me out of the blue that autumn and told me to get off my arse and ring Richard Cotterill, an old friend of his, who was directing *Richard II* for the Prospect Theatre Company. Richard had been a bright spark in the Cambridge Footlights, and was fast gaining a reputation as the new-kid-on-the-block director in London. It was typical of Charles that he knew all of this – he somehow made it his business to keep a finger on the pulse in these matters.

'Of course I will.'

'Do it now,' said Charles and put the phone down.

So I did. I had no idea what I was calling about because Charles didn't tell me. Cotterill was teaming up with Toby Robertson, who was to direct Christopher Marlowe's *Edward II*. These two plays were to open the Edinburgh Festival, tour England and parts of Europe before ending up at the Piccadilly Theatre in London's West End. The two principal players were to be Ian McKellen and Timothy West. Not a bad cast for an actor straight out of the blocks.

I turned up, as ordered, at the Donmar rehearsal rooms in Covent Garden to audition. Looking back, it was a scary moment and I should have behaved a lot better. If I passed the audition I would become what is known as an acting ASM. I didn't know what it meant, so, while I was hanging around waiting to do my bit, I asked some bloke who seemed to be organising operations. He looked at me as if I was something from the bottom of a pond, but he did at least fill me in.

'Young man,' he said, 'if you survive today, you will be carrying a spear and making cups of tea for the following twelve months.'

'Oh, very funny,' I replied, thinking: Great sense of humour. 'What do you do, then?'

'I am the company manager,' he replied, 'and I shall look forward to whipping you into shape every single day – if you survive.'

Within seconds I was called in to audition.

'We'd like you to do your classical piece now, Mr Havers.'

'Certainly.' I stepped forward to centre stage, stood smartly to attention and then slowly, very slowly, with my imaginary spear, I went to the 'at ease' position. I held it for quite a long time.

'What the hell are you playing at?' someone yelled.

'This is my classical piece. Isn't this all I'll be doing for the next twelve months – oh, and making cups of tea, of course?'

Cheeky little shit – God knows how I got the job. Maybe it was because they only paid five pounds a week and no one else would do it. But do it I did, and I never regretted a single moment of what happened to me that year. Almost everything I have learned about the business I'm in, I learned in those twelve months.

It was a bloody hot summer and rehearsing in the dusty old Donmar studio was practically intolerable at times. It was going to be hard enough doing one full-length Shakespeare piece, but to tack on another Elizabethan tragedy was asking a lot of everyone involved. Mostly, I sat at the back watching, listening and learning. The company manager, Clive Wiseman, ruled us eight ASMs as though we were at boot camp and I hated him to begin with. Being the youngest, I got all the worst tasks, but I decided to keep my head down and do exactly what I was told. At one stage, this meant getting the 'key to the grid'. Off I went in search of the blasted key. Of course, it didn't exist – it's a famous theatrical wind-up, but hell, you only have to learn it once. To this day no one knows what the key actually is – a theatre myth that sounds wonderfully technical but in fact is total rubbish.

The thing that really kept me going was watching Ian McKellen and Timothy West at work. I remember one extremely hot afternoon watching Ian receive the news of Gavaston's death halfway through *Edward II*. The pain seemed to come from deep inside him as he let out an animal yell. It just confirmed how much I wanted to be an actor myself, and if I could be half as good as he was I reckoned I'd be all right.

During the final run-through of the play, it became clear that Robert Eddison, one of the distinguished members of the company, still didn't have a proper grasp of his lines. Actually, he didn't seem to know them at all. I started to panic for him: it was only three nights before we opened at the Forum Theatre, Billingham.

Billingham wasn't the prettiest place in the world, but it boasted a brand-new theatre which could seat over twelve hundred people, and Toby and Richard had decided this would be the place to unleash our two plays on an unsuspecting audience prior to the big one at the Edinburgh Festival. I think it all went rather well on the first night and, by some extraordinary fluke, Robert Eddison remembered every single word. Not a bad wheeze, I thought. Maybe I should play that game myself – pretend I don't know it and then at the last minute become DLP (that's Dead Letter Perfect).

The next morning we were all called in for 'notes' by Richard Cotterill. I got bawled out for something I don't even remember doing, like standing in the wrong place at the wrong time – reminiscent of Nowton Court and being beaten for something I didn't know I'd done. Clearly, I managed not to do whatever it was I'd done again, as it was immediately forgotten. I think sometimes directors take their frustrations out on the 'pond life' junior members of the cast because the stars are above criticism. No one cared or noticed what we did really, so the odd bollocking was considered fair game and it certainly kept me on my toes.

Come Friday night and five successful performances to a mostly full theatre, we were all very pleased with ourselves and went off to a nightclub to celebrate. The Four Tops were in town and there they were playing live – everyone went bananas. The girl next to me was screaming and yelling and dancing and jiving, so of course I spent the whole evening trying to impress her.

'What's a bloke like you doing in a place like this?'

'Well, I'm starring in a new Shakespeare production, actually.'

'Oh, that's nice,' she said. 'What's 'e like?'

Clearly she thought the Bard was still with us. I looked at her in astonishment. She was quite sexy, in a Cruella De Ville sort of way. Eventually, she asked me back to her place and of course I said yes, so we leaped on a night bus and headed miles out of town. 'Oh blimey,' I thought, 'this better be worth it.' We got off the bus and walked for what seemed like for ever. 'Oh, Christ, this is a long way for a hot dog.' We got to her place, and she asked if I wanted a cup of tea.

'Christ, haven't you got anything stronger?' I asked.

She rummaged for what seemed like hours in the nether regions of a cupboard and emerged brandishing a tin of Nescafé. I looked around as I considered which was the less offensive – tea or coffee – and my jaw dropped in awe. I was completely surrounded by Roy Orbison. He was everywhere: on the ceiling, on the walls, even on the floor – there was a rug knitted as Roy Orbison. Suddenly, 'Pretty Woman' blasted out of her gramophone.

'I hope you like him,' she said, ''cos I love him more than life itself. In fact, I'm in love with him.'

I couldn't possibly compete with Roy so I buggered off, out of the door, down the steps and into the street. It was four o'clock in the morning. No dinner, practically nothing to drink, and I certainly hadn't got my leg over. Worst of all, I didn't know where the hell I was. I started walking. City Centre was the sign I followed, and by some extraordinarily brilliant piece of navigation, I was in my digs by six fifteen.

The landlady was banging on my door by ten o'clock. 'The theatre people want to know where you are.'

Oh, shit! I was supposed to be there by nine thirty. Richard Cotterill berated me in front of the entire company for at least five minutes. He reduced me to the size of a mosquito – I think he wanted me to burst into tears. All I could hear was 'Pretty Woman' pounding in my head. Fuck him, I thought, and fuck her too – and fuck Roy most of all.

Edinburgh – just the most beautiful place. People say it's the Paris of the north. Bollocks. It's up there on its own, no need for comparisons. It was my first time and to be there for the Festival is the greatest way to discover it. We were to perform both plays at the Assembly Rooms, not exactly a theatre, but a most impressive space nonetheless. There is no proscenium arch, for a start. The stage is thrust out, so the audience is on all three sides. There were no proper entrances or exits – they had to be built – and there were no backstage dressing-room areas or greenrooms to rest in. All this made life a lot harder for the ASMs, but it didn't matter. What with making fifty-six cups of tea at the interval and carrying my banner, and also being in the King's army and Bolingbroke's rebel force, there wasn't a lot of time for oneself anyway.

The only serious problem I had was where to lay my head. Digs during the Festival were harder to get than cup final tickets. I found a night here and a night there, and at one point I was thinking of sleeping on a park bench in the theatre grounds. Six pounds a week ruled out a suite at the Balmoral Hotel. Then I got a lucky break. Towards the end of *Richard II* there's a scene set in the Duke of York's garden. The director decided they should eat during this scene and real food was laid out on a Tudor table. It's almost impossible to act and eat, so apart from a couple of nibbles the rest was mine. As I cleared away the leftovers at the end of the scene, I popped them all into a plastic bag I kept under my doublet. When the play was over, I'd sneak off into a quiet corner of the building to devour my spoils. On one of these excursions, I found myself in what seemed to be an annex of Edinburgh University. Yes, the Assembly Rooms backed on to the university, and I was in the private bedroom area. There must have been thirty or forty unoccupied rooms, seeing as everyone was on summer vacation. There were bathrooms, too. I was made. I moved into my new digs that night and slept in glorious comfort and isolation. Soon, though, in my cups, I mentioned my sleeping arrangements to a couple of mates, and, within what seemed like minutes, Timothy West and three others moved in. Colonisation was complete. It felt rather like a school dormitory, but I felt so lucky to be spending some time with Tim – he was incredibly generous and giving professionally, and gave me lots of advice. We were also getting something for nothing which gave us enormous pleasure as we regarded our payslips with dismay.

We were a sell-out for the whole six weeks that we were there. I don't suppose one single ticket holder noticed me, but Phil and a couple of other friends had made the journey up from London to see me, so at least I accounted for three tickets sold.

'Fantastic,' they said afterwards. 'Ian McKellen is just breathtaking, and Timothy West is superb.'

'Er . . . what about me?'

'Oh yes – were you actually in it?' asked Phil. Little shit.

'Of course I'm in it. I'm the guy who threw the spear at Ian.'

'Oh, right. You were brilliant,' he said.

'Thank you very much,' I replied. And there started a code of conduct between actor and friend. If you go and see an actor friend in a play, and you go backstage afterwards, you must say, you *will* say, how brilliant he or she was. It doesn't matter how terrible it was or how terrible they were, you will say: 'Brilliant, you were brilliant.'

Just as I'd got the hang of Edinburgh it was time to leave. We'd been a great success and being part of that success, even though I'd only carried a spear and made endless cups of tea, meant I'd been asked to see countless other plays and revues. Not bad for my first professional outing.

Now the serious stuff kicked in. We took both plays on a twenty-week tour of all the major theatres in the British Isles; hard work for the actors – and even harder work for the acting ASMs. Not only did I do the usual graft, but now I had to help get the shows into each theatre on a Sunday and also get them out on a Saturday night. It meant there was virtually no time off at all. Each city came as quite a shock to me. I hadn't realised I lived in such a big country. Cambridge was fine – I could get my brain round that, but Doncaster, Plymouth, Cardiff and Liverpool . . . God, Liverpool! At the time, I hoped I'd never have to return there. Fourteen years later, I ran my heart and soul out there, but that's a different story.

The hardest part for me was getting myself physically from one city to the next. Whoever arranged the tour had evidently never looked at a map. It made perfect sense to them to send us from Edinburgh to Plymouth, on to Glasgow and from there to Norwich. That was fine sitting behind a desk, but try doing it on British Rail – a bloody nightmare! One of my fellow ASMs, Michael Howarth, had a motorbike with a sidecar. 'Fancy a lift, Nige?' 'Fantastic,' I said as we set off from Brighton to Newcastle at three in the morning, in January. A couple of hours later, 'Holy Mother Mary, I can't feel my face,' I yelled at him. That journey was the longest seventeen hours of my life. It took days to coax my hands out of their white-knuckled claw position, and I walked like John Wayne for weeks. I never biked it again.

Next stop: central Europe. The people of Bratislava were gagging for the Bard. We were well behind the Iron Curtain, which was exciting and scary all at the same time. We were first given a lecture by a geeky-looking man from the Foreign Office.

'Now, you're to change any money you need at the border, and not be persuaded to do the same with any black-market money touts. The same applies to buying clothes and other goods. You only shop in government-owned stores. And, whatever you do, avoid the prostitutes loitering in the hotel lobby – you will recognise them by the significantly shorter hemlines and large quantities of make up.'

'Right,' Michael and I whispered to each other, 'that means we'll change money with the highest bidder, buy our stuff on street corners and get lucky with the first bird we see hanging around in the hotel – this sounds like it's going to be a bloody good laugh.'

And it was. Within the first couple of hours, I'd sold the jeans I was wearing for eighty pounds, about eight weeks' wages. The only small drawback was that the roubles I was paid in had slightly less value than Monopoly money outside the country. I can still hear the howls of laughter from the man at the bureau de change, when I tried to change them back into sterling at Heathrow.

The hotel we stayed in looked like a bank. The rooms were huge and hideous, but for the first time on this tour I had a bed and my own bathroom. Completely white it was – white floor, white walls, white ceiling, even white taps. I felt like I was in a morgue. Saturday night we'd finished the show, and it was time to party. The next morning we were off to Vienna at the crack of dawn, but so what? We were determined to find out how Bratislava rocked and rolled. We soon discovered that it didn't do either, and we ended up in a grotty little restaurant having a strange row with some local drunks. It seemed that they were insinuating that we Brits couldn't hold our drink.

'OK you, we now have very big competition – right now.'

'All right, you commie bastard!'

With that Clive, our company manager, selected me to be the drinking competitor. Me! Christ, I could hardly sink a pint without falling over. But there I was, standing opposite this Balkan mountain with three pints of wine in front of me. I drank the first one without taking a breath. He was already on his second. By the time I hit the third he'd finished his and was drinking a brandy. I'd lost. I'd also lost the plot. For some extraordinary reason, Clive had asked me to look after his briefcase, saying, 'I can't leave this in my hotel room, that Foreign Office bloke told me to keep it with me at all times. It's your responsibility now, so for Christ's sake don't fuck up. Every company member's passport is in there, and if you lose them we'll be stuck behind this bloody curtain till we're sixty.' After three pints of wine I didn't give a shit about that briefcase – or about anything. All I wanted to do was get into my bed, cuddling a bottle of aspirin. Clive and the rest of the gang had to carry the loser home. As we walked up the steps to the hotel lobby, avoiding the advances of the glamorous hookers, I suddenly realised I'd lost something important.

'Pashports,' I spluttered.

'What's he on about?'

'Paaarshports.'

Clive went white. 'Oh my God! What have you done with them?'

'I zink aive left them shumwhere.'

He interrogated me for five minutes, becoming increasingly frantic.

'Under zher table,' I said, pointing to the ceiling.

'You're coming with me.'

Somehow we retraced our steps to the restaurant.

Of course it had long since closed, so we started banging on the door. 'Letsh shrow stones at the windowze.' We did so, nearly breaking a couple in the process. Eventually, a light came on – we'd managed to wake someone.

He knew exactly why we were there. 'You vill be needing zis,' and he handed me Clive's briefcase. Saved by an eighteen-stone communist bar steward.

It took me the whole of the next week in Vienna to be my old self again. Pity, really, because Vienna is a lovely place – or so they told me. I had to do the show every night, of course; it practically killed me. I remember the audience all applauding in unison. To begin with this is very unnerving – you think they're slow-handclapping and giving you the bird, but that's just the way they do things there. I could get out of my costume and out of the stage door before they finished. They must have loved us. And I loved them – or rather I loved their chocolate cake and champagne, a treat from the management on our last day.

Our tour was over and we headed home. We hit the West

End like a ship in full sail. A year and a half after that cheeky audition, I walked into my dressing room (actually, eight of us sharing) hardly able to breathe for excitement. My first proper job and I'd ended up in the West End. I had to pinch myself to make sure it was real. The West End! It was the Piccadilly Theatre and we got rave reviews for both plays. Ian McKellen was going to be the next big thing, they all said. Critics sometimes do get it right. To top it all, my wages had gone up to fifteen pounds a week. That was enough to rent a room in a flat with an old friend from Market Harborough, Paul Raben.

Out of the blue one day, Dad called me. 'What are you doing for lunch tomorrow?'

I checked there was no matinee. 'Nothing,' I said.

'Come and have lunch at the Garrick.'

When I got there, I saw Dad standing at the bar with Michael Caine, one of many actor friends he had met there. He introduced me as his son. 'Hello, son,' Michael said. (Funnily enough, he said that to me again fifteen years later in a movie. But that's another story.) Dad told him that I was 'starring' in *Richard II* and *Edward II*.

'Oh, I'll come and see it, son,' Michael said.

'Thursday night?' I asked.

'Perfect,' he replied.

He never turned up. I'd told everyone he was coming. Another lesson learned.

Shock, horror, the notice went up one Friday afternoon. Now, 'the notice' is what all actors in the theatre dread. It is a notice to close, and it gives the actors two weeks to pack their bags and find a new job. We were sold out, so that couldn't be the reason . . . It transpired that Ian had been offered the part of Flashman in a movie and he was desperate to do it. He wanted to be a movie star. It took him a few more years than he thought, but he got there in the end. Perseverance does pay off. We were all disconsolate, but there was nothing we could do. At least we went out on a high, with people queuing round the block for returns.

It had been almost two years of doing two plays day in, day out with hardly a day off. A real baptism of fire and I'd come through it. Not only that but I'd loved doing it, every step of the way. I'd made a lot of new friends – all older than me, all more experienced than me – but most important of all I'd learned to keep quiet and watch, listen and learn. I also discovered that I could remain standing after three pints of bitter. I could still manage a conversation after four. In other words, I could drink like a man. That's a very important thing for an actor.

Chapter 6

Conduct Unbecoming

Charles Blackburn kept in touch with my father on and off throughout his life. 'What's Nigel up to?' and 'I hope he's doing some theatre. Actors should really only do theatre. The rest provides pocket money.' As well as advocating the importance of theatre, he maintained that actors should live in a garret and suffer for their art. Bollocks to that. My current address was 14 Brunswick Gardens, smack in the middle of the Royal Borough of Kensington. Luckily, Paul was kind enough to give me 'mate's rates' for this exclusive penthouse pad and I rented the second bedroom for five pounds a week, all inclusive.

I had wheels, too. My mother's old Ford Anglia had been duly passed down to Phil, and then to me – what was left of it. When he handed me the keys and 'waved goodbye to the old girl', the tank was empty, the sump without any oil at all and the battery as dry as a martini.

'What do you mean, she looks fucked? She's good for at least a couple of hundred thousand.'

'Couple of hundred thousand inches,' I thought.

I slowly nurtured her back to life, and she was parked outside number 14, nestling between Jaguars and Aston Martins, as if born to it.

As my newly acquired agent had gone a bit quiet on me, something all actors have to put up with from time to time, I decided I'd better find some temporary means of survival. A local advertising agency in Kensington needed a copywriter, and I applied and somehow got the job. It sounds a lot grander than it was. All I really had to do was get in early and make tea for everybody – would I ever get away from making tea for everybody? Occasionally, they asked my opinion about some useless piece of copy they'd come up with. 'Absolutely bloody brilliant,' I always said. On one occasion it was a photograph of two sausages sitting on a plate. Above the top sausage was written 'Porky and Best'. 'My God, that really is bloody brilliant.' I couldn't possibly come up with anything better than that. I only lasted a couple of weeks, but something good did come out of it. The receptionist was called Joy and, oh, what a joy she was: pretty, blonde and looking in need of a good meal. She was an orphan and had been brought up in one of the Dr Barnardo homes – the sort of girl, I thought, who needed a bit of looking after. I had a new girlfriend, a new bird, and she looked fantastic in her tiny miniskirt and air-force, blue-suede Biba boots.

One little problem. My bedroom had the smallest of single beds, obviously designed by a monastic dwarf. If Joy stayed the night, I'd have to sleep on the floor. Bugger that! And it was off to Barker's in Kensington High Street to rectify the situation. I'd forgotten to measure the room, so found myself saying to the salesman, 'Well, it's about so big, and this long . . . roughly . . . I think.' Next day, my new baby arrived. She slipped into place like a glove – so well, in fact, that there was no room whatsoever either side. My bedroom truly was a bed room; in fact, I had to make the bed while lying on it. So what? Nothing but happy memories.

Paul Raben was the most bizarre creature. He never seemed to work; he didn't have to. Somehow, somewhere, there was always plenty of cash. He spent most mornings lying in bed reading P. G. Wodehouse, smoking Consulate cigarettes and drinking Lucozade. 'This is bloody funny, isn't it?' he'd say. 'Just listen to this,' and he'd read out whole chunks of *Right Ho, Jeeves* brilliantly.

'Christ, you should be an actor,' I said.

'Don't be ridiculous, that's a job for poofs,' he said, cleaning the barrels of a twenty-eight-thousand-pound Purdey shotgun.

We rubbed along like this for months, Paul playing with his barrels, me playing with my birds – a marriage made in heaven.

Sitting around the flat without a job in sight is a hazardous occupation. My friend Andrew Brudenell-Bruce lived in the heart of Newmarket and became a dangerous ally. Around ten o'clock every morning he rang up and told me where to place my bets. Silver Tongue in the three thirty at Newmarket or Fisherman's Creek in the two fifteen at Sandown – all absolutely hopeless and eating away at what little savings I had. 'I've really go to stop this,' I thought.

The phone woke me on a Saturday morning at eight forty-five a.m. Far too early to take it, but for some reason I did. 'Hello.'

'I haven't woken you, have I?' Andrew said.

'No, of course not.' The first lie of the day.

'This is serious,' he said, 'very, very serious. You've got to go to the bank and draw out eighteen pounds right now.'

Oh, Christ, I thought. This really *is* serious.

'OK, so now you walk back up Kensington Church Street and into Coral's and put the lot on the following two horses.'

I wrote them down and, zombie-like, did as I was told. By nine thirty I was back in bed and fast asleep. I forgot all about it. I went about the usual Saturday, doing this and that.

Five o'clock that afternoon Andrew was on the phone again. 'Did you do what I told you?'

'Er, oh, yes, I think I did.'

'Good man. Now go down to Coral's – and take a friend, the biggest friend you have. You might need some protection.' He put the phone down.

'Bollocks, he's winding me up,' I thought. But I scampered down to Church Street and stood in a queue. I produced my betting slip.

The clerk peered over his half-rimmed glasses. 'Was this your idea?'

'Yeah, 'course it was.'

He turned round and fiddled in the till. 'Right, that's one thousand four hundred and eighty-five pounds.'

The air was sucked right out of me. I just about managed 'Jesus!'

Back home I sat on the double bed and threw the whole wedge up in the air. 'Wow!' I felt like the man who broke the bank at Monte Carlo.

Paul told me to make sure I bought something with the cash. I didn't need telling twice, and went straight out and got a portable TV, a suit, a couple of shirts, a tie and a pair of shoes.

The rest I gave straight back to the bookies over the next couple of weeks – lost the lot. Oh well, very unemployed but very well dressed.

Things were getting a bit desperate. I sat by the phone, willing the 'newly acquired agent' to ring. I didn't dare turn on the recently acquired TV in case I caught a glimpse of the racing. No, I was going to be very disciplined: I shall be in my garret, and I will only eat bread and cheese, and I will suffer for my art.

My greatest asset was my availability. And my greatest asset remained intact throughout that winter. I did my bit at being a waiter in a hamburger joint in Knightsbridge. I opted to do the night shift – it paid double. I hated every second. If I got the wrong sauce on the hamburger the customer screamed and I threw it back at the chef. It was rinsed under the tap and another sauce slapped on the top. We both spat on it, and I returned it. The complainers were mostly American so we didn't care. The more I fucked up, the better the tip.

I did my bit washing cars, serving drinks at cocktail parties, in fact, anything I could lay my hands on, and still no word from the now not so newly acquired agent. Going to the pub of an evening, I could make a pint last all night as I contemplated going back to my old copywriting job and spending my future composing punchy copy for pork pies. 'If this isn't the best pork pie in the world, I'll eat my hat.' Pork pie hat – geddit? Bollocks. Better stick to acting.

Mr Micawber had nothing on me. I was waiting for something to turn up. Eventually it did. My agent rang me and told me to get my arse to the Queen's Theatre in Shaftesbury Avenue pronto, to audition for the part of a subaltern in a play called *Conduct Unbecoming*. Auditions were pretty thin on the ground, so I wasn't going to argue. The play had been packing them in for six months and it was time for a cast change. I had the right voice and came from the right background, and they offered me the job there and then. They also asked whether I'd be interested in understudying the lead, which was then being played by Mark Wynter. If I was, they promised to up my salary by fifty per cent. I agreed, but that wasn't why. It was for the chance of Mark Wynter being struck down by some mystery virus and, therefore, my chance to play the lead in a West End play. Everything was agreed, the contracts were signed, and the next thing I knew we were rehearsing at the Queen's Theatre all through that autumn.

The play centres round a regiment stationed in India during the Raj. Very disciplined they are, too, working hard and playing even harder. High jinx are often encouraged to let off steam, pig sticking being the favoured pastime. Unfortunately, one night one of these games gets out of hand and results in an accusation of rape made by one of the junior wives. The second act consists almost entirely of the resulting court martial. My character was one of the five officers on the enquiry board. We all five sat at a long table, directly facing the audience, and I was at the adjutant's right hand. I only had one line in every four hundred.

After a month or so of doing this, it became bloody difficult to stay awake. It's not that I was tired, I was just bored. Bored out of my mind. Sitting there listening to the adjutant drone on night after night was enough to drive anyone to despair. Paul Jones, who played the prosecuting officer, tried to pep things up a bit, but even he found it tough going. I'd signed up for a year, and though it was steady work, the idea of eleven more months of this . . . Something had to be done. I'd become good friends with the actor sitting on the adjutant's left, Michael

Fleming; he had a wicked sense of humour. A notepad and pencil were always placed in front of each of us to make notes during the trial. To keep ourselves amused, Michael and I passed notes behind the adjutant's back. I would appear to have had a brainwave and write furiously on my pad. In fact, I'd be writing something along the lines of 'What are you doing after the show? Fancy a pint at the Old Vic?' I'd surreptitiously tear off the page and roll it up into my left hand, which I then very gently let drop to my side. Michael spied this manoeuvre and would drop his right hand to his side. The exchange took place behind the adjutant's back, unseen by the audience. Michael would read the note and reply, 'Pint sounds good. Fancy a fuck?' This kept us amused for some time.

For some bizarre reason, a television commercial at that time for Bournvita chocolate had cast an actor who looked like Richard III doing a very good imitation of Laurence Olivier: 'This chocolate is so dark, it's almost wick-ed. Methinks I liiike it.' It became a catchphrase around the dressing room, so much so that I went out and bought a mini-bar of Bournvita chocolate with one purpose in mind. During the show, I pretended to write something on my pad. Hand went down to the normal delivery position. Michael's hand came out for the drop. He smiled, he liiiked it. He then proceeded to eat it, which practically spiralled me out of control. The following night he had a little something for me. The drop was made. It was a two-and-a-half-pound bar of Cadbury's chocolate.

How he'd got it on stage I've no idea, but it was going to be a bugger to get it off. I sat there terrified. If you're wearing mess kit there aren't a lot of places to hide a bloody great bar of chocolate. He must have set it on stage before the second act started – the bastard. I managed to wriggle it slowly under my extremely tight waistcoat. It started to melt and I could feel the chocolate running into my balls. Chocolate balls, I thought; I'll never live that down. The rest of the cast were pissing themselves. Something serious had to be done.

Between the matinee and the evening show that Saturday, I sauntered into Fortnum & Mason. 'Do you have any large sausages?' I enquired.

'Indeed we have, sir, a very special saveloy. Would that be what sir is looking for?'

Bugger me, it was huge. 'It would be exactly what sir is looking for.'

Next stop the chemist next to the stage door. 'Um, a packet of three, please.'

In the corner of my dressing room I surgically eased the saveloy safely into a condom. This felt good. I slipped my jacket on and slid the sausage up my sleeve. By now I had told everyone in the cast what I intended to do. The trial was well under way and the Saturday night audience were hanging on every word. It was a full house and the adjutant was giving it plenty. I glanced at Michael. He knew I had something important for him. My hand went down into the pass-over position and my outrageous banger slipped dutifully down my sleeve and nestled sweetly in my hand. Michael reached over. I didn't bother to watch his face. He took possession, but immediately passed it back. I heard a sudden intake of breath. He was desperately trying to hold on to some sort of sanity. I glanced over: tears were streaming down his face, he was like a kettle waiting to go off. Suddenly, all hell let loose and he burst into an outrageous cackle of laughter. The rest of the cast immediately followed suit, except for Paul Jones and the adjutant, neither of whom had the slightest idea of what was going on.

'I do not find this case amusing' was the only thing poor Paul could think of. In fact, it was the worst thing he could have said, we all of us erupted. It stopped the show. When the scene finally ended I still had the stupendous saveloy in my hand. Christ, I thought, I'd better get rid of this! I tossed it high, right up into the roof of the theatre, waited and ... nothing. It stayed up there – to this day, I imagine. I ran from the theatre that night like a blue-arsed fly, but it wasn't all over. Monday morning I got a call from the company manager: 'Donald Albery will see you in his office at eleven thirty.' Oh my God, I knew what it would be about.

I was shown into his rooms. He sat at a desk raised a foot above the rest of the room like some sort of a throne.

'I understand from my company manager that you managed to stop the show in the second act on Saturday night in front of a full house. Is this true?'

Now, when I'm put in a position when I should be utterly terrified, a very bizarre thing happens to me. I find it the funniest thing that could possibly happen. 'Yes, it's absolutely true,' I said, bursting into uncontrollable laughter.

I was put on probation for the next two months.

'If I hear so much as another squeak out of you, I'll make it my business to see that you never work in the West End again.'

I turned and opened the door to leave, tears of laughter still pouring down my face.

When I told Michael, he shook me by the hand. 'What a result!' he said.

'Does this mean we'd better behave?' I asked.

'Well, probably best to, at least until after Christmas.'

On Christmas Eve, Michael produced a fully decorated miniature Christmas tree from under his mess waistcoat and placed it by the notepad in front of him. It was the first sign of misconduct since the night of the long saveloy.

Behaving well can really get on a bloke's tits. I was always wary that someone in the company would do a wind-up on me, so one night when I was told there was someone called Adrian at the stage door to meet me, I didn't believe a word of it. But Adrian turned out to be Adrienne, a really pretty girl who'd come to see the play on her own, just for the experience, and it wasn't a wind-up. 'It's the first time I've ever seen a drama,' she told me, standing at the stage door in her high-heeled, thigh-length boots, 'and I really loved it. I've always wanted to be an actress myself.' It was the perfect opportunity to invite a girl out for a drink and a serious chat about how to get on in theatre. She duly obliged, and we ended up having a quiet drink in a little bar in Soho. She was a hat-check girl in a Vidal Sassoon hairdressing salon. Perfect, I thought. I also thought it was about time to show her how big my bed was.

'Lovely boots you're wearing,' I said as she slipped out of her bra and knickers.

Next thing, I saw her getting into bed wearing them.

'What's that all about?' I asked.

'Oh, I thought you said keep your boots on.' And that's exactly what she did.

The leading actress in *Conduct Unbecoming* was Maxine Audley. To be honest, I'd never heard of her when I joined the company, but Mum and Dad knew all about her. She was a grande dame of her time and a fantastic actress. Slightly over the top in manner, both on and off the stage, she was dark, voluptuous and magnificently sultry. The sort of woman who could have anything she wanted at the snap of her perfectly manicured fingers. At one stage, that turned out to be me. Snap. I was in her dressing room between shows on a Wednesday afternoon doing whatever she asked me to, and I mean anything and everything. Quite a learning curve, one could say. This went on for some time, always on a Wednesday, and sometimes on a Saturday as well. One spring afternoon I sauntered into her dressing room, still in my officer's kit, only to find a similarly clad new member of the cast rehearsing what I had perfected over the last few months. My time was up. She blew me a kiss and I slid away. Snap. Actually, I was rather relieved. Her demands were more exhausting than I'd realised. I needed a rest, both from her and from the play, and soon enough the play came to the end of its run and my unbecoming conduct was over, and there I was, back in Brunswick Gardens listening to Paul and P. G. Wodehouse.

Chapter 7

Anything but Acting

In 1973, I had a tremendous urge. I didn't need to see a doctor, I needed to see a travel agent. I desperately wanted to go to Los Angeles. The only stumbling block was that I had absolutely no money at all. I had the odd bit of work, but I wasn't exactly saving. I had to rack my brains as to how to raise the money. I'd worked out that the trip would cost around two hundred and fifty quid – that's airfares and motel with a tiny bit left for eating (not high on my agenda). Unusually, I had a flash of inspiration. My grandfather, God bless him, had pots of money and, having retired as a high-court judge a few years earlier, was kicking his heels a bit.

Several months before this I'd filmed a TV special for Lew Grade at ATV. Richard Widmark played Benjamin Franklin and it was directed by a very nice American guy who took quite a shine to me. He kept telling me that going to LA would 'work out just great for you'. 'Why not?' I thought. LA – God it even sounded cool.

So here I was, thinking of tapping into Grandpa's coffers. But he was known in family circles to be as tight as a camel's arse in a sandstorm. I rang his house and spoke to Nanny Harwood, his housekeeper, who'd been part-time nanny to Phil and me. She was tough as old boots and had often made me sit on the potty until I produced something – anything; I'd sometimes sat there till lunchtime. Anyway, she was pleased to see me a week later when she came into Grandpa's study, bringing a tea tray heaving with sandwiches and cakes.

I hadn't been there for years. It was like a film set: books, paintings, ceiling a rusty yellow, rather like a pub, and I could see why. He had a fag burning in the ashtray on a side table, a cigar on its last legs propped up in a teacup and, as he greeted me, he lit a pipe. Not bad for a chap who lived to ninety-four. I perched rather nervously on the edge of a lumpy sofa. He said nothing, just got up and walked over to his desk in a cloud of smoke. A lot of scrabbling about went on.

'How much do you want?' he said.

How the fuck did he know? 'Er, well, how does five hundred quid sound?' I said. I don't know why, but my brain, with an instinctive understanding of sharp business practice, doubled the amount I needed without even consulting me.

Silence.

Another huge cloud of smoke later he handed me a cheque for five hundred pounds.

'What's it for?' he said.

'I want to go to LA,' I replied.

'Bloody good idea' was the response. He banged on and on about how America was the place to be if you wanted to be in

Grandpa – wearing the uniform that he wore
to sentence Ruth Ellis to death in 1955

Mum and Dad soon after they were married

The clan in the early sixties: Dad, Auntie B, Uncle Jo, Auntie B Two, Grandpa, Mum,
Uncle Tony, Auntie Liz, Uncle David

Second Lieutenant Havers at the end of the war. Three times the ship he was serving on was torpedoed, three times he survived

My father in his first year at Corpus Christi College, Cambridge – this is the photo he used to hand out to his girlfriends; he liked to think he bore more than a passing resemblance to Leslie Howard

My father, his Scotch and the sofa protecting me from the terrors of the first episode of *Dr Who*

Two young Haverses: me and my brother in our innocent youth

Monkeying around in Gibraltar, 1958

Wedding Day: me, Mum, Caro and Di – my mother-in-law

Me in my MG, my pride and joy

Helloooo… desperately earnest young man for hire. My first Spotlight photo

Man on a horse. During filming of *A Horseman Riding By* in Devon, 1978

Dame Judi the lesbian truck driver... One of my favourite theatrical wind-ups

The Importance of Flirting with Lady Bracknell... Playing Algy, 1982

A thespian moment: with Caro, Simon Williams and his first wife, and Anthony Andrews

Four little maids from school… after having seen a production of *The Mikado*. (From left to right: Ben Cross, Daniel Gerroll, me, Nicholas Farrell)

All those months of training finally paid off

With Alice Krige. That dressing-gown was specially made for me by Turnbull and Asser – I still have it

The iconic picture of the film

Cast and crew photograph taken by Terry Donovan (also includes several members of the Royal Ballet Company who unexpectedly came to keep us company). No sign of Ben who'd gone for a run; Peter Egan takes centre stage; harder to spot – Ruby Wax, Nicholas Farrell and Ian Charleson

At the premiere – where I congratulated Her Majesty on one of her horses having a win that day

Caro and Kate, aged seven

the movies, about how every young actor should poke their nose around and how I should grab the chance if I wanted to learn anything about the industry. Everything he said to me that afternoon has in some way or another become true – he always was a canny old bugger. I was, of course, on cloud nine by this time, and I just wanted to get the hell out of there before he changed his mind. As I reached the door, having thanked him a million times, I heard, 'You'll have to pay me back, of course.' Sod it, that wasn't part of the deal at all.

'Absolutely,' I winced.

'How about a pound a week?' he said. 'And I suggest you keep a diary. I need to know everything that happens to you over there.'

By this stage I would have agreed to public castration in Harrods Food Hall. I was at the travel agent's within the hour and on my way before you could say 'Sunset Boulevard'. The funny thing was, when he died a few years later, his will said, 'Nigel needn't pay back the remaining sum of two hundred and eighty-five pounds from private loan.'

'Loan? *Loan?*' my father barked at me some days later. 'How in God's name did you manage that?' Apparently, he'd been trying for years to squeeze a few bob out of the old man.

'Maybe,' I said, 'you just didn't have enough charm.'

That went down well.

I didn't realise how far it was. A lot further than the farthest place I'd ever been to – which was probably St Tropez. It seemed to take for ever, but I'd never been in a jumbo jet so the whole thing was an extraordinary experience. I must have had balls of steel because I didn't even reserve somewhere to stay. I got myself into a motel on Sunset Strip, about the seediest place one could possibly end up, like something out of *Psycho*. I had two contacts in LA, the first of whom was 'The Director' from Lew Grade who had taken a shine to me. He was amazed and delighted I was in town and invited me to lunch 'today'.

Now, I'm jet-lagged and utterly open-mouthed about this place, but I'm off to the Brown Derby to have lunch with this fabulous director. The Brown Derby had been the place to lunch since Fred and Ginger tapped into the entrance lobby and the King was still alive. It was all dark panelling and faux masters – desperately trying to be the Garrick Club and completely failing. I knew, because at the time I was the Garrick's youngest member. (Dad proposed me and my grandfather, Sir Cecil Havers, seconded me – no, that's a lie, Kenneth More did.)

Anyway, there I was, munching away on soft-shell crab and sipping a deliciously cold chardonnay when I thought I felt a hand on my thigh. Christ! Who in the hell was this? It was our 'Director'. It had never crossed my mind that he might be a shirt-lifter – I suppose in America there's a different set of rules, different lighthouse signals. Would I like to come back to his 'fabulous' place and see how Californians live? Not bloody likely, I thought, or rather, 'How absolutely fabulous of you to ask, but I've got a very important audition this afternoon.' Well, would I like to have lunch with him on Sunday at the Farmers Market, an absolute must if you're in LA? I didn't know how to deal with that one. I've never been any good at saying no, so I found myself agreeing to meet at the north entrance on Sunday. It turned out to be a great day – he never had a go again and showed me some fabulous sights, including watching them make cashew butter – it seems silly now, but I was amazed and bought bloody jars of the stuff. Ugh!

The next day, I was off to Santa Barbara to stay the night

with my second LA contact, my friend – new best friend – Brad Dillman. I worshipped this guy, a sort of movie star in so much as I had seen him in a couple of films. I'd just worked with him at Elstree in a really awful low-grade TV film and he was married to Susie Parker – *Susie Parker*. My mother was so excited. I'd never heard of her, but apparently in the not-too-distant past she had been a really beautiful model. This alone was worth the trip.

Santa Barbara is a really pretty place about three hours' drive north of LA along the Pacific Coast Highway. Everything about that smacks of cool. So I'm in the rental car (not cool), but the shades were on and the Eagles blaring – I'm doing great. They lived in a spectacular house: it reeked of pots of money. Maybe LA is the place to be after all? And Susie – darling Susie – she was pretty in a mumsy way. About six-thirty they announced dinner would be served. Dinner? I'd just sunk a couple of dry martinis and was gearing up for the impossible third. Dinner? That's LA.

'What's your golf like?' inquired Brad.

'Absolutely extraordinary,' I slurred.

'What do you play off?'

This got me. 'Erm, oh eight – ish.' Big mistake. Never – and I mean never – pretend you're better at golf than you are. Eighteen would have been a lie, twenty-six more like it. It was so embarrassing the next day at his 'little local' golf course, the most stunning course I had ever played. The clubhouse was at the end of a long driveway and every fairway, every green, had that just-cut look. As we swung into the members' carpark in Brad's convertible Corniche, I noticed a rather dashing couple on their way to the first tee. They were wearing his and hers designer golf outfits, hanging out of their snappy electric golf cart. These guys don't have trolleys, they have the Ferrari of the fairway. I was hacking about in bushes, spluttering, 'I don't know what's going on – this has never happened to me before.' Brad looked on open-mouthed. 'You have played this game before?' he said after I managed to drive the ball off the tee, hit the ladies' marker box and land twenty yards behind us. 'I won the junior competition at Royal Worlington,' I lied.

It was the longest eighteen holes in the history of golf. I longed for the last one, finally putting in for at least twenty-six over par in near-darkness.

Back in LA, I was 'hooked' up to an agent – Brad's agent. Huge office. Many, many people working away. At what? I wondered as I was frogmarched past row upon row of people on the phone. Sitting opposite 'the front man' I was spellbound by an open-necked white shirt, dazzlingly white teeth and a deep-brown hairy chest sporting a Navajo Indian medallion.

'Oh my God, he's perfect for this role. Nancy, Jake, get your asses in here and take a look at this boy.'

'Oh my God,' they all say in unison, 'you're perfect for this role.'

What role? What the hell are they talking about? There they all were, mincing about in the front man's office and I was about to land the best role in movie history.

Except for one thing: I never heard from them again.

It's directors, producers and agents who lie for a living, not us poor truthful actors, and the Americans are the world champions. Alan Parker rather cheekily once said of David Puttnam, '"Hello," he lied.' I think he was just summing up the business, but it was a bit rich coming from a director.

* * *

My time was up and I reluctantly flew east. Home. Before I left, though, I did manage to take myself to one of the most famous bars in town, the Polo Lounge at the Bel Air Hotel. One drink cost as much as dinner – very LA, very me, I thought. And there I found my first star. I spotted Orson Welles, an enormously big man in every sense, and while I was having a pee on the way out there he was again, having a pee next to me. At least there was a story to take to Grandpa! I couldn't have made that up.

Soon my time with Prospect, sharing the stage with the great and the good, became a rather distant memory. I knew things were bound to change and change they did, with a vengeance. There was no work around, so I had to look somewhere else to earn a penny and pay the rent. Thank God for Denis Haynes. The father of one of my friends, Denis was a wine merchant, one of the few professions that can always do with an extra pair of untrained hands, and he was quite happy to throw me into the cellar of one of his shops, André Simon Wines in Davies Street, smack in the heart of the West End of London. It wasn't a bad job, primarily because I had access to something I hold in high esteem: decent red wine . . . and white wine, champagne and various liqueurs. I started off stacking wine in the cellar, but after a week or two, drifted up into the shop itself and started selling direct to the customers.

I thought I'd only be there for a few weeks, so six months later it was a bit of a shock when Denis asked me whether I'd like to go on a wine course. He was an extremely decent chap and decided that whoever worked for him needed to have a pretty good knowledge of the product they were trying to sell. I think he thought I was becoming more permanent than I actually wanted to, but hey, I was keen to learn about wine, so off I went. It was probably the best education I've ever had – the most useful and certainly the most expensive. Give your taste buds that sort of make-over and you'll understand what I mean. However, despite enjoying the research, the job was only meant to be a stop-gap, so when autumn became Christmas, and Christmas became spring, I was distinctly unamused at the prospect of spending the summer wrapping bottles. I was bored and frustrated.

That explains why one afternoon I was glancing through the classified section of *Private Eye*. The words 'new models needed for young female photographer – please send photo. Box Number' etc., etc. leaped off the page at me. I'll give it a try, I thought; and I whizzed off a couple of photos of me in full military regalia, fresh from my stint on jury duty in *Conduct Unbecoming*.

A week went by and I heard nothing. In fact, I'd forgotten all about it when one sunny afternoon a rather pretty girl walked into the shop.

'What is madam looking for? A bottle of bubbly, or perhaps something smoother, like a bottle of Pichon Longueville '66?'

'Neither,' she replied. 'I'm looking for someone called Nigel Havers.'

Now, I can get a bit shy on these occasions because I never know what I'm letting myself in for. Did I know the girl? Had I had a 'moment' with her? Was she pregnant? All those questions flashed through my brain in a microsecond.

'I'll just go and see if I can find him,' and I scuttled out to the back office. A few moments to collect my thoughts and I decided she was a complete stranger, so I re-emerged confidently as Nigel Havers. This must have confused her.

'Do you have a twin?' she said.

'Not as far as I know. Now, how can I help you?'

'That's weird . . . Anyway, I've come about the advertisement. You sent me your photograph. My name is Tuppy Owens, my studio is in Hays Mews, just around the corner, and I'd like you to come and do some photographic work with me tomorrow afternoon. I'll offer you a fee of fifty pounds – how does that sound?'

'That sounds very nice indeed. Thank you very much,' I said. 'I'll be there as soon as I close the shop – five thirty-ish. Is that OK?'

The following afternoon, I stood naked in her studio. I'd had a shower to remove the cellar dust, and there I stood, stark bollock naked, in front of a girl I'd only met the previous day – pretty good going, I thought. After I'd posed for a couple of rolls of film in all kinds of positions, Tuppy announced that another model would be arriving shortly.

'What sort of model?' I asked.

'Don't worry,' Tuppy said, 'she's very pretty, and you're going to get on fine.'

Everything was looking up. 'What do you want us to do?'

'I want you to pretend you're fucking her.'

'Oh, OK,' I said, as if I was asked to do that every day. And that's how I spent the rest of the evening, pretending to fuck this pretty girl, whose name I never caught. We didn't say much to each other, either: she spoke no English at all and my Croatian wasn't up to much. I have to say with my hand on my heart that it was the most enjoyable fifty pounds I've ever earned. Many years later, walking down Forty-second Street in New York, I saw a huge billboard: 'Behind the Green Baize Door. Triple XXX. Directed by Tuppy Owens.' Damn it, I thought, another glittering career that slipped through my fingers. If only ... No, get a grip.

Tuppy seemed quite pleased with my first effort. 'Why don't you come back and do some more?'

I would have done, but for the fact that I'd become very attached to my new girlfriend, Carolyn. She'd suggested that we move in together, as we'd found a little studio flat off the King's Road in Beaufort Street. Nude modelling and new live-in girlfriend didn't have quite the right ring to it, so Tuppy got the elbow and Caro got a new flatmate.

I'd never lived with a girl before, and it had all happened quite quickly. I'd gone to Cambridge a few weeks before to see Clive Wiseman, who had been the company manager on *Richard II*, my first theatre work. He had a new production on at the Arts Theatre and I jumped at the chance to see him again and spend a few days with Phil in his digs, reacquainting myself with one of my favourite roles, that of undergraduate manqué. I thoroughly enjoyed the play and afterwards had dinner with Clive and his girlfriend – Caro. I thought she was fabulous. Unlike any of my previous girlfriends, Caro was quite quiet. She had the longest, most beautiful legs this side of Hollywood, and sleepy eyes that were very sexy. She was also funny and warm and I was totally smitten. I managed to get her phone number – sorry, Clive – and we had dinner the next week. Bingo! We really hit it off and became inseparable pretty much from that moment.

Caro shared a flat in Sutherland Avenue with another girl and two Siamese cats, Bomb and Fanny. The cats made the move to Fulham, but we left the girl behind. Caro had a full-time job, which meant we could make the rent as I floated around in full domestic goddess mode. I cooked and cleaned,

I even hoovered and dusted – I loved it. For the first time, I was going out with someone who was a few years older than me, and it gave the relationship a certain maturity that I'd never had with anyone else. We didn't just talk about *Top of the Pops* or Carnaby Street. We also discussed politics, literature and what our aims and aspirations were. Life took on a different meaning. I admired the way she worked hard, and I found her opinions challenging. I couldn't wait for her to get back in the evening. We settled into shared domesticity and were totally happy, with just one slight cloud that refused to blow over: I still couldn't get a job.

Nipping out one day to get a pint of milk and some hoover bags I practically knocked over some poor sod walking up the front steps.

'So sorry,' I said.

'No problem, mate. Hang on, you're the actor, aren't you?'

I'd been carrying a spear and sitting at a table not saying much for the best part of two years, so, oh boy, this was a real shot in the arm, a big confidence booster.

'Yes, absolutely. Er, which play did you see? Was it *Richard II*?'

'What? Oh, no, can't stand Shakespeare. I know you're an actor because you don't do anything. You're always here, up and down these bloody stairs, never up to much. It all adds up. You must be an actor.'

'Very good, Sherlock,' I said. He chuckled and asked me if I fancied doing a bit of work for a change. 'Please. Anything,' I replied.

'OK, meet me tomorrow, six a.m., room 601, sixth floor, BBC Radio 2 in Portland Place. And don't be late,' he said as he turned and ran up the stairs.

Hallelujah, a job!

Needless to say, I didn't make it by six; it was nearer six fifteen when, just as I was about to bang on the door, the name above the room number caught my eye: Jimmy Young. Oh my God, please, no. Terry Wogan would have been OK, Ed Stewart just about, but JY . . . My grandmother adored JY. How could I possibly tell my friends? I took a deep breath and went in anyway.

The usual principles applied: head down, listen and learn. As it turned out, Charles Thompson, my friend from the front steps and the show's producer, proved to be a hell of a guy to work for. He was a trained journalist and had a keen eye for a story. Between getting him the full English breakfast and endless cups of tea before even the birds fell out of bed, I watched him pull the show together brilliantly. Charles briefed JY every morning just before it started. The programme ran from eleven thirty a.m. for two hours and was a mixture of music and chat, either with guests on the telephone or in the studio. It was all pretty lightweight stuff, but exactly what the public wanted. They loved JY and before long so did I. I thought he was the consummate broadcaster: totally professional, informative, chatty and, above all, slightly bonkers – exactly what you need to engage all ages.

After a week or two, I was allowed to swallow as much information from the morning papers as possible, and then turn the odd idiosyncratic story into a possible feature on the programme. I didn't always succeed in getting my 'find' included, but it was great fun trying.

One day, I managed to set up a telephone interview with a man from Caracas. Apparently, this chap had caught the biggest sailfish in the history of catching sailfish – it was the size of a small bungalow. I briefed JY, wrote the questions for him, got the chap on the phone all the way from South America and live on-air JY asked him the first question.

'So tell me, José, where did you catch this fish?'

'I no catch this fish. My brother-in-law friend, he catch fish.'

'How big was it?' JY asked, looking daggers at me through the studio glass.

'Ees no big. He threw it back in sea.'

Never believe anything you read in the papers.

About this time, Margaret Thatcher was elected to lead the opposition – the first female leader of any political party. Dad was shadow attorney-general at the time, having served as solicitor-general for quite a few years under Edward Heath. Between the two of us, we thought it would be a good idea to get her on the JY show – good for him, bloody good for me. At the following Monday morning production meeting I threw this little pebble into the pond.

JY was having none of it. 'I don't do politics – you all know that,' and we moved on to the next item. By the end of the meeting, though, Charles had been ruminating.

'Hang on a minute, Jim, this Maggie Thatcher idea might be rather a coup.' And within five minutes, he'd persuaded JY to have her on.

The next morning, I was dispatched to the House of Commons with twenty possible questions for her. I arrived at her office and was shown straight in – none of the usual waiting. I introduced myself, handed her the questions and sat down opposite her. She looked extraordinary: elegant, piercing eyes, and rather sexy. Sounds strange but it's true.

I waited and I waited.

She looked up. 'I will answer questions one, seven, nine, twelve, thirteen and fifteen. Thank you.'

And that was it. But we got her on the show.

She arrived that Friday and was ushered into the studio to meet JY. He melted, and there started a professional love affair which lasted twenty-five years. She was brilliant on the show, direct, quick-witted and surprisingly funny. More interestingly, JY was superb, better than I'd ever seen him. This mid-morning, kitchen-sink politics was exactly what he could excel at, and he grabbed it with both hands. It wasn't only that, though. He flirted outrageously with her, and that made for one hell of a good radio programme. At the end of the show, at the post-mortem meeting, JY grinned from ear to ear. 'Let's do that more often,' he said.

We did. In fact, the JY prog became one of the most influential platforms for politicians for the next twenty years. I'd like to take the credit for that, but I really can't. Good ideas never belong entirely to one person. Everything has to fall into place at exactly the same moment. In this case, Charles had to like the idea, he then had to persuade JY to take it on, then Maggie had to agree, and, most importantly, the show had to be a success; there are lots of ingredients in 'the making of an idea'.

The JY show was really good to me. I could come and go pretty much as I wanted or, in my case, needed. I got the occasional little acting job on telly, but worked for JY most of the time. Coming down in the lift one day from the office to the studio, something I had to do twenty times or so during the show, I found myself surrounded by actors. They were recording a new drama in a studio next to ours. For the first time in my life I thought of myself as a researcher, not as an actor, and I realised I'd been using the job as a comfort zone. It came as a horrible shock. It was time to get back to treading the boards. That afternoon, I told them I was leaving – for good.

Charles very kindly asked me whether I'd like to produce one of the shows in my final week. I jumped at the chance, and had a great time doing it. At the end of the programme, JY looked at me through the glass and did a thumbs-up to say, 'Well done.' He then removed his headphones, which were temporarily attached to his toupee. He always wore one. In fact, he had three, the first one for 'I need a haircut', the second for 'I've had a haircut' and the third for 'I don't need a haircut'. This particular day he was wearing 'I need a haircut'. It came as such a shock – the top of his head looked like a hot-cross bun, toupee tape like noughts and crosses. He didn't notice until he looked up and saw my expression of horror. He scrabbled about in panic and stuck the dead cat back on top of his head. Unfortunately, he didn't quite line it up straight. That's how I will always remember him: kind, extremely generous and looking like an animal had crawled on to his head and died.

On 25 October 1974, Caro and I got married. It was a pretty quiet affair as neither of us wanted a big fuss, but it was a really happy day with our families and close friends. At the reception afterwards, my aunt, the illustrious lawyer Dame Elizabeth Butler-Sloss – at that time head of the Family Division – arrived and apologised for being so late. 'I'm so sorry,' she said. 'I've been up to my ears in divorce all day.' I glanced at Caro, who looked a bit shell-shocked, and turned back to Auntie Liz. She had a twinkle in her eye and a big grin on her face. Caro got the joke, of course.

After a few more drinks we fell into the Honeymoon Suite at Brown's Hotel. The manager was a great friend of my mother and father so I managed to get it at a knock-down rate.

No time for a honeymoon – couldn't afford it, anyway – so it was back to work the following Monday, trying to find some impressively bizarre facts and figures for JY before I left.

In 1979, Margaret Thatcher became prime minister and JY and I felt we deserved much of the credit! Suddenly, Dad really was attorney-general. He worked round the clock and loved every minute of it. One weekend, Caro and I went home to Suffolk. There was quite a high-profile guest list – a few politicians and, most fun of all, my godfather Brian Plaice. He'd served in the navy with Dad and they were the best of friends. At times, Dad could be a bit pompous – 'Maggie this, Maggie that' – and Brian was the one chap who could take the piss.

This Friday night, Dad was on a particularly high horse about some political issue that was all over the press, and none of us agreed with him. Next morning, Brian and I decided to put the cat among the pigeons. About ten o'clock, I walked up the road to the phone box in the village and rang home. With a handkerchief over the mouthpiece I asked to speak to Sir Michael.

Eventually, he came to the phone. 'Yes?' he said. 'Who is this?'

'It's the BBC *Panorama* programme,' I said in my best received pronunciation. 'We'd very much like to come and do an interview with y—'

'I know what you want to talk to me about,' he said, interrupting. 'You'd better come along, then. What time can you make it?'

'Er, two o'clock any good?'

'Ridiculous. Right in the middle of lunch.'

'I'm so sorry, it's the only time we can do it – we're up against a deadline.'

I heard a huge sigh of exasperation. 'Oh, well, I suppose that will have to do,' and with that he put the phone down. Of course, I had to phone him back to 'find out' where he lived, and he proceeded to give me detailed instructions.

As I swung into the drawing room half an hour later, I caught Dad's eye and he said, 'Your lot are coming to interview me this afternoon.'

'My lot?'

'Well, the bloody BBC.'

It was a very hot summer's day and Dad's usual attire would have been extremely informal – linen trousers, open-necked shirt, that sort of thing. He changed out of this into a stiff collar and dark, thick suit. He sat at lunch, refusing any cocktail offered. We chatted, vaguely ignoring him. I could see his mind was elsewhere. By two fifteen, he was tapping his heels and getting into quite a lather.

'Where the hell are your lot?' he said.

'Haven't got a clue,' I replied.

About twenty past two, I sneaked up to the phone box again. 'Sorry, Sir Michael, we seem to have got lost.'

'Well, where the bloody hell are you?'

'Somewhere called Wickhambrook.'

He gave me very detailed instructions how to get home. I had to really control myself from pissing myself with laughter. I shot back without being noticed.

'This is ridiculous,' he said at three fifteen. 'The BBC couldn't even run a bath.'

By three thirty, it was time to put him out of his misery. 'Dad . . . erm, that phone call . . . it was me.'

'What the hell are you talking about?'

'All that *Panorama* stuff, it was me, Dad. I was taking the piss.'

The whole table collapsed. Dad's face remained

expressionless. He looked me right in the eye. 'Go and get me a very large whisky,' he said, and he never mentioned it again. Brian, of course, never owned up to having been part of it. I was about to include him, but one look at the dangerous glint in Dad's eye told me, 'Least said, soonest mended.'

Apart from a couple of tellys here and there, I was still skating on thin ice jobwise. I'd go up for a part, but never managed to get beyond round two of the auditions, apart from a movie called *The Go-Between*. I usually got into the last three, but somehow didn't make the cut. It's a devastating phone call when the agent tells you, 'You haven't got it.' I allow myself twenty-four hours to sulk, and then never think of it again. It's on to the next, whatever/whenever that will be.

Andrew Brudenell-Bruce introduced me to Frank Lowe, the fastest-rising advertising executive in the country. He ran a company called CDP, and they were riding higher than the rest of them put together.

'Know anything about wine?' he asked me.

'Matter of fact, I do,' I said. I knew Denis Haynes would come up trumps.

'You wouldn't mind sorting out our cellar, would you?'

'Of course not.' And I ended up in the bowels of the office in Howland Street for the best part of four months. I got paid top dollar – actually, I organised my own salary and no one seemed to mind. It was probably the best cellar in London at the time so there wasn't much hardship, not when Frank would ask me to test-drive a bottle of Latour '66. 'Drinking now,' I'd say, and drink it they did. Frank was endlessly kind and generous to me, even offered me a job as an advertising executive, but, just before it became too tempting, I got a fantastic job and I had to go and tell Frank that I was leaving.

'You can't be,' he said. 'We need you here. Anyway, what job is this?'

'It's *Nicholas Nickleby*.'

'And what part do they want you to play?' he asked.

'Well, um, Nicholas Nickleby.'

'Christ, you'd better do it.'

Wackford Squeers, you'd better watch out.

Chapter 8

A Play or Two

One question I'm often asked is: 'Which do you prefer, theatre or television?' I answer: 'When I'm doing television, I wish I was in a play. When I'm in a play, I wish I was doing television.' Funnily enough, that's the truth. Well, half a truth. I never really had the choice. You see, I'm what John Hurt describes as a 'letterbox actor'. That is to say, I sit at home waiting for a script to come through the letterbox. I pick it up, I read it, and nine times out of ten I do it – whatever it is, television or theatre.

One sultry morning in 1977, my letterbox was in full swing. I weighed the envelope. This could be the big one. I ripped it open. *Man and Superman*. Jesus! This sounds good. Hang on a minute, it's by George Bernard Shaw. That didn't have the Hollywood ring about it I secretly craved. On closer inspection, the part I was being offered wasn't going to save the planet. Octavius Robinson is 'an uncommonly nice-looking young fellow. He must, one thinks, be the jeune premier; for it is not within reason to suppose that a second such attractive male figure should appear in one story.' That's how Shaw described the chap and I wasn't going to argue.

The Royal Shakespeare Company had been invited to open the very first Malvern Festival, the brainchild of Sir Ian Hunter (he became known as Mr Festival, having already created the Edinburgh and Bath festivals, among others). It consists of a series of artistic events held annually, and the works of prestigious musicians, poets, writers and film-makers are performed in various locations throughout the glorious Malvern Hills.

The undoubted highlight of that first year was to be the presence of Yehudi Menuhin. Ian was also a renowned manager, and had managed Menuhin for many years, so the great man would be there to perform during our short tour. Reason enough by itself to take the part, I thought, but another huge plus was the fabulous cast for our play: Richard Pasco, Susan Hampshire and Nicky Henson, for a kick-off.

The more I read about the play, the more I realised that it was really quite something, so I did what I always do when confronted by the classics. I put on a tie and went to the Garrick Club. I climbed the stairs to the top of the building, to the library. It contains manuscripts and reviews going back to the time of Garrick himself, and it is an invaluable way of gaining a feel for the play and, more importantly, one's own character. In my experience, there is always one character in every play who steals the attention and hogs the reviews, and sometimes it's a character who is on stage for precisely five minutes. Flipping the coin, there are some characters who get totally ignored or generally cop a stinker. After a bit of research, it was obvious that my part was stinker material. That stood out a mile, and didn't do much for my confidence. Nevertheless, I went off to rehearsal determined to try to reverse the process.

The play was being produced by Eddie Kulukundis. Eddie is one of the most charming and generous men I have ever met. He went on to marry the star of our show, Susan Hampshire, and is now considered to be part of the backbone of British theatre. Eddie's way of working was basically to have a few parties. So we'd have a party before rehearsals began, a party once rehearsals had finished, an opening-night party, a party after the first week and a party to celebrate the first month, and that was just for starters.

We were to be directed by Clifford Williams who was a noted authority on Shaw, so the four-week rehearsal period was a wonderful learning curve spent with a real master. 'Doing Shaw' is a bit like 'doing Shakespeare' in so much as they both require an enormous amount of discipline. Actors can't do it in a colloquial manner; it just doesn't work. We're not doing *EastEnders* or *Coronation Street* – that requires a different kind of skill. In the opening scene, Octavius has this to say: 'Well, Anne has a most exquisite nature, but she is so accustomed to be in the thick of that sort of thing that she thinks a man's character incomplete if he is not ambitious, and she knows if she married me she would have to reason herself out of being ashamed of me for not being a big success of some kind.' Quite a sentence. It requires the actor to do two things. First of all, you have to make sense of it and drive the thought to the end of the sentence. Secondly, you have to fill your lungs with air in order to get through the bloody thing. You can, of course, take tiny top-ups now and again, short intakes of breath which no one notices. But, by and large, breathing is what it's all about.

Octavius is on stage pretty much the whole time, so I had

my work cut out, especially as I had not a single funny line – as I said, a real stinker. I spent a lot of time providing a feed for Nicky Henson, who played the chauffeur, plenty of listening to Alan Pasco's Tanner, and just the occasional relief when I flirted with Susan Hampshire. Nicky kept saying, 'You're going to be great in this; you'll knock 'em dead.' Knock 'em dead? What was he talking about? Put 'em to sleep more like.

We rehearsed mainly in London, arriving in Malvern in time for the technical rehearsals. Those are when all the elements that make up the production are fitted together for the first time – the stage set, the props, the lighting, the sound, etc. For a play, this normally takes about two days. For a musical, it's nearer two weeks.

One day during a break, I wandered out into the garden to have a fag. The Malvern Theatre is built right next to the Winter Gardens, a fine Edwardian concert hall, and they both back on to beautiful gardens and rolling lawns. I stretched out on the grass and lit up.

All of a sudden I froze. A solo violin was playing in the concert hall, the windows wide open, the sound floating towards me. Elgar, as English as fish and chips, mustard and cress, and a lot better for you. I leaped up and walked towards an open window. There was Yehudi Menuhin, rehearsing on his own. I perched on the ledge, as the sun started to go down, listening to the greatest violinist the world has ever known coaxing notes of such beauty out of his little wooden instrument, knowing that I would remember the moment for ever – my own personal concert as I gazed up at the hills where Elgar had found such inspiration many years before.

The opening night came, and because of the importance of the occasion, not to mention the weight of the RSC, we were reviewed by all the national newspapers. It will come as no surprise to learn that the chauffeur stole it. I got no mention at all. My plus-fours were ridiculed in passing, but other than that, zip. Susan Hampshire 'doesn't read reviews'. Apparently, Judi Dench doesn't, either. Actually, I have it on very good authority that Judi really doesn't – hell, she doesn't even read the play she's offered, or the film script that lands on her desk. She doesn't need to, she can do anything. I, on the other hand, do anything without knowing if I can, and read the reviews. That means I'm a bloody fool. Anyway, you only remember the bad reviews, never the good, and I've had my share of both.

In those days, you signed up for what was known as 'the run of the play', which could be anything up to two years – not like now, when a three-month stint is more the norm. After Malvern, we went to Brighton and Bath before settling into the Savoy Theatre, London, where we played for a year. It was a fabulous time for me. Not only did I have a secure and incredibly fulfilling night job, but Caro had discovered that she was pregnant, and it was wonderful to be able to spend some time at home in our house in Applegarth Road, Brook Green. I loved the fact that we now had a bit of cash to spend on preparing for the baby's arrival. We both pottered around 'nesting' contentedly by day, and *Man and Superman* continued to play to packed houses by night.

Our daughter, Kate, arrived with perfect timing, between the matinee and the evening show on 13 August 1977. We named her after Katherine Hepburn, an actress we both admired tremendously, in the hope that she would grow up to be beautiful and feisty like her namesake. She hasn't disappointed on either count! I used to do my share of the feeds, including the early-morning one, to give Caro a bit of a breather. I loved that quiet, intimate moment with my new daughter, and I became an expert on the early-morning comings and goings on Brook Green – and I'm not just talking about the milkman.

It's a fact that the longer one stays in a play, the harder it becomes to remember the lines. Simon Callow was once at the National Theatre in a play directed by John Dexter. It had been running for some time when John decided to check up on things. As the lights went down, Simon strode confidently centre stage. Nothing happened. He'd forgotten the first line of the play. In fact, he'd forgotten where he was; it could have been Christmas for all he knew. Eventually, he got a prompt. When the interval came, John rushed backstage to issue the appropriate bollocking, and Simon's response was: 'OK, but how long do I have to remember it for?'

The other hazard is being unable to go on, for whatever reason, and letting the understudy do it for you. It's their chance to prove that the director has missed an opportunity and every actor's worst fear is that his understudy will do a much better job – part of the actor's insecurity, I suppose. The only time I had to phone in sick was when I lost my voice.

My mate Andrew Brudenell-Bruce had decided to pursue a career in the wine business, and I was doing whatever I could to help him set up a company. The first coup was going to an auction where Andrew bought thirty cases of Château Latour 1966. He had to ring the bank from the auction room to secure an overdraft, made possible by the fact that Andrew already had a buyer, none other than Frank Lowe.

Spurred on by this success, he discovered a fabulous private cellar for sale in the basement of a house in Regent's Park. The old boy had died, and when his children searched the house they found this little goldmine. Not that they knew how much gold it was. Andrew lost no time in buying up the lot. He asked me to help him clear it on a freezing cold morning in mid-November. After a few hours of humping cases up from the cellar to the pavement, I could feel the tell-tale soreness in the back of my throat, but chose to ignore it, mainly because we had attracted the interest of an elderly chap who was wandering past wearing a hat and a canary-yellow scarf. It was Ralph Richardson, one of my favourite actors of all time. Andrew and I introduced ourselves and he was utterly charming. We chatted about this and that, and he kindly appeared to be most interested in the play. 'Jolly good writer, that Shaw chap, but he does go on a bit.' He was on his way to a pet shop in Marylebone High Street. 'I'm going to buy some seeds for José.'

'Anyone we should know?' I enquired.

He told me he'd just come back from filming in South America. While there, he'd fallen in love with a parrot in the market one Saturday and decided to buy him and bring him back to England. On leaving the country, Immigration grabbed him and the parrot. 'Where are the parrot papers?' Ralph had to fill in a huge form. He handed it back. 'What is the parrot's name?' they snapped. 'This parrot has no name,' Ralph replied. 'With no name, he no leave the country.' Ralph filled in the form again. 'I name this parrot José Parrot,' and with that José was allowed to leave and now resided very comfortably in a Nash house in Regent's Park.

At this point, I noticed that Ralph was carrying a large book under his right arm. 'What's with the Spanish dictionary?' I asked.

'José doesn't speak a lot of English, so I thought I'd learn to speak a bit of Spanish.'

Andrew offered him a bottle of Château Petrus, which he was justifiably thrilled with, and he wandered off into the mists of Marylebone, a heavy tome under one arm and a priceless bottle under the other.

By the time I got to the theatre, I sounded as if I had been given a whiff of laughing gas. I did the show, but my Popeye-like tones caused a bit of hilarity in the stalls and on the stage. By the end, I was totally silent but for a rather pathetic wheeze. The following morning, I was sent to Dr Punt – that really was his name – a famous Harley Street ENT specialist.

'Stick your tongue out,' he said. He grabbed it with both hands and stuck his head down my throat. 'Laryngitis,' he said. 'Bend over and take your pants down.' He stuck a horse syringe full of penicillin into my backside.

I couldn't sit down. For a very long time. But I only missed the one night – no understudy was getting his hands on my part, stinker or not.

Susan and I had a very difficult scene towards the end of the play which we always struggled with.

ANNE (throwing up her hands): Oh, Tavy, Tavy, Ricky Ticky Tavy [that's me!], Heaven help the woman who marries you!

OCTAVIUS (his passion reviving at the name): Oh why, why, why do you say that? Don't torment me, I don't understand.

ANNE: Suppose she were to tell fibs and lay snares for men?

OCTAVIUS: Do you think I could marry such a woman – I who have known and loved you?

ANNE: Hm! Well, at all events she wouldn't let you if she were wise. So that's settled. And now I can't talk any more. Say you forgive me, and that the subject is closed.

OCTAVIUS: I have nothing to forgive; and the subject is closed.
And if the wound is open, at least you shall never see it
bleed.

ANNE: Poetic to the last, Tavy. Goodbye dear. (She pats his
cheek; has an impulse to kiss him, and then another impulse
of distaste which prevents her; finally runs away through the
garden into the villa.)

See what I mean?

I knew that Martin Jarvis had played Octavius several years
before, so, despite the fact that I didn't know him, I decided
to give him a ring for some advice. Susan had worked with him
before and knew him.

'I know exactly what you're going to ask me,' he said. He
was very polite and charming, but said he couldn't help much
as he hadn't been able to make it work, either. It seems to me
that nobody ever has done.

What was obvious about the scene was that it required
both actors to engage in what I can only describe as a mental
dance round each other. It was like walking on ice, and required
the lightest of touches; otherwise you crashed through the ice
and murdered the moment. In any acting, the vital thing is
to listen acutely, in order to make the responses real, and by
the end of our run, Susan and I felt we had done as well as
we could with our scene, and had enjoyed the nightly challenge
of getting it right.

Finally, we came to the end of the run – or rather we came
to the end of the audience, but for most of that year we had
done pretty good business. Our last Saturday turned out to be
Richard Pasco's birthday, so the rest of us decided to send him
a strippergram. It was a thoroughly inappropriate gesture, as he

was very strait-laced in a rather endearing and old-fashioned way. It made us all laugh wildly and meant that we finished the run on a wave of high spirits – and, of course, another of Eddie's parties. I was sad to say goodbye to the Savoy – it's a funny old theatre, rather out on a limb compared to the rest of theatre land and part of a hotel to boot, but it's a beautiful Art Deco building and I had grown extremely attached to my 'second home', despite the very uncomfortable backstage conditions and a hellishly cramped dressing room.

Acting at the National Theatre is not something one can plan. It's considered a sort of earning-one's-spurs moment, and you always dream of the day when they put in the call, so when it actually happened, I practically fainted.

Peter Hall was on the line asking if I would be interested in playing Algernon in his upcoming production of *The Importance of Being Earnest*. Is the Pope a Catholic? Am I an actor? Luckily for me, I happened to have the right sort of look, be the right age and be in the right place at very much the right time. What made the whole thing absolutely perfect was that Judi Dench was to play Lady Bracknell. In fact, the entire cast was made in heaven: Zoë Wanamaker, Anna Massey and Paul Rogers, with Martin Jarvis playing Earnest. I was excited and terrified all at the same time, and not only that but we were in repertoire, alternating *The Importance* with another play, Harold Pinter's *Other Places*, for the full season, which meant at least a year. Although I knew *The Importance* would be well up and running by the time I had to tackle my lines for the Pinter, I had a quick glance at my part in it anyway and saw that at one stage I had a sort of monologue which went on for over twenty pages. I had absolutely no idea how I was going to keep my head above water, not forgetting the fact that we had a noisy toddler at home whose idea of fun was to bellow at full throttle around three in the morning, in an effort to rouse her comatose parents for a spot of hide and seek and a very long story.

I decided to bury my head in the sand, and concentrate on one thing at a time. Looking back to the first day of rehearsals, I remember being slightly anxious, but not the gibbering wreck that I'd be today – the confidence of youth, I suppose. Peter Hall introduced us all at the read-through, where there must have been over fifty people about to listen to my first stumbling effort. Read-throughs are almost as terrifying as first nights. To begin with, you don't really know anybody, so all the actors are sniffing around each other, and I always feel I have to give a complete performance to justify being cast in the first place. Added to that, the entire crew turns up; that is to say, all the make-up, costume, administration departments – you name it, they turn up. It's as if they really want to wind you up. The National Theatre has about three times more than anybody else in those departments, so it's safe to say that that first read-through was an extremely personal affair between me and my underpants.

Judi was instinctively brilliant, and seemed to have nailed the absolute essence of Lady B at the outset. I gathered later that in fact she had terrible trouble getting a feel for her, especially as she was so much younger (being at that time only forty-eight) than the previous famous portrayals, but when you think about it, Lady Bracknell has a young daughter, so Judi was probably just about spot on.

After the read-through we were shown a model of the Act I set, designed by John Bury. As we gazed at it, I could hear Judi hissing through her teeth – she wasn't enjoying what she was seeing. Neither was I. Algernon's apartment in Albany looked faintly ludicrous: odd sofas and chairs and, to cap it all, a dark-blue Perspex floor. Perspex? 'Very Edwardian,' I muttered to Judi. John Bury elaborately removed the model's back walls to reveal tiny potted plants. 'This is for Act Two, the garden scene.'

'And will the blue Perspex work as a lawn?' enquired Judi.

'Oh, don't worry,' John replied, 'the floor will turn green to signify that you are outside.'

It never did, and it was an absolute death-trap. Every night the unwary could hurtle down the shining Perspex at high speed, and end up in someone's lap in row H of the stalls.

'Another fabulous production buggered by the set,' Judi summarised succinctly.

Oscar Wilde is notoriously difficult to get right – even worse than old GBS. In fact, Peter offered a case of champagne to anyone who managed to deliver a word-perfect performance. Many came close, but it was never won. In the middle of rehearsals, Peter went off to direct some Wagner at Bayreuth, so Judi decided to go on holiday for a couple of weeks. This was rather unexpected, but looking back I think it would be a good plan to implement today. Rehearsals are a very intense period. Everyone is trying to get the play on its feet, and you can only do that if you have the text under your belt. For some reason, having a gap in the middle of a rehearsal period makes the learning process much easier.

Judi came back full of beans and with what appeared to be a renewed understanding of her character. The rest of us weren't allowed to take any time off, and just trudged on, which meant that instead of my normal anxiety as the opening night approached, I was fed up with the wait and couldn't have been keener to get going for real. We previewed at a friends' matinee the day before we opened. In the first scene, I had to eat a cucumber sandwich, and when I came to pick the damn thing up, I saw it was the size of a doorstop. There was nothing for it; I had to cram it into my mouth. Martin Jarvis rambled on.

JACK: My dear Algy, you talk exactly as if you were a dentist. It is very vulgar to talk like a dentist when one isn't a dentist. It produces a false impression.
ALGERNON: [I'm supposed to speak here] Umm, errmm, ommr, gulp . . . [A chunk of cucumber sandwich shot straight into Martin's face. It got a huge laugh]. Well, that is exactly what dentists always do. [Another big laugh.]

The opening scene of the play is a potential minefield. Brilliantly written, it requires real dexterity to get it right. We had one great advantage: Peter Hall. For example, he explained the relevance of the cigarette case inscribed 'From little Cecily, with her fondest love to her dear Uncle Jack'. The whole exchange works brilliantly, but there's an in-joke built into the sequence. Oscar Wilde often gave boyfriends an inscribed cigarette case. Armed with this sort of information, the scene becomes much more of a game to play than a piece of acting to do. The fun of it makes it work.

We eventually opened to mostly rave notices. The audiences laughed themselves sick, which was great – it was very infectious and they carried us along with their enthusiasm. Funny old thing, comedy. It's all about timing, something I don't think anyone can teach; either you have it or you don't. What makes it harder than serious drama is that you not only have to listen to your fellow actors, but also to the audience. If they laugh (and you pray that they will) there's a gap while they laugh which the actor has to fill. 'The harder they laugh, the more serious you have to be,' Peter told us, and boy, was he right.

We were a sell-out, and this carried on as the weeks went by. However, there were two words that kept me from getting carried away: Harold Pinter. Our rehearsals for his play were due to start very soon. One day, I bumped into him in the theatre. 'How's it going, Nigel? Managed to learn it yet?' Of course I hadn't so much as looked at it. 'Almost,' I mumbled. The thought of it was a real erection-killer, and it hung over me like that bloody sword everyone always goes on about.

Eventually, there was nothing for it. I had to knuckle down. When I got going properly it wasn't nearly as bad as I'd thought it would be. The writing is so brilliant that it stuck in the brain with much less effort than I'd feared. I ended up on a train on the way to Poole to meet Caro, Kate and other friends on a Sunday morning. There I was, clutching my script, totally immersed in Harold Pinter's mind: 'This is a place of creatures, up and down stairs. Creatures of the rhythmic splits, the rhythmic sideswipes, the rums and roulettes, the macaroni tatters, the dumplings and jam mayonnaise, a catapulting ordure of gross and ramshackle shenanigans, open-ended paraphernalia.' I looked up to find the carriage full of people staring at me. I realised that I'd been talking aloud.

Rehearsals for *Other Places* coincided with the publication of Peter Hall's *Diaries*. This shouldn't have been an earth-shattering event as far as I was concerned, but in the event it certainly was. Peter talked in the book about Harold's affair with Antonia Fraser (who was later to become his wife). This was pretty much an open secret among most people who would be remotely interested, but Harold felt that Peter had betrayed him cruelly by not seeking his permission to mention it. They had a huge row, resulting in an arctic silence which famously lasted for about ten years.

Harold insisted on directing his play himself. This was a daunting prospect, made more complicated by the fact that the National was obligated to take a few productions on tour each year, and this meant us. So right in the middle of our opening month with *The Importance*, off we went to Norwich. Harold came up for his rehearsals, which took place each day at the Assembly Rooms, next to the theatre. He used to sit on a small chair with an ashtray and a glass on a table beside him and a bottle of white wine on the floor, which was replaced when necessary. Dressed in black from head to toe. Black hair, black glasses, black polo neck, black suit, black shoes. The original 'Man in Black'. I found him terrifying to begin with, but after a day or two I realised that he was not only extremely articulate but also kind and affectionate and, most of all, extraordinarily encouraging. From my research, I knew that he hated being asked what something he'd written meant. His reply was always, 'Whatever you want it to mean,' so I avoided that elephant trap and worked hard at pretending I knew what I was doing, assuming that he would correct me when he saw fit.

I noticed that women fell under his charismatic spell – so did I. He was surprisingly tactile, but there was always an undercurrent of risk about him that crackled round him like electricity.

We had to get back to London to open the play, so Oscar Wilde was put on the back burner for a few weeks while we got Mr Pinter up and running. There was no sign of Peter; he was keeping his head well down. We were all getting very nervous. The opening night loomed ever closer, and then suddenly it was upon us. There were only five of us in the cast and when the time came to do the usual dress run before the opening show, Harold suddenly said, 'Do you all really need this dress rehearsal?' I had never been asked that before and judging by the others' faces, nor had they, but we jumped at the chance of avoiding it and all said a definite 'No'. We just lay about on the stage chatting with Harold, who out of the blue said, 'The critics all hate me, so they'll hate you, too, I'm afraid. Just remember, it's not you at all, it's me, so my advice is to just go out there and think, "Fuck 'em!"' That really appealed to Judi.

The National is made up of three different theatres. The Olivier is the largest, seating twelve hundred people, and has a thrust stage, which means the stage is pushed out into the audience, who sit on three sides of it. The Lyttelton, which seats nine hundred, is a proscenium-arch theatre, the most conventional style of theatre we have in this country, with a 'picture-frame' arch between stage and audience, big stage curtains, and so on – perfect for *The Importance of Being Earnest*. The third and smallest is the Cottesloe, which doesn't have a stage at all – it's just a space which the director and producer can play with at will. For *Other Places*, Harold had decided this was the perfect space, and the set sat in the middle of the theatre while we were surrounded by the audience.

So there I was on the first night, knees trembling and mouth as dry as the Gobi Desert. I had to make my way out in the darkness and sit down in a chair before the lights came up. I looked at the audience. 'Fuck 'em,' I thought. 'Fuck the lot of 'em, especially fuck the fucking critics. You're right, Harold, they can all go fuck themselves.' While this was going on in my head, nothing was coming out of my mouth. Caro was sitting near the front. 'Oh Christ, he can't even remember his first line – we're in for a long night.' She had helped me learn my lines and knew how daunting it all was. She needn't have worried, I didn't forget a word. Nor did anyone else. We took the curtain call at the end muttering, 'Fuck 'em,' to each other under our breath. Harold came rushing round. He was chirpy as a cricket, and off we went to his house in Holland Park for a fabulous party.

'I thought you were all wonderful,' he said, 'and who gives a damn what they say? Little shits.'

About half past twelve I heard the front door bell, and Harold shuffled out into the hall. A few minutes later, he came back with a bundle of newspapers. For a man who didn't give a damn, he had more than a passing interest in what they might say. We held our breath. After watching him riffle through each newspaper – it was a special Pinter moment – he put them back on the table.

'The best reviews I've ever had in my life.'

A big cheer went up. The rest of the evening is a blank.

The trouble with first-night parties is that you wake up the following morning pleading with the Alka Seltzer not to fizz too hard, and facing the stark reality that you have to do it all over again that night. And the following night. In fact, for the next fucking year. In the run-up to the opening night you focus solely on that event. It's as if it's the only performance, and it's the paracetamol-fuelled 'morning after' that really starts my hands trembling. But with practice, and with time, both plays became habit, and I soon became accustomed to the added workload, juggling both without mishap. Both plays were full every night, and it was incredibly stimulating and a real buzz to be involved. There was no reason to suppose that anything would upset the apple cart – no reason at all. Of course, that was assuming that I didn't have a moment of crazed stupidity and agree to do a bit of filming during the day.

The BBC had decided to do a dramatisation of C. P. Snow's trilogy *Strangers and Brothers*, to be filmed almost entirely in Cambridge. Really handy for the South Bank. It had what would now be regarded as a 'really interesting' cast, including Anthony Hopkins, Tom Wilkinson and Cheri Lunghi, and it was just too good to pass up. Looking back, it was somewhat ambitious to think that I could cope with driving up to Cambridge after the theatre, getting up at the crack of dawn for a full day's filming and driving back to London in time for curtain up at seven thirty.

I managed OK to begin with, but slowly and surely things began to fall apart. For one thing, I was released from filming later and later, and used to spend the journey back in a state of hysterical panic that I was going to be late. It wasn't as if the director and producer didn't know I was on stage at seven thirty – they just always wanted that extra mile. 'Nigel, just one more take . . . You'll still be in plenty of time.' Another take. 'God, that was just so nearly perfect . . . just one more.' During the third take an aeroplane screws up the last few lines. 'Sorry, Nige, look, that aeroplane really fucked us. Sorry. One more take.' By this time, I was shitting myself. And as if that wasn't bad enough, I was also totally exhausted, and started forgetting which theatre I was in on which night – or even what day it was, arriving at the theatre on a Sunday and wondering whether there had been a bomb scare to account for the locked stage door.

Things came to a head one night in *Other Places*. I had been filming in Cambridge as usual until the last minute, and just made 'the half'. The half is old theatrical bollocks for when you have to sign in at the stage door of the theatre. If the play starts at seven thirty, the half is at six fifty-five, because Act I beginners are called to the stage at seven twenty-five. It's a rule and it mustn't be broken. Dare to be late for the half, and when you arrive you may find your understudy wearing your costume, for he will surely take your place.

In a scene towards the end of the play, Anna Massey had a short speech which I always found incredibly sad, and which often made me cry. On this night, I started crying even before she started, and suddenly found that I couldn't stop. I started to sob uncontrollably. Anna looked rather startled at first, moving swiftly from anxious concern to controlled panic when she realised that I really couldn't control myself. 'Get a grip,' she hissed. I continued to cry, terrible sobbing and snivelling noises instead of the speech I was supposed to make. 'Nigel! Get on with it!'

I slowly clawed my way back into the speech, wiping my nose on the back of my sleeve, no handkerchief in sight. I really didn't know where I was. I knew I was missing my mum, and worried about what was happening to my life . . . hang on a minute, that's Harold Pinter's mind I'm in . . . oh God, there's an audience looking at me. I snapped to, and managed somehow to make it to the interval. I stumbled off the stage in a haze of snot and tears.

As fate would have it, Harold had decided to drop in that night, to check how things were going, and I got a hell of a shock when he appeared in my dressing room. He had heard whispers in the audience – people were wondering if it really was part of the play, or was I having a breakdown? He was very concerned, and was worried that I was ill. I must have looked like death, standing there at the door of my dressing room. Harold put his arms round me. 'Terrifying to watch,' he said.

'Blistering intensity. I don't think I've ever seen anything like that before.' He never said whether it was good or bad, but I've never lost control like that again. Harold told me later that Olivier always said, 'A tired actor is a great actor.' That night I was exhausted, so . . .

Other Places is actually a trilogy of plays, all of which were performed each night. *Family Voices* – mine – was first up, and the second one was called *Victoria Station*. It was a two-hander between Martin Jarvis and Paul Rogers. Martin had by this time become a good mate of mine, and we soon realised that once our plays had both finished, if we got our skates on, we had exactly the right amount of time to leave the theatre, cross Waterloo Bridge, have a huge dry martini at the Waldorf and be back ready for the curtain call (slightly pissed) before the third play, *A Kind of Alaska*, had finished. It was a wonderful challenge, not something we did every time, but if we thought we'd turned in a particularly good bit of work – hey, let's go for it.

One Saturday night, we were both totally parched, having done a matinee as well as the evening show, and the first martini hardly touched the sides. 'The other half?' Martin asked. It didn't need a reply, and a lot of shaking and stirring went on. We savoured the second – too much so: we missed the curtain call altogether, and got backstage just as Judi was leaving. 'I know,' she said, 'it was a two-martini evening, huh?' Martin came to an abrupt halt, and I slammed into the back of him. 'Perfect,' she said. 'What a girl!' we both cried. Mind you, it was a good thing I'd finished with C. P. Snow by then, or I'd never have managed even one.

Martin was also in *The Importance*. We had become new best friends, and just ripe for getting up to no good. I soon realised that early on in the play, there was a perfect 'corpsing moment'.

Corpsing is the theatrical term for unscheduled laughing on stage – a cardinal sin – and, being the childish lot that we are, we're always inventing new challenges to try and force a good corpse out of our fellow cast members.

During the first act of *The Importance*, there is a scene in Algernon's rooms in Albany. Lady Bracknell, my Aunt Agatha, arrives with Jack (played by Martin), who proceeds to ask for her daughter Gwendoline's hand in marriage. She finds this outrageous and leaves in a huff. I'm off stage at this moment, playing the piano and, cruelly, decide to play 'Here Comes the Bride'. Of course, I'm not actually playing anything – that's on a tape somewhere else coming through a loudspeaker – so basically I'm twiddling my thumbs, thinking up naughty things to do.

Jack, at this point, has to walk upstage, look into the wings, and shout to me to stop playing immediately. I knew this was a perfect moment to corpse Martin. There was a production at the National at the time which involved someone dressing up like Carmen Miranda. I arranged with my dresser that when Martin looked into the wings, I'd be standing there dressed entirely like her, including the banana hat. Mart pissed himself. It was fantastic. This became an elaborate nightly challenge, with me having to think up more and more ridiculous costumes. Sometimes it took hours to organise. It became even more important than the play itself, and a lot of effort and time went into it.

One night, after what I'd thought was one of my better efforts, Mart said, 'Nige, I'm sorry to say this, but I think tonight's effort was a bit . . . pedestrian, shall we say.'

'Pedestrian? What do you mean, "pedestrian"? It took me all afternoon.'

It was time to up the ante. I'd been through most of the

costumes involved in every production, so they'd lost their shine. Out of the blue it came to me – a flash of inspiration.

Before the curtain went up, Mart was striding confidently around the set in his frock coat and fancy boots. 'So what's in store for me tonight?'

'Er, actually,' I said, 'I didn't have much time today, so . . .'

He gave me the oh-so-confident look that says, 'Nothing can corpse me now.'

Huh, I thought, we'll see.

Lady Bracknell swept out of my digs. I started playing. Martin lunged upstage, and peered into the wings.

'For God's sake, Algy, stop playing that—' Nothing further emerged. I was standing there naked. Totally naked.

With the help of three dressers I managed to get back on stage within five seconds. I thought Martin was going to die – he was purple in the face and hyperventilating. He couldn't speak. At all. For minutes. I made up a bit of Oscar Wilde – rather well, I thought. 'Pedestrian' was a word Mart never used again.

I took pity on him after that. He told me he was worried about his heart, but I couldn't resist one last crack at him. When we took the play out on the road for a few more dates, we ended up in the King's Theatre, Glasgow, which had a much smaller stage than the Lyttelton's, so our set was squeezed in, leaving only inches of room in the wings. On the first night there, when Mart came up to do his usual shouting at me, I was only inches away from him, rather than yards. We both found this rather odd and off-putting, but funny at the same time. It was also a perfect opportunity for a definitive corpse.

I'd noticed that a tramp used to hang around at the stage door. Not the best place for a tramp to hang around, I'd thought:

what was he going to get from an actor? However, he was my inspiration. Having done my bit in Act I, I whipped off stage and down the stairs to the stage door. He was there as usual. I pressed a tenner into his hand and said, 'Follow me.' He duly obeyed, and we clattered up the steps together. Jesus, I could smell the alcohol oozing from his every pore.

'Now,' I whispered, almost holding my breath, 'just stand here, and when I tell you, say, "Good evening, Mr Jarvis."'

'Nae problem,' he wheezed.

We waited silently together. 'For God's sake, Algy, stop—'

'Good evening, Mr Jarvis,' my new friend belched. Their noses were practically interlocked. Mart exploded. Unfortunately, so did I. I came on stage a gibbering wreck. I've no idea to this day how we managed to finish the scene.

The rest of the week was spent trying to recover. After the final Saturday matinee, I decided to stay at the theatre until the evening show and have a snooze. I was a bit knackered and needed a quick recharge to deal with getting back to London and doing the Pinter on Monday night. I stretched out and soon fell into a deep sleep, only to be woken up what seemed like minutes later by Martin wandering into my dressing room, fully dressed for Act I, Scene I.

'What's going on?' I said.

'Look at the time,' he replied. I grabbed my watch, and saw to my horror that it was twelve minutes to curtain up. Total panic. I grabbed the curlers and rammed them into my hair – they were required to make my hair suitably foppish – and had managed to drag on about half of my costume when to my horror I heard the opening music. 'Jesus, how did that happen? Where's the time gone? Jesus, I'm going to be "off".' I grabbed my jacket, tore down the stairs, yanking out the curlers, hair still attached, screaming, 'Fuck, fuck, fuck!' – straight out of *Four Weddings and a Funeral*.

To get on stage from the right-hand side, I had to run down even more steps into the basement, under the stage, and up the other side. Tearing across the bowels of the theatre, I heard the opening music come to a grinding halt. My heart sank. The show had started without me. I burst out into the lights, jacket done up all wrong, both shoes unlaced and one stubborn curler dangling across my right eye. I looked up to see the entire cast waiting for me. The curtain was in behind them while they howled with laughter. Martin had put all the clocks in the theatre back one hour. He'd sneaked into my dressing room while I snored like a train and adjusted my wristwatch. He'd got me good and proper. It was the best wind-up I'd ever seen, and I was proud to be part of it.

It was a very happy year and a half. We were in two beautifully written and challenging plays, which were constantly full, and I was also lucky enough to work with wonderful people. With only a few weeks to go, I knew I was going to miss them enormously. I also wanted to know what any of us were going to do next.

'I think I'm doing a sit-com for the BBC,' Mart said. Zoë Wanamaker was off to do a movie. What was I going to do? Walking to the bar for a quick pint after the show one evening, I heard the following coming over the tanoy system: 'Miss Dench and Miss Massey, rehearsal time for tomorrow for *The Crew* is ten thirty in studio two. Thank you.' *The Crew*? What crew?

Mart and I sank a pint, hissing about how we should know about this play. Who's written it? Who's directing it? We know who's in it – or do we? Will there be parts in it for us? We're at the National Theatre, for Christ's sake. Aren't we part of the crew?

Next day, the two of us burst into Judi's dressing room.

'What the fuck's this all about?' I said. I saw Anna roosting behind her, preening with pure theatrical pleasure.

'Oh, didn't we tell you, darling? We're doing this new David Hare play. Not only that, he's directing it as well.'

'And it's a two-hander,' Anna piped up. 'Theatrical bliss.'

'What's it about?' Mart said.

'Quite simply,' Judi said, 'it's about two lesbian truck drivers.'

'Christ, that'll pack 'em in,' I sneered as we left the room.

Every time I was in the theatre there seemed to be endless calls for Miss Dench and Miss Massey and *The Crew*. Drove us mad. One day, I bumped into David Hare in the corridor and, bugger me, he was wearing a T-shirt with 'The Crew' written all over his chest.

'How's it going?' I asked nonchalantly.

'It's a daily joy for me to work with such talent. My words leap off the page like a beautiful waterfall.'

'So you're on to a winner, then?'

'With a cast like that, you tell me,' he replied, wandering off towards rehearsal room two. On the back of the T-shirt, in huge letters, was 'MASSEY/DENCH'. It reminded me of some strange tractor – yeah, lesbian truck drivers, this could well be a hit.

Funnily enough, it was all bollocks. There was no play, there were no rehearsals, there was nothing. Nothing but air. The perfect play. To this day, Judi maintains they're on the cusp of doing it. The last thing I heard, it was being made into a film. She even sent me a photograph to prove it. There she is, leaning out of a huge Eddie Stobart megatruck, fag dangling from her lips. There's Anna, leaning over her right shoulder with a face like a mad wrestler's. In the foreground stands David Hare in that bloody T-shirt, doing a bit of directing. Absolute bollocks. Total fun. God, when this business is good it's out of this world.

Entr'acte

Dressing-room Tales

The other day I added up the amount of time I've spent in dressing rooms dotted about the world. It comes to well over seven years. That's a hell of a lot of time in my book. Unfortunately, it's well over seven years spent in mostly filthy surroundings that beggar belief. So much so that I'm embarrassed if anyone comes round after a performance to tell me how awful I was or whatever. However much money is spent decorating a theatre front of house, they'll compensate by ignoring backstage. It's as if they're putting two fingers up to the people who actually work in the theatre, and in my opinion that makes theatre owners fucking bastards. I don't mean that, of course – if I did I'd never work in the theatre again, but I'm trying to get a point across. Why oh why do we most of the time have to roost in conditions that a dormouse would find unacceptable?

This brings me neatly to dressing-room number one at the

Hippodrome Theatre, Bristol. I was on tour with a play called *Art*, with Barry Foster and Roger Lloyd Pack. The famous West End producer David Pugh had decided to take a gamble and put a quirky little three-hander into a huge auditorium. The gamble paid off, thank God, and we were pretty much sold out in a theatre which seats nearly two thousand. That's big business for any theatre.

I arrived at the stage door on a Monday afternoon to 'check in' to my new dressing room, and was greeted by the stage doorman (that's the chap who looks after the stage door and generally watches television on a small screen all day long) with 'Can I help?'

'I'm looking for my dressing room.'

'And you are . . . ?'

Now, it's not that I'm conceited or arrogant or think my face is familiar to everyone on this planet, it's just that there'd been a poster hanging opposite him for at least two weeks with my bloody great face staring at him, so maybe he should have known who I was. That put me in a fantastic mood, just right for giving it all that night. I staggered into my new abode, my home from home for the next week, carrying my bits and pieces, and started to unpack.

I always have to have a radio – who can live without Radio 4? A smelly candle is also essential – most dressing rooms don't smell too good. A spot of make-up, mostly for show because you don't need to wear make-up these days unless you're doing a character part, and then I look around for something to stretch out on. Fuck all there – looks like we're in for a fun week. It's round about this time that I'd expect the theatre manager to pay a visit. He's the guy who runs the entire operation, and he'll know exactly how much money has already come in.

On this occasion I knew the take was pretty fantastic and he was on course for a record-breaking week. But did he come to see me? Of course not. In fact, he never came at all. Made me feel a million dollars. I got a bit of my own back, though. That week an ITV crew came to film me in my warren for a series called *Stars in Their Dressing Rooms*, and I didn't take any prisoners. I talked directly to camera and told it like it was.

Not a million miles from Bristol is a place called Bath. The Theatre Royal there is one of the prettiest I've ever had the pleasure of working in, and it's the opposite of everything I've said about Bristol. The star's dressing room is one of the most comfortable and elegant spaces an actor is ever likely to find. When the theatre was re-decorated in 1982, the board of directors obviously decided that actors and crew were worth investing in. Alec Guinness came to see the restoration and was shown into dressing room number one. He was wearing a beautiful cashmere camel coat. He swept into the dressing room with a 'Wonderful, darling!' Alas, they'd forgotten to warn him that the paint on the claret-coloured walls hadn't properly dried. He ended up looking as though he'd completed a scene from *Macbeth*.

'Not to worry,' he said, 'it's a definite improvement.'

The star's dressing room is now known as the Sir Alec Guinness Room.

The most glamorous of all dressing rooms is at the Royal Albert Hall. Typically, I was only allowed one night in it. My friend Debbie Wiseman, a brilliant composer, had asked me to recite two Oscar Wilde short stories which she had set to music, rather like *Peter and the Wolf*, and we were performing them with the

Royal Philharmonic Orchestra. I was greeted at the stage door like royalty and ushered into the 'conductor's dressing room'. It was rather like being in a major suite aboard the QEII. I could have set up camp for a week.

Unfortunately, all I had time to do was change, go on stage, perform and leave. I didn't even have time to enjoy all the free goodies. Forget the acting, I thought, I'll be signing up for conducting night classes.

Llandudno. A dressing-room nightmare, something out of a horror film and then multiplied by ten. On our tour of *Art*, the only poster that was defaced was the one outside the stage door at Llandudno. Some very smart chap had put an F in front of *Art*. By God, that's funny, we all thought – original, too. Maybe he should write a play. The stage door weren't expecting us. I think they thought it was wrestling that week. The dressing room itself hadn't been cleaned for five weeks. They'd had a run of *Jesus Christ Superstar* and I was in Jesus's room, and Jesus wasn't tidy. The shower looked like JC had been crucified *Psycho*-style. I left. 'I'll be back when it's stopped looking like an abattoir,' I said. Some poor sod spent hours with the Harpic, but it never quite lost its battleground tinge.

London's glittering West End. There's nothing glittering about the dressing rooms. Checking into the Wyndham Theatre for our first spell of *Art*, Malcolm Storrey, Ron Cook and I sniffed around the rooms. Ron went upstairs, which left Malcolm and me tossing a coin. I got the shower (either boiling or freezing), Malcolm got the bed. I noticed many months later, when Madonna decided to tread the boards, that my old dressing room had been turned into a tart's boudoir. 'Oh, spending some money now are we?' I said to the theatre manager. 'No, no,' he said, 'we were going to redecorate anyway.' Bollocks.

The Albery Theatre is directly opposite Wyndham's. Quite grand, the basement dressing rooms, but with one fairly major fault: when it rains they flood. The summer Ardal O'Hanlon and I were there, it rained most of the time. I had that damp look about me during most of the run of the play.

The Whitehall Theatre boasts some really nasty dressing rooms. You climb sixty odd stairs from the stage to the dressing room, only to find a hovel that a chicken would reject. At one stage, the hot water packed up in the entire building. 'When's it going to be fixed?' I asked plaintively that night. I was filming during the day at the time, and doing the show at night, so a shower before the show was imperative. 'It'll be done by tomorrow, don't worry.' Six weeks of cold showers put me in a bad mood pretty much every night. Eventually, I got hold of the main man. 'Is that Howard Panter's office?' 'Yes, can I help?' 'Could you tell Mr Panter if there's no hot water at the Whitehall Theatre by tomorrow night, he'll be an actor short? Thank you.' The following evening, I had my first hot shower in all that time. Howard had the grace to send us a few bottles of wine. They didn't need chilling, backstage was always freezing cold.

There's no excuse for the National Theatre getting it wrong, but get it wrong they did. Every tiny dressing room faces on to a courtyard, so you can see what's going on in everybody else's space. Fun if you're Judi Dench and Anna Massey. Every time I looked up from my little desk in front of my little mirror to look out of my little window, I'd see them pointing, or just poking their noses in my direction. This was too good an opportunity to miss. I had the most fantastic dresser, Ralph, who looked after me like an owner looks after a Crufts winner. He would run the basin full of hot water; he would guide me to the stage and greet me when I came off – the perfect batman, the finest dresser.

'Ralph,' I said, 'we have to do something outrageous.'

'Do you have anything in mind, sir?' he enquired, Jeeves-style.

'I think it should be of a sexual nature. We know how much that will outrage the dear things.'

'Indeed, sir.' Accordingly, Ralph purchased a life-sized blow-up sex doll, complete with pubic hair. That evening we secretly took it in turns to blow her up. When she was fully inflated, I introduced her to a small but over-excited audience. I kissed her, I fondled her and I finally disappeared out of sight inside her. Judi and Anna needed medical attention. Point made.

Another problem with the National is that, as it has not one but three theatres, there are more actors than dressing rooms, which means occasionally one has to double up and share on odd nights. When I was performing in *The Importance of Being Earnest* in the Lyttelton, I sometimes found an actor from one of the other theatres holed up in what I thought was my little dressing room. This really hacked me off.

Nick Jones used to come crashing in, carrying his racing bike over his shoulder.

'Evening, all,' he'd say as he sat down, burped and farted, and then pissed himself laughing. 'Better an empty flat than an unwelcome lodger.'

I always had to get out of the way as quickly as possible, and would scramble past him, tripping over his fucking bicycle.

'Listen, mate,' I'd say, 'there's a perfectly good bicycle park round the corner' etc., etc. He never listened to me, but I'd secretly wheel the damn thing out while he was on stage, and shove it up against the emergency exit.

During my stint at the National, there were two things I did during the evening. First, I had just enough time during the first interval to nip over to the Olivier Theatre wings and listen to 'Rocking the Boat' from *Guys and Dolls* – fantastic. Secondly, I had just enough time to pay a seven-and-a-half-minute visit to Judi's dressing room and catch up on a bit of gossip. She was often doing a bit of tapestry. Contrary to popular perception, Lady Bracknell is only on stage for about twenty minutes out of a total of nearly three hours. Judi was getting very good at tapestry.

'This one's for you,' she said one day. I looked over her shoulder – it looked like Greek hieroglyphics. She watched me out of the corner of her eye.

'What's it say?'

'It says: Fuckemfuckemfuckemfuckemfuckemfuckemfuckem-fuckemfuckemfuckem.'

Chapter 9

Life on the Box

When I first turned professional, about a thousand years ago, the only way we were allowed to work was to hold a British Equity card. A small thing that meant a great deal. I trotted off to the Equity offices in Harley Street and became a provisional member. It was sort of like getting your provisional driving licence. In order to gain your full licence, you had to prove that you had worked in the theatre for more than forty weeks. Forty weeks is quite a long time, but thanks to what seemed like a lifetime with Prospect, I was the proud owner of a fully paid-up British Equity card.

I was hungry for a little bit of television experience. Everybody wanted to be on the box. Three-quarters of the nation was glued to it every night, and what a wonderful and bewildering choice the viewers had. There was BBC 1 and BBC 2 and ITV, and that was it. Mum and Dad mostly listened to the Home Service, better known now as Radio 4, but if you got on the telly you could pretty much guarantee that half the country would get a glimpse of your face.

Actually, I don't think many people got much of a glimpse on my first outing: I was covered in armour from head to foot. I tried to sneak the visor up for a couple of scenes, but someone snapped it back in place. Given the success of Prospect's *Edward II*, the BBC, in their wisdom, decided the nation was ready for it on the small screen. It's a raw and thrilling piece of drama, and, apart from its rarity value, there's a riveting scene at the end of the play when Edward is murdered in his prison cell. Not your run-of-the-mill murder, either. Someone lets him have it with a red-hot poker up his arse. Perfect pre-watershed television for 1970. The audience got a glimpse of Ian McKellen's arse, and I got my first glimpse of how television works.

It was also my first glimpse of life in a television studio – and not any old studio, but the Holy Grail itself, BBC Television Centre, Wood Lane, London. I was really impressed by the sheer size of the building. Not only was it crammed full of offices, corridors, meeting rooms and restaurants and bars, but it had five huge studios, each serviced by its own wardrobe, make-up and prop departments. Then there were the camera departments. Every studio contained five huge video cameras, film cameras for location filming and special cameras for filming sport. Welcome to the BBC.

I found myself in what's known as the 'blue assembly area', Studio 2A, a huge thing housing sets, lighting and five cameras in all, with unseen people in the dark upstairs gallery pressing the buttons that decreed which camera was being used and when. I remember I was paid one hundred and twenty six pounds for the entire job, which was the equivalent of about twenty weeks in the theatre! Of course, as in the theatre production,

I had a non-speaking part, which gave me lots of opportunity to learn the most valuable skill of work in a studio – the art of hanging around for hours.

In those days, most things on TV were shot on tape. When you shoot on tape you have to record it on to a machine. There were only two in the building, so each production had to book its recording slot. Ours was at night, so we would camera rehearse all day, and then, when our three-hour slot arrived, we would produce one and a half hours' worth of cut TV each night, a massive output which would be unheard of today. It was in colour, but it was very grainy and old-fashioned compared to what we are used to now. All the interior scenes were shot on tape, but as soon as the story required an exterior scene we disappeared to the location – which could be anywhere from Gretna Green to Land's End – and shot on film. When you put the two together, tape and film, it looked a bit ridiculous. They couldn't possibly match, as one looks clean and lacking in atmosphere, while the other (film) looks grainy and stuffed full of atmosphere. Nobody noticed or complained, though; that was the way it was – for the next thirty years.

The cast was the same as for the theatre tour, so there we were, all eight ASMs, vying for position and desperate to be in shot. I had to do a fight scene and I pretended that I couldn't see and asked to take my helmet off. Of course, the director saw right through my pathetic ploy.

'You've been doing it all year with it on.'

Bugger.

The great thing was that, whether in shot or not, I was getting paid more than I had ever got before. Also, *Edward* proved to be incredibly popular, so we got these wonderful things called repeat fees; just as the bank balance was accelerating towards the red zone, a cheque for, say, forty-two pounds would suddenly appear and scoop me from the jaws of the poorhouse.

I love watching football matches. It's a sort of bonding thing, not necessarily between males, but anyone who fancies an afternoon screaming, fighting, smashing chairs and generally behaving like a fucking lunatic. I support Fulham, something I've kept pretty secret until now. The thing is, if you tell someone you're a Fulham supporter, they roll around laughing.

In the spring of 1971, my brother and I went to Craven Cottage to scream support for our local lads, and boy, did we scream. We lost, of course, but my throat was bloody sore at the end of it. I gave my neck a rub and discovered to the right of my Adam's apple a rather large lump.

'Phil, what the hell's this?'

He prodded and poked at this plum-like thing sticking out of my neck. 'I've no idea, but you'd better go and see Dr Riddle.'

Dr Riddle was our family doctor and a really nice guy. He was the sort of doctor who'd give you a jab of penicillin with one hand and a large gin and tonic with the other, while lighting up and offering you a Piccadilly cigarette – untipped, of course.

He looked at my neck and then looked at me. Straight in the eyes. 'What are you doing tomorrow?'

'As a matter of fact, I start rehearsing a new TV play, if that's OK with you,' I answered, rather smugly.

'Not tomorrow you don't.' He picked up the phone. 'Would you wait outside for a second?' No gin and tonic. Things were looking pretty serious.

At nine thirty the following morning I turned up at St Thomas's Hospital in London.

'You'd better get a move on, Mr Havers. Room 202 – the surgeon will be there in twenty minutes.'

Surgeon? What do they mean, 'surgeon'? Christ, this really is serious.

Mr Alexander was a tall fastidious-looking man, beautifully dressed from top to toe. 'This little lump you've got here needs to be whipped out as soon as possible. In fact, I'm going to have a crack at it tomorrow morning. Let me tell you what's going on. A lump like this can mean one of two things. One, it's a lump of no importance and I'll throw it in the bin. Two, it's a nasty lump which comes under the name of cancer. If it's number two, I might have to take other bits out around it, and that might mean losing your voice box. All right, I'll see you tomorrow.'

Right, I thought. Number two doesn't sound too good. I'm trying to be an actor, and silent films are a thing of the past. I looked down at my hands; I was shaking like a leaf. Dear God, if there is one, please help me here.

The next morning I was taking a shower before slipping into my attractively skimpy, open-backed operating robe, and I thought, I feel so good, so fit. How will I feel by the end of the day? Absolutely shocking was the answer.

I woke up, if you can call it that, to several anxious faces round the bed, but I did notice one thing – they were smiling. And I could speak. There is a God.

Apparently, during the seven-hour operation, as soon as the lump had been removed it was taken for analysis. Everybody waited for two and a half hours. 'Benign' was the answer and they clamped my neck back together.

I was supposed to be Andrew Brudenell-Bruce's best man in five days time. I'll make it, I kept saying to myself, I'll make it.

I didn't, of course, but they made it to me. They came directly after the wedding ceremony and before the reception. I was sitting in a chair at the time, looking like a grumpy old man. They leaped straight into my bed and probably created their first child. I didn't care what they did – I just felt so happy to be alive.

My rather impressive scar is still there. Sometimes I tell people it's the result of a fencing accident, an altercation with a grizzly bear or even a medical experiment that went wrong. At the end of the day, it always reminds me of my little brush with death. People often say, 'Treat every day as if it was your last, and treasure every moment.' It's impossible to do that, of course, but if I ever get complacent I just run my finger across my scar.

The big TV hit of the mid-seventies was *Upstairs, Downstairs*. The show was the brainchild of Eileen Atkins and Jean Marsh, two of our most respected actresses. As with all good ideas, the simpler the better. The main star of the show was the house in Eaton Square. Upstairs lived the Bellamy family. Downstairs lived their staff. And that was pretty much it. Every week a new story unfolded, and the series gripped the nation. Every actor's ambition was to be in it. Although I was no exception, I was actually getting to be quite busy. The BBC in those days put on a series of wonderful plays, from Mikhail Bulgakov's *The White Guard* to Terence Rattigan's glorious *French Without Tears* – quite a literary leap in anyone's imagination. We rehearsed these plays just as in the theatre and then shot each act in one take, something utterly unheard of today. You ended up being able to perform the play as if you actually were in a theatre. I quite often thought it was a bit of a waste not sliding into the Garrick Theatre and doing a short run. We could easily have done it – opportunity missed.

Anyway, after a year or so, I got a call from the *Upstairs, Downstairs* production office asking me to do a couple of episodes, playing a character called Peter Dinmont. Hang on, I thought, isn't that some kind of dog? Were they barking up the wrong tree? Actually, I didn't care; I just wanted to be part of it, even if it was daunting to join such an established and popular show. The whole nation had taken the show's characters to heart, and the actors had become household names. I already knew Simon Williams, who played James Bellamy, the patriarch's eldest son – I had met him doing a charity gig a couple of years before and we enjoyed each other's irreverent sense of humour – but the rest were total strangers. Well, all but one – Anthony Andrews. Back in those days, Anthony and I always seemed to be gunning for the same roles, and he seemed to be doing distinctly better. When I read the first episode, I realised that his part was bigger than mine. That really pissed me off. One thing I noticed about Anthony was that he always acted the part of the big star, and as a result he got treated like one. We were to rehearse in a large room on the south side of Chelsea Barracks – quite in keeping with the production, I thought – and on the first day, Anthony arrived in a Bentley. How he could afford it, God only knows. I took the tube. Damn it, I'd always wanted a Bentley. And why did he have to be so good-looking? (I still want to put my fist through a window when I hear that *Brideshead* music. I'd tried to sabotage his audition for that piece, elbowing him out of the way at every opportunity. To no avail, blast it. And he was brilliant, I have to admit.)

Now, where was I? Oh yes, the first day of *Upstairs, Downstairs* – very scary indeed. The director was Bill Bain, known as 'Do It Again Bain' because 'Do it again' seemed to be all he ever said, but this method managed to conjure up some of the best and most memorable TV performances ever given: without a doubt those characters are for ever part of the lives of a certain generation of box watchers. The entire country was in love with Georgina, played by Lesley-Anne Down. I was no exception. I tried to flirt with her at every opportunity. One day, she invited me back to her place for tea. I was nearly sick with excitement – until I realised that Jackie Tong was coming with us, and she really did mean tea. Lesley-Anne was happily living with Bruce Robinson at that time. After a brief career as an actor, Bruce had decided a more profitable future lay in scriptwriting, and he even threw me a script one day, telling me, 'There's quite a nice part in it for you.' He was dead right, it was a great part, but he couldn't find the money or the people who wanted to do it. Ten years later, he did manage it, but unfortunately I was too old for the part by then. It was called *Withnail and I*. Richard E. Grant is for ever grateful – actually that's a lie: he couldn't give a toss.

One day during a break in filming, Lesley-Anne and I had a heated argument about, of all things, Harrods. I maintained that it was a well-known fact that one could order absolutely anything from Harrods. She insisted I was talking bollocks, so to prove my point I rang 'the best department store in the world' and asked for the pet department.

'I'd like to buy an elephant, please,' I said.

'Of course, sir. Would you prefer African or Indian?'

I think that proved my point.

Upstairs, Downstairs finally came to the end of its run. It was still phenomenally successful, but, as with all great shows, it was best to 'leave them wanting more'. It was back to the theatre for me: eight weeks touring in a play called *George and Margaret*, directed by Nigel Patrick and starring Dora Bryan.

'We'll be coming into the West End with this super little show,' the producer told us all on our last night on the road. 'It's just a matter of which super little theatre to put our show into.'

My reaction now to that sort of bullshit would be 'Bollocks,' but back then I was as green as an apple and said, 'Wow! Shaftesbury Avenue here I come.'

While I twiddled my thumbs, dreaming of my name in lights – albeit very small ones – my agent rang me. 'Get your arse over to John Gorrie's office at London Weekend Television studios, ten thirty sharp tomorrow morning.'

John Gorrie was a very famous and extremely successful television director (and many years later was to be one of my daughter Kate's godfathers). He was about to start work on a TV mini-series called *Edward VII*. I turned up smack on time, but with a little apprehension. John turned out to be a really charming and friendly man who thought I was perfect for the part of Lord Frederick Crichton, a close friend of the young prince.

'We start filming next month,' he told me. 'How does that suit you?'

'Well, the thing is,' I blurted out, 'I'm going to be up Shaftesbury Avenue.'

'What are you doing up there?' he asked.

'A play with Dora Bryan. We haven't got the theatre yet, but the producer says we're on our way.'

'No, no, Nigel, don't worry about that. I'll see you at rehearsals on Tuesday week.'

He was right, of course: I never heard another word from the play's producer, who must have disappeared into very thin theatrical air. Goodbye *George and Margaret*, hello *Edward VII*.

The part of Edward as a young man was played by Charles Sturridge. This was only his second job as an actor and he was really up for it. It was a big break for him and he wasn't going to waste it – or was he? Every day I saw him watching John, eagle-eyed. He seemed to pay as much attention to what was going on behind the camera as to what was going on in front of it. On the last Friday of rehearsals before we went off to film, John Gorrie took us out to lunch. It was quite a heavy-duty affair and all the cast were there – Annette Crosby, Robert Hardy, Francesca Annis, even John Gielgud, all squeezed round a table in some strange Italian restaurant in the West End.

The art of directing was discussed at length by Gielgud.

'Very few actors can do both acting and directing,' he announced haughtily.

Out of the blue Charles responded, 'Actually, I want to direct.'

All eyes turned on him.

'If you want to be a director, Charles,' said Mr Gorrie, 'you must think that whatever piece you're acting in at the time, you could direct better than the director.'

There was a silence you could cut with a knife.

'I want to be a director.'

Another silence.

Then Robert Hardy fell off his chair laughing. 'You see,' he said to John, 'you're not that good.'

By the way, John was right – and so was Charles, who went on to direct *Brideshead Revisited* in 1981 to extraordinary critical acclaim.

Filming *Edward* was fun from beginning to end. I applied the same rules as before: listen and learn; and with a cast like that it was a full-time job. Everyone has a John Gielgud story and I'm no exception. At least mine's short and to the point. While sitting around waiting to do something, like being in the background of a scene, all the oldies would sit in their director's chairs with their names printed on the back, trying to be the first to complete that day's *Times* crossword. I'd be observing this, perched on a wooden crate behind them. Robert Hardy was pretty good, but not as swift as Annette. Pencils tapped their front teeth, ankles crossed and uncrossed, as they furiously delved into their literary upbringing. Francesca would turn as if to ask me for help.

'I'm not good at this,' I said truthfully.

Suddenly, like a Victorian explosion, sideburns and whiskers quivering, Sir John would fling his paper high into the air: 'I'm finished, quite finished, dear boy.' And with that he would saunter off towards the catering truck, lighting another cigarette in a professorial puff of smoke. The rest of the oldies would be crestfallen.

This happened day after day. It was only after a few of these vignettes that I picked up the tossed newspaper with its immaculately completed crossword. I began to study it. Now believe me, I was honest when I said I was no good at them, but even I knew that 'Redgrave' wasn't the answer to fifteen across: 'Cut cost – on a shoestring (8)'. It got better, much better. Twenty down: 'He's a lumberjack (7)' – 'Sweetie'. The whole thing was total bollocks. Everything fitted perfectly, it was just all bollocks. What a brilliant man, just my sort of crossword.

Old *Edward* turned out to be rather a success. People love that sort of drama; they always have and they always will, especially when it's well written, well directed and, though I say it myself, well acted. It did nothing but good for all of us. Charles, true to his word, decided that acting was for fools and he went up north to Manchester, to study the art of directing.

By an extraordinary coincidence, I followed him. Not to direct, but to do a six-part Granada Television series called *A Raging Calm* by Stan Barstow, an everyday story of northern folk. I was amazed to be involved, but, reading the scripts carefully, I saw I was to be a bit of southern relief. The show's great appeal to me was a chance to work with Alan Badel and Michael Williams: I could learn something from them.

All the rehearsing and filming was to be done in Manchester, which meant finding digs for at least three to four months. Typically, I never bothered to investigate this properly, so found myself staying in a B&B over a pub called the Brown Bull on the outskirts of the city. It didn't get much worse than this, I thought, until I opened the bedside table drawer to find a tube of KY Jelly and a sprinkling of pubic hair. Time to find some proper digs. Thank God for Charles Sturridge.

'I'll only stay a night or two,' I told him. 'Just till I sort myself out.'

Three months later I was still there. God bless him.

Manchester became my second home for the following few years: *Crown Court*, *The Nearly Man* and all sorts of other good and interesting plays and series came my way from Granada TV. I was slowly crawling up the cast lists, playing slightly better parts all the time. Every time I got a new job up there, the only fly in the ointment was where to stay. The Brown Bull had burned down long ago – caused by an explosive tube of KY, no doubt – and other digs were equally oily. I couldn't keep staying with Charles and the only hotel worth staying in was the Midland Hotel, a grand old Victorian railway hotel, but that cost an arm and a leg.

Vicky Williams, a great friend and companion who was working with me, suggested I should move in with her and Yvonne.

'Who's Yvonne?'

'That's totally immaterial, and anyway you'll be fine with her.'

'How many bedrooms?' I asked.

'Well, there's mine and Yvonne's.'

'So where do I sleep?'

'With Yvonne, you idiot.'

I suggested that it would probably be best if I met Yvonne – she could have a look at me and I could have a jolly good butcher's at her. After rehearsals the following evening, we all met at the Film Exchange, our local boozer behind the television studios.

'This is Yvonne,' Vicky said.

Digs sorted: she was fantastic. She looked a bit like a rock chick, all long blond hair, boobs and legs, and really clever and fun, too. This was too much. There had to be a catch.

'Where do I sleep?' I asked innocently.

'With me,' she replied, and that was that (I should perhaps mention that this was before Caro and I were married).

There was just one tiny little, ever so small, hardly worth mentioning blot on the landscape: Yvonne was the local leader and fully paid-up member of the Workers Revolutionary Party – quite an interesting bunch one way or another. In a nutshell, it was a Marxist party hell bent on teaching the working classes to overcome the terrible poison in our society that is capitalism. At the time, my father was attorney-general and a cabinet member of the Conservative government. That miniscule fact, I thought, would be best kept to myself if I wanted a roof over my head, and so it was never mentioned. If Yvonne asked about my background, I told her I didn't have one really and it wasn't worth mentioning, anyway. This was all fine by her, and so I found myself one Saturday afternoon standing outside Old Trafford football stadium handing out leaflets promoting death to the upper classes to the sixty thousand punters on their way to see their heroes.

'WRP – you know it makes sense!' I shouted in my newly acquired northern accent. 'It's the only way forward for all of us.'

I prayed I didn't bump into anyone I knew. I was mostly ignored, but occasionally someone would clap me on the back. 'Good lad. Keep up the good work.' Blimey, I thought, there really are people out there who agree with this bollocks.

'How's it going?' Yvonne would ask, running over from the other side of the stadium.

'Brilliant,' I'd reply. 'I've gone through all my leaflets – this place is heaving with supporters.' Thus guaranteeing another week in my super deluxe digs.

The following Sunday, we were lying in bed reading the papers. I'd made the coffee and toast, and felt as chirpy as a cricket.

'Good God,' Yvonne said, 'there's a bloke in the paper here with the same name as you.'

'Really?' I said.

'Yeah, and you'll never guess what he's up to. Not only is he the fucking attorney-general, he's also prosecuting the Guildford bombers. Bastard.'

'How about that?' I said without thinking. 'That's my dad.'

Exactly the same thing happens when you light the blue touchpaper before the firework explodes. I can't exactly remember what happened, but what I can remember is that within what seemed like seconds, I was out in the street with my few belongings. I never saw Yvonne again. I'm glad really; not for me – I can look after myself – but for her. If anyone had found out that she was sleeping with the son of the Tory cabinet member responsible for bringing Irish revolutionaries to justice, she would have been taken out and been given a roasting that would have made tarring and feathering look like a tea party.

On the whole, Manchester was good to me. Eventually, though, the people who ran the drama department at Granada TV began to drift away or retire, so my allies were disappearing. One of the last plays I did there was *The Portland Millions*, a wonderful piece of Victorian hokum, part of a series called *Victorian Scandals*. Patricia Hayes played a dotty old woman, in other words not a million miles from herself. She was on a murder charge and I was the young brief given the unenviable task of defending her, but the main reason for singling this play out was that it was there that I met Richard Wilson, who was playing the feared prosecutor, stern and pompous at every turn. He turned out to be one of the nicest men I've ever met. We instantly became friends and we remain so to this day – Kate gained another godfather.

Not long afterwards, my letterbox produced *The Glittering Prizes* by Frederick Raphael. It sent a shiver up my spine – the right sort of shiver. I swear to God, if I was sent a script like that today, the same shiver would go up an older spine. How lucky can one get? I thought, as I ripped open the envelope and pulled out the mighty tome. It did everything it said on the can. Six hours of television heaven. Two great directors, Waris Hussein and Rob Knights, one superb producer, Mark Shivas, and an Oscar-winning writer. The summer disappeared in a flash and we all found ourselves on a coach trip to Norfolk – an end-of-shoot party chez Raphael; he lived in a beautiful Elizabethan house surrounded by a moat.

After a huge glass of champagne, I wandered round the house and spotted what looked like a queue waiting to go to the loo. As I got closer, I realised it was a queue waiting to touch an Oscar. I joined it and waited my turn. Eventually, I held that little gold statue.

'The nearest you'll get?' It was Tom Conti.

'I reckon so.' I replied. 'What about you?'

'I'm going to give it a damn good shot,' he said.

He's nearly there, at least he's been nominated. I'm not letting go, I'm still going to give it a jolly good shot myself.

The next thud from the letterbox produced another corker. As I ripped open the envelope, the name Dennis Potter screamed out. Reading the script was a fascinating experience – it was unlike any television piece I'd ever read before. He was a great aficionado of the classic thirties popular songs and found an extraordinary story to weave the two elements of music and drama together. Each character would have to mime to one of these songs in the middle of a scene, an amazingly bold thing to do. It was called *Pennies from Heaven*.

Bob Hoskins played a travelling salesman who sold sheet music to shops up and down the country. He was married to Gemma Craven, who stayed at home generally pampering herself. I played a travelling salesman selling pampering stuff, who managed to get into her house to do the business. I had to mime to 'Smoke Gets in Your Eyes', undressing Gemma as I did it – an unforgettable experience. Cheryl Campbell played Bob's mad mistress on the road (shades of *Bonnie and Clyde*). It sounds crazy and it was.

During rehearsals early on, one hot Friday afternoon, Piers Haggard, the director, was beginning to get on Bob Hoskins's tits.

'Why are you doing that?' he yelled at Bob.

'Because you fucking told me to.'

'Well, do it like this.' And so it went on.

I entirely agreed with Bob. Piers had a habit of making you do it one way, and then denying he'd ever said that and making you do it completely differently the next day – bloody annoying.

Bob was really losing it now – a bead of sweat trickled down his brow. Go on, I thought, do something drastic, but make sure you do it in character. Quick as a flash, he grabbed Piers by the throat. The fact that Piers was six foot three and Bob five foot six made not the slightest difference.

'If you get through this thing intact it'll be a fucking miracle.' Piers looked sheepish. He'd got the message.

We all went to a screening the week before it was due to be transmitted. I sat there open-mouthed. Not because I thought it was brilliant, but because I didn't know quite what to make of it. Was it going to work? No one had a clue. It was probably one of the greatest critical successes the BBC have ever had. I was only in a tiny bit of it, but it was one hell of show to have been part of. Every year I still receive a shilling or two, part of my repeat fees. It will soon be thirty years of one pound twenty-eight pences. It's not the money that counts, it's the fact that people are still watching it.

Quite a few people were also watching another series on television, *Angels*, a drama about nurses and what they get up to. Riveting stuff. Actually, it's just the sort of riveting stuff that television does really well, getting behind the ward, having a look under the skin of the nursing profession. I spent quite a lot of my only episode in bed with one of the nurses, and everything they say about them is true – in television terms, I mean. My episode was directed by a very nice guy called Christopher Barry, and on the grapevine I learned that he was going to be directing *Nicholas Nickleby* for the BBC, starting in the coming weeks.

By my reckoning there was a pretty good part for a chap who was in his early twenties, spoke with a straightforward voice and didn't mind running around and getting himself into all sorts of trouble. The part was of course Nicholas Nickleby and I was going to have a good crack at convincing my new best friend, Christopher, that I was the man for him.

Basically, without letting on that I knew what was afoot, I was up his arse for the entire shoot. 'Oh God, Christopher, that's so brilliant – what a brilliant idea!' and 'Christopher, you are just the best,' and even 'I don't think I've ever worked with anyone as, as . . . as you.' He lapped it up.

'Nigel, I want you to keep this under your hat, but I've been asked to direct *Nicholas Nickleby* for the BBC and I'm considering you for the main role. As I said, keep this to yourself, please.'

I did some of my best acting. 'Oh my God, what can I say? I'm . . . I'm, well, flabbergasted.'

He winked at me and it was our little secret.

God, I'd have given anything to play the part. We finished filming and Christopher very kindly asked the cast and crew back to his house near Marlow for a party. It was a very pretty cottage with a lovely garden and, would you believe, a swimming pool. So there we all were, eating, drinking, laughing round the pool, when for some extraordinary reason I thought it would be 'bloody amusing' to throw Christopher into his pool. What a laugh, eh? I thought as I tossed him in. He plunged into the deep end, glass of wine in his left hand, sausage roll in his right. Bosh! He surfaced, and as he spluttered and gasped for air, I noticed something was amiss. Where moments ago there had been hair, the top of his head was now pink and smooth and shining like a peach. As we pulled him from the water I noticed something furry had surfaced. It was joined by a half-eaten sausage roll. I can say goodbye to *Nicholas Nickleby*, I thought. Bugger.

But Christopher was bigger than a toupee and put the whole thing behind him – or on top of him. I got the part. This was it, the breakthrough I'd been working towards. I was to play the lead role in a major BBC production – wow! Of course, by this time I was back working with Frank Lowe, but I knew he would understand that this was my big break and give me his blessing. I was hardly God's gift to advertising after all. The following week, my agent, Michael Whitehall, brokered the deal. He rang me afterwards with some rather alarming news.

'As the programme goes out before six in the evening, they are only prepared to pay sixty per cent of the normal fee,' he told me.

'In which case,' I said, 'I will give them sixty per cent of my normal performance.'

Quite bold, I thought. But it did the trick.

We were soon up and running and I was in heaven. The cast was huge and I was in awe of pretty much all of them. An actor called Peter Bourke and his wife, Kate Nicholls, were to play Smike and Kate Nickleby. I knew them both already, and it was interesting how the chemistry we had off screen helped pull the whole piece together. These three characters drive the story along, and with Dickens it goes at a hell of a lick. Also in the cast were Derek Godfrey, Derek Francis, Liz Smith, Patricia Routledge and Freddie Jones, to name but a few, and when we sat down to read all six episodes through it looked like an A–Z of British television talent.

The first week, we shot a lot of scenes on the *Oliver!* set at Shepperton Studios. When they made that musical version of *Oliver Twist*, the producers had built a huge Dickensian London set, and when they finished filming they decided to keep it and hire it out to other film productions. So there I was with Freddie Jones, rehearsing a long tracking shot that covered about six pages of dialogue. It was directly after lunch and I think Freddie had opted for the liquid variety. That meant a trip to the pub, thereby avoiding film catering. After a couple of notes from our director, we did the first take. Someone shouted, 'Cut!' at the end and I stopped. Freddie didn't. He kept walking, muttering to himself, and eventually came to the end of the set. At which point he unzipped his flies, which took about five minutes as he had so many layers of Victorian costume, and peed against a cardboard lamppost. 'Actor unloading,' he barked. It brought the house down.

Playing a leading role is a very different experience from playing a supporting role. For a start, it means you'll probably be in almost every scene. That in itself gives you a huge advantage over everyone else. Not just because you have more exposure, but more importantly, because of the nature of the game, you get better. You're doing it more and your heartbeat goes down on each take. I found myself more relaxed in front of the camera. I also found out something more important. I could really get under the skin of a character. It's a private thing and I pretend that I don't, but in truth I do, and it's a lovely place to be. I began to really like Nicholas and to hate the people who were mean and cruel to him and his sister and his friends. In one particular scene, when Wackford Squeers, the headmaster of Dotheboys Hall, was being particularly beastly to Smike, I nearly thumped him with all my might. Good thing I stopped myself: I might have killed him. Christ! It was only Derek Francis, one of the country's most loved television actors. Acting can really play tricks on the mind.

The other advantage of being the leading man is that you have some say in the product. Only a tiny bit to begin with, but people started to listen to what I had to say. I also liked 'leading the company', which really means looking after your fellow actors, and standing up for them if the need arises. I was better at that than at being head boy at my prep school. Maybe all that time I had been preparing for this, and I was damned if I wasn't going to enjoy it.

Nicholas Nickleby was shown on BBC 1 on Sunday afternoons in the winter of 1977, the perfect time for a family to watch one of the jewels in Dickens's crown. No one at the BBC could say how many people watched it – they didn't have ratings in those days – but judging by the number of comments that came my way in Boots and WHSmith, it wasn't doing too badly. It was therefore deemed a success and might have had something to do with my letterbox working overtime – the first three episodes out of thirteen of a new BBC 1 drama, *A Horseman Riding By*, by R. F. Delderfield. It read like a dream and there I was sitting in one of those big offices in TV Centre talking to producers and directors about playing the leading role.

'Thanks for coming in.' (No need to thank me, I was dying to come and meet you.) 'What do you think of the scripts?' (You're asking me?)

'Well, I thought the scripts were . . . What can I say? I thought the scripts were fantastic.'

'Who do you think would be good to play your wife?' (They're actually asking me who I'd like to play another part – incredible!) And so it went on. I was beginning to enjoy this.

Our producer was a wonderful man called Ken Riddington. I'd never met a man who worried as much as Ken did. If he didn't have anything to worry about, he'd invent something. I had the feeling during the first few weeks of rehearsal that he was a bit worried about casting me. As usual, we filmed all the interior scenes for the first three episodes in studios at TV Centre. They were rehearsed over several weeks and then filmed over several days. At our last run-through before we went into the studio, I watched Ken out of the corner of my eye. He was biting his nails. At the end, he went into a huddle with the director, Philip Dudley. After ten minutes or so, he addressed the assembled company.

'Well, I have to say I'm not worried about a thing. I think it's going to be terrific.'

Looking back, I remember being worried myself. This was my biggest leading role so far, thirteen hours of television, and I didn't want to make a mess of it. The recordings went without a hitch. Even the camera crew said to me, 'Can't wait to record the next lot.' Always a good sign.

We were off to Devon next to film the exterior scenes. Caro and Kate stayed at home to begin with, as Kate was only a few months old, but we'd arranged to rent a cottage later on, and they were to join me. The first-episode fee of four hundred pounds bought four new wheels – a third-hand British Racing Green MGB. An old mate of mine, Robin Hawdon, a wonderful actor and writer, wanted to get rid of it and I snapped it up. So there I was, roof down, collar up, hair vertical, gunning down the M4, mid-afternoon on a beautiful, sunny spring Sunday, on my way to Salcombe Bay in Devon. The Tides Reach Hotel wasn't exactly a five-star experience, but it did have a good view and I was greeted by Philip, our director, with open arms.

'Hello, darling, how was the drive?'

'Fine,' I said. 'Are you OK?'

'Perfick.'

'Oh my God, he's pissed,' I thought. I unpacked and wandered down to the bar. Philip was buying another round.

'Whaddaya want, darling?'

If you can't beat 'em, join 'em. 'A bucket of wine please, darling.'

And so it went on, and on, and on . . . It ended up with just three of us, Philip, me and Edwina, the first assistant director.

She suddenly realised it was time for bed. 'Off you go, for Christ's sake,' she said. 'You've got to be up in three hours.'

What seemed like minutes later, I was in the make-up wagon, feeling like death warmed up. I didn't see Philip. The first shot I had to do was to drive a horse and trap round a bend in a forest clearing. The camera was positioned by the side of the bend so that I would appear and pass as close to it as I possibly could, going at a hell of a lick. I sat in the trap, holding the reins, waiting for action. I could hardly lift my arms, I felt so weak. Before Edwina could shout anything, the horse lifted its tail, farted and followed through with panache.

'Action!' somebody shouted. The horse continued its business. I knew in a split second that I was going to be sick. Barf! 'Action, for Christ's sake!'

'I'm being sick,' I spluttered. The whole thing was fucking chaos.

Philip had the constitution of an ox and I couldn't possibly keep up with him. Every night after filming, he migrated straight to the bar. Actors take a little longer to get there – they have to shed costumes and make-up.

Some evenings, I bribed the hotel staff to let me in through a side door, and went straight up to my room.

'Where'sh Nigel?' Philip would say.

No one had any idea that I was tucked up and asleep by nine o'clock. For a man who lived entirely on liquid, Philip was one fine director, and never missed a beat. Sober in the day, legless by night. Actually, that's not entirely true: he used to wander around the location with a can of Seven-Up first thing in the morning. On one occasion, feeling a bit parched after running up and down a hill ten times, I took a slug from his can. Seven-Up? Twenty-Seven-Up more like – neat vodka. The way to go, I thought.

We were all gearing ourselves up for a ten-day night shoot. Now, night shoots are horrible things. Suddenly you're supposed to sleep in the day and work all night, but that's the way it goes. There was one episode which pretty much revolved around a ship being wrecked and what happened afterwards. I was supposed to rescue people and generally act like a hero, which required being in the water most evenings – pretty miserable, but I knew it was going to look fantastic.

There were many planning meetings with the camera crew, director, producer, etc. You have to plan much more elaborately for night filming, for several reasons. First of all, people generally lose their temper much more quickly. Secondly, you can't see much in the dark, so it's best to do things in a military manner. Thirdly, and most importantly of all, time seems to fly quicker at night than it does during the day. Philip was on top of the whole thing. The only thing he wasn't on top of was his drinking routine. He drank at night, and couldn't get it into his brain to get completely pissed during the day. Halfway through the first night shoot, he passed out. Edwina took over the reins and carried on seamlessly. Philip occasionally woke up, shouted, 'I waaaan you tooo mooooooove the camera!' and slumped back into his chair. After a while we paid no attention to him, unless he did this in the middle of a take.

'Shut up, Philip!' I would shout.

'Awright, daahling,' he'd belch as he disappeared down the back of a sand dune.

All thirteen episodes took the best part of a year to make. The most alarming thing to me was that while we were filming episode nine, episode one was being broadcast on BBC 1 on Sunday evening. What if people hated it? What if the critics weren't on our side? As it turned out, I needn't have worried. Delderfield wrote skin-deep novels – there's nothing too deep about the plot or any of the characters, and in my opinion this makes the best kind of television drama. It was one hell of an experience, and I enjoyed every second of it. Whatever happened from now on, I was looking at life with a different perspective. I was out of the First Division and into the Premiership.

Chapter 10

Chariots of Fire

'Can you run?'

I looked at my alarm clock; it was nine a.m. Why the hell was my agent calling me at nine a.m.? He's never awake before ten.

'What do you mean, can I run? Of course I can run. Can you?' It's a bit like asking an actor if he can ride, swim, dance or speak Chinese. The answer is always 'Of course I can.'

Half an hour later, I was running down Queensgate, turning right into Queensgate Mews South and up the cobbled stones to David Puttnam's house. I had no idea who the hell he was, I was just collecting a script, any old script as far as I was concerned. As I turned to leave, a voice said, 'You'll have to sign for that.' Now, a script you have to sign for generally means it's a little bit more serious, so as I retraced my steps, walking this time, I looked at the opening page: *Chariots of*

Fire. What does that mean? I wondered. Is it a space movie? Maybe it's a religious thing. I started to read it on the hoof. I got to Kensington Gardens, sat down and finished it. I have to be in this film, I thought. It's the best thing I've read since the old King died.

I knew instinctively which part I'd be auditioning for – the toff, the aristocrat, that one with the blond hair, the part I'd been playing for years and had got pretty much strapped down. But here was a golden opportunity to play something completely different. One of the other characters in the film was a prickly Jewish athlete with a chip on his shoulder the length of the M1. Let me at him, I thought.

For the audition, I had to meet the director, Hugh Hudson. I was told to present myself at his office. This turned out to be a rather gorgeous drawing room in Covent Garden, furnished with enormous comfortable sofas, coffee-table books and discreet lighting. Hugh was sprawled on one of the sofas in his habitually languid manner, and this most casual of auditions turned into hours of chat.

He must have thought I was a complete prat when I announced that I wanted the part of Harold Abrahams. 'Er, well,' he said, 'unfortunately you neither look nor are Jewish, so we might have a problem.'

'I don't see why. Isn't that what acting is all about?' I said rather pompously. Of course I didn't get the part and the script was returned.

Caro had given up work at this point to look after Kate full time, so when I told her what I'd done, I got one hell of a bollocking and the cold shoulder for days, until, luckily, the phone rang – again at nine a.m. Their first choice for Lord Andrew Lindsay had been another actor, Patrick Ryecart. It hadn't worked out, so Michael was asked to give my butt a verbal kicking and tell me to reapply for the part. Oh, thank you, God, and please stop me indulging in actorish bollocks in future. Looking back, I marvel at my stupidity in thinking that I could possibly have passed myself off as the darkly brooding Jewish sprinter.

The parts of Harold Abrahams and Eric Liddell went to Ben Cross and Ian Charleson. Both gave such staggeringly good performances that they became irrevocably identified with their roles long after many other successes. Ben mirrors the dark intelligence and slightly chippy outsider mentality that was so vital for the part. He is also fiercely competitive and set about becoming a world-class athlete with frightening determination.

If anything, Ian had the harder task in portraying someone without flaws, but his angelic, if somewhat eccentric, nature made him a perfect choice, and that smile, which seemed to be lit from within, is one of the most lasting and heart-rending images of the film. For his audition, he arrived clutching a copy of the Bible. 'I've read half of it – I think it's rather good,' he said. The part was immediately his.

The making of *Chariots of Fire* is a fairy tale. David Puttnam's romantic nature makes him firmly believe that the spirit of the saintly Eric Liddell watched over us during filming and delivered us from all kinds of disasters. It certainly was a magical experience; and, as we all know, it doesn't do to deconstruct magic with logic. Just let it be, it's there for us to wonder at. With hindsight, it's easy to say that we caught the zeitgeist of the nation, emerging, as we were, into a frenzy of Thatcherism after years of debilitating strikes and the three-day week. In fact, Maggie Thatcher was later to adopt the film's message of individual endeavour and triumph, much to the fury of our resolutely lefty director!

But at the time we were just turning a modest little story into a film, with no money, a rookie director and, in the main, totally unknown actors – not the most obvious route to four Oscars, you have to agree. Of course, the one thing we did have was an absolute belter of a script, something which even the bluntest knife in the box was quick to recognise as special. Maybe, just maybe . . .

On a personal level, after a shaky start, things proceeded to go swiftly downhill. I was invited back to meet David Puttnam for a briefing on the film in general and my part in particular. I was shown in by a rather luscious blonde. When I was ushered in to see David, he asked if I would like some coffee.

'No, thanks, your secretary has already looked after me very well – what a cracker.'

'I think you must mean my wife, Patsy,' he said rather tersely.

Bugger, I thought, I've blown it again; but luckily no harm was done. He explained that we would be on the absolute minimum pay and that the budget certainly wouldn't stretch to covering wages during the training, but as a gesture of goodwill he would give the four main characters two and a half per cent each of his percentage. 'You won't make a bean, but at least you can ask for something similar on your next film and, well, let's face it, you never know.'

'Can you run?' didn't seem like such a stupid question as I unzipped my new tracksuit. There was quite a group of us – deathly pale and spindly, no hint of a muscle between us. We had been told to report to Chiswick Athletics Club, bang next door to the cemetery – which I thought I might be visiting on a permanent basis after a couple of days' training. Hugh and David wanted us to be entirely convincing and therefore decreed that we should have three months training prior to the start of filming. The man charged with knocking us into shape was a dour Scot called Tom McNab. His face was a picture as he watched us assemble, and his expression became more and more disbelieving as we started to jog round the track. If I tell you that Richard Griffiths was one of our number you begin to get the picture. I could hear Tom thinking, 'You've got to be kidding.' Warning bells sounded with his first piece of advice: 'Eat some breakfast before you get here, just so's you have something to throw up later.'

Once round the track and I needed to sit down. 'This is going to take a bit of extracurricular,' I thought. A couple of years earlier, I'd done a charity gig with Alan Pascoe, who was an Olympic sprint silver medallist in 1972. Nothing ventured, I rang him up for some advice and he agreed to give me an hour's free tuition. Both my cheek and his generosity still amaze me, but he really helped a lot, and I started to believe I could do it. We didn't know it at the time, but apparently Hugh was hidden somewhere in the bushes as Tom slowly – very slowly – started to knock us into shape. He'd watch through his binoculars, rather like a trainer on Newmarket Heath watching his Derby hopefuls being put through their paces.

I was subjected to the extra torture of having to learn to hurdle. As a schoolboy, I'd quite enjoyed running, but I'd drawn the line at hurdling – rather like rowing, it made me want to clench my legs together as certain bits of my body that I was quite keen on got squished in my imagination, but the funny thing about practice is that it really does make perfect and suddenly one day – I got it. Boy, did I get it. Rather like acting, you can go on learning for ever, but there is always that breakthrough moment when you think, 'Yes!'

One day, I decided to show off to Ben (the competition between us was getting pretty fierce). We'd been training hard all day at a new stadium in north London, and I was beginning to feel like a real pro. A voice inside my head kept saying, 'Go on, just one more lap.'

'You want to see something special?' I yelled across to Ben, who was still pounding out hundred-yard laps.

'Sure' he said. 'Show us what you've got.'

I could feel myself flying over the hurdles. Thirteen strides between flights. I could do it with my eyes closed. Just as I reached Ferrari speed, I clipped the fourth hurdle and crashed and burned. It hurt like hell – I had dislocated my shoulder. I lay on the tarmac, unable to move, thinking, that's it – I've blown it, all for a bit of useless showing off. A pro knows when to stop practising, when he feels tired. An amateur, I discovered, carries on to the death, and this felt like mine.

Tom took one look at me and rang for an ambulance. At the same time, he jammed a Mars bar in my hand and said, 'Get that down you – a sugar hit will take care of the shock.' I tried to hold the chocolate up to my mouth and suddenly saw that my hand was sitting at a very jaunty angle indeed. Surely I couldn't have broken my wrist as well? My shoulder really hurt like hell, so I suppose this seemed minor in comparison. Bloody hell, I thought, if I have to have a plaster cast on my wrist, I'll be off the film. I pulled my sleeve down and kept quiet. Even in hospital, I managed to hide the wrist from view, despite having to sit for an hour and a half in screaming agony before they could give me a general anaesthetic and reset my shoulder. They would have done it instantly, but Tom's Mars bar blew the 'nil by mouth' rule right out of the water. Anyway, I kept my mouth shut and my wrist out of sight. I was so determined to stay on the film, I'd have put up with anything.

Tom had gone home once it became clear that I would be back in training without too much delay, and I was beginning to wonder where I was, and how the hell I was going to get home, when Ben walked in. Boy, was I glad to see him, and as he eased me into the passenger seat of his vintage Jaguar, he handed me a huge joint. 'This should do the trick,' he said, and indeed it did.

Of course, Caro hadn't got a clue where I was or what had happened. She was less than amused when I walked in several hours late, stoned out of my brain, bandaged up like a mummy, giggling like a moron saying, 'Dadah! Broken wrist!' She'd only got a quarter of the way through her 'irresponsible, selfish git' speech when it became obvious that the narcotic effect was beginning to wear off and I was starting to suffer. The hand protruding from the plaster cast was completely black, and was throbbing like hell.

The speech was put on hold for a more receptive audience and, not for the first time, Caro took charge of the situation, gently shielding my arm from potential knocks, and making sure there was a pillow underneath it during the night. She immediately understood my fear that the part would be taken away from me, and did everything she could to help speed up the healing of my battered bones. What a star. My Florence Nightingale.

Once I got back in training, I had to concentrate like never before in case I fell on either my professionally mended shoulder or my still-broken wrist. The thought of it makes me sweat a bit, even now, but Tom never found out and I actually managed to improve my hurdling in double-quick time.

Just before filming started, David took us to a private screening of *Lawrence of Arabia*. Afterwards, he gave us a really inspiring talk about how he wanted our film to have that epic feel about it, the triumph of human endeavour and all that. He also taught us the power of the close-up. 'Never forget,' he said, 'that when your face is measuring thirty feet by seventy feet up there on the screen, less is very definitely more: stillness is the key.' Afterwards, he took us all out for dinner and we heard for the first time the origins of what we were about to try to create.

Several years before, he had been working in California and staying with friends there. One day, he was struck down with some ghastly stomach bug and ended up stuck in bed staring at the ceiling. Looking through the shelves for some reading matter, he settled on *The Official History of the Olympic Games*. He started reading without much enthusiasm, but one paragraph caught his eye – the little story of Eric Liddell, a devout Christian, refusing to run in the hundred yards final on a Sunday, and Lord Burghley (Lindsay in the film), who had won a medal already in the hurdles, giving up his place in the four hundred yards final so that Liddell could compete in it – it fell on a weekday.

David couldn't stop thinking about it, so when he got home he approached the AAA for more information. Incredibly, they handed over four scrapbooks, contemporary ones of the time, which provided much of the information he needed for a cracking good screenplay, and for this he knew just the guy, Colin Welland, actor, writer and sports freak.

Fired up by this fantastic evening, I drove home in my old banger with Ben, Ian and Nick Farrell, who played Aubrey Montague, through whose eyes the film for the most part is seen. (Incidentally, Aubrey himself also provided a lot of original material for the script.) It was late and we needed to be up early, but we were all too excited to sleep. We sat for hours, the windows steaming up around us, discussing everything that had happened so far, and wondering whether the film was going to be any good, who on earth would ever want to watch it or even if it was actually going to get made in the first place. David had told us that he'd already had to mortgage his house to help fund it after his original backers pulled out. Luckily, Mohammed Fayed had agreed to put money into the project, on condition that his son Dodi could be on board as an executive producer. This didn't mean much to us at the time, but we decided on that cold night, in our smoke-filled and rather clammy Ford Fiesta, that, either way, we certainly weren't going to make much money. Still, at least it would look good on the CV for future work. Which proved that none of us knew our arses from our elbows.

Shooting began in Cambridge. One of the first things Hugh did was to hire a load of extras from the local athletics club in order to film one of my qualifying races. Obviously,

I had to come either first or second, and Hugh only wanted to film the last hundred yards or so. For the first take, I was positioned ten metres in front, the logic being that the pros would just about be catching me at the line. They didn't catch me. Five metres – they didn't catch me. Level – I came second. What a magic moment! I thought Tom was going to burst with pride. He'd pulled off a minor miracle. Of course, all the pros muttered stuff about training not having started yet, lack of this, lack of that. Yeah, yeah! Suck it up fellas.

The magic was in full swing when filming started in earnest. The first day, filming Ben's arrival at university, the sun came out for the first time in weeks, bathing the impossibly beautiful university buildings in a golden glow. One of the interior scenes required an enormous crane for a hugely complicated continuous take which started miles up in the air and swung down to the ground. These things are notoriously time-consuming, and usually the crew becomes a bit edgy as take after take goes west. By five o'clock, nothing had been shot that could be used. By five fifteen, they had the full six minutes in the can. It went like clockwork – the shot worked perfectly first time.

Of course, even fairy tales have the odd nightmare thrown in, and this one was a hell of a bombshell. The Dean suddenly reviewed his decision to let us film there and decided to turf us out – lock, stock and pretty stunned barrel.

'The script is outrageous. It accuses us of being anti-Semitic,' he wailed.

'Well, you were,' David Puttnam replied.

Honesty was clearly not the best policy, and the door was swiftly slammed in our faces. David was beside himself and as a last resort asked if my dad could intervene. Dad had been up at Cambridge after serving in the Royal Navy during the war and was by now attorney-general, but the Dean was having none of it – we had to go.

Many years later, I was asked to be joint starter of the *Chariots of Fire* Charity Fun Run, with Sebastian Coe and Steve Cram re-enacting the famous quad race. They were brilliant, and really entered into the spirit of the thing, with Seb managing, like Harold all those years before, to beat the clock. I happened to sit next to the Dean at lunch, and gave him both barrels about the stupidity of the decision, bearing in mind we were going to shoot the scenes anyway, we just had to pretend that somewhere else was Cambridge. To my surprise, he was totally on my side, and said he had regretted it ever since. Those scenes were eventually shot at Eton and everyone agreed that, if anything, Eton looked better than the real thing!

The scene that everyone remembers most is, of course, the opening one of us running down the beach, accompanied by 'that music'. Actually, Hugh had originally wanted another piece of Vangelis music for that scene, and they had rather a stand-off about it. Vangelis insisted that he could produce something better. Eventually, Hugh agreed to let him give it a go – a wise decision. It was played over the loudspeaker on the beach to inspire us for our run, and it has continued to inspire countless people in every walk of life ever since.

One of the earliest scenes to be filmed was running on the beach at St Andrews, and I think that was where Eric Liddell's ghost started to get busy. One continuous take of all the main actors running barefoot in sub-zero temperatures for over a mile – madness. Any one of us could have injured himself, and money was really tight and didn't allow for re-shoots. The director of photography, David Watkin, decided to use slow motion together with high-definition film, which is very expensive. If you watch it again, you will see that each drop of water is incredibly crisply defined, and the slow motion creates a shot of David Lean-type brilliance. As when Omar Sharif emerges in dreamlike fashion from that desert mirage in *Lawrence of Arabia*, on first sight we resemble small turnstones pecking about in the sand, and only gradually do we come into focus – me grinning like a lunatic and trying to pretend that my lungs weren't bursting. It took three takes before Hugh was happy. We were exhausted by this stage and not at all keen to go again, not to mention the fact that no one relished going over budget so early on.

When David and Hugh looked at the rushes the next day, disaster: a hair had got into the lens, making the whole day's filming useless. We had to do the whole thing over again a week later. On the first attempt, the sea had been calm and rather lethargic, but on the second, a slight squall had blown in, creating a much more dramatic background of white horses and sunlight dancing on the blustery waves. Was that just luck?

We had a great first assistant director called Jonathan Benson, whose catchphrase was: 'Cut! Very good in many ways – but shall we do it again? Thank you.' One day, we were about to do a shot on the lawn in front of the St Andrews Golf Club House. 'Action!' shouted Benson. 'No, just wait a second, there's a lady teeing up at the first and she's hit the ball . . . into the rough. Frightful shot. And . . . action!' Priceless.

Filming in Scotland, especially all the Highland Games

sequences with Ian Charleson, was magical. I turned up pretty well every day, even though I wasn't actually involved in the filming. It was just a pleasure to watch Ian working. He had such charm about him and a smile that would melt the polar ice cap. In one scene, he was surrounded by a pack of young would-be athletes. I'm convinced that they thought he was Eric Liddell by the end of the day, such was the power of his performance.

On our last Sunday in Edinburgh, our day off, Ian called me far too early in the morning. 'Did I wake you?' he asked.

'No, of course not,' I lied (it's very often the first lie of the day).

'Do you want to have a walk around my city before we go?'

There wasn't a nook or cranny in that beautiful place that Ian didn't know about. We walked for miles, and I listened for hours, until the sun set and we sat nursing a pint opposite the old Assembly Rooms – quite a day. I remember Ian this way, kind, compassionate, very amusing and very, very naughty. They don't make 'em like that any more.

If all goes well, one of the really good things about filming is the close bond that forms between everyone on set, and in this instance it was particularly true. Everything felt easy and comfortable – we knew each other so well after those months of pain in training – it really was a close-knit bunch.

On our last night in Edinburgh, the hotel fire alarm went off at two in the morning. We all emerged into the courtyard, bleary-eyed and wrapped in hastily grabbed blankets. None of us had thought to collect up any valuables. No one, that is, apart from Milena Canonero, the costume designer, who had grabbed all the costumes she had in her room and was sitting in a corner calmly sewing one of our running shirts. There was no way she was letting those costumes out of her sight, and she was preparing to sew away all night to get everything ready for shooting next day. Actually, it turned out that there was no fire after all, it was just someone's smoke alarm getting a bit above itself.

We found our Olympic Stadium in Liverpool – not the obvious twin of Paris, I grant you, but it wasn't at all bad. The track was surfaced in tarmac, which didn't exist back in 1924, so it had to be covered in grass before we could start filming. Unfortunately, May was proving to be unseasonably warm and some bright spark forgot to do the watering. I found myself summoned to David's suite at the Adelphi Hotel. For the second time, he asked if Dad could come to the rescue. There was no money available for more grass; surely Dad could come up with a few readies? I promised to telephone him.

'Are you out of your tiny mind?' was the decidedly frosty response.

'Dad is really sorry, he'd give his right arm to be able to help, but he just doesn't have the spare.'

Back to the drawing board – we needed money fast. A plan of genius suddenly erupted in my brain – Eric Liddell wrote it on a postcard and floated it before my eyes – Dodi! Fayed Senior had got us out of a hole all those months ago, so we couldn't go back to him, but what about Fayed Junior?

I persuaded David to give him a call. He chatted about the weather in Paris, where Dodi was staying with his girlfriend, and generally talked a lot of bollocks, and then David popped the question.

Dodi took no persuading and business was done very swiftly that day. A cheque arrived by return.

We had all been looking forward to the arrival of the

Americans – rather like in the war, we felt once they were on board things would roll along with a bit more zip. Unfortunately, the reverse was true. David and Hugh were staying up town in the rather grand Adelphi Hotel, whereas we low-life actors were stashed in the Atlantic Towers, perfectly nice, just not as nice. Blow me if the Yanks weren't put into the Adelphi. What's going on? we thought, and a niggle of resentment set in. They also seemed to be rather off-hand and aloof on set, especially Brad Davis who played the charismatic American sprinter Jackson Scholz. Brad had starred in Alan Parker's brilliant *Midnight Express* a few years before and I had been especially looking forward to meeting him, but he seemed to go out of his way to ignore us.

One evening back at the hotel, the phone rang and it was Brad inviting us all over for a drink.

'Tell them they can go fuck themselves,' Ben growled rather ungraciously from the corner.

'We'd love to,' I said, and off we went.

It turned out that Hugh had been deliberately pitting Brit against Yank in order to get the feeling of antagonism he wanted on film. Once we started talking and realised what had been going on, we had a riotous evening and ended up the best of friends. Hugh did a lot of winding up during filming. He once persuaded me to have an enormous and very public row with him over something pretty trivial. I had to get very worked up, and it ended with Hugh throwing me off the set. Ben, of course, was incensed on my behalf, and took Hugh to task for his behaviour. Ben worked himself up into a right old lather, and suddenly we heard, 'Action!' It was exactly how Hugh wanted Ben to be in the scene – his scheme had worked perfectly.

For the stadium shots, we needed around five thousand

extras every day for two weeks and there was no way we had enough money to pay them. David came up with a scheme of breathtaking brilliance. He advertised on local television and radio: 'Come and be an extra on the British Film of the Year! Breakfast and lunch free, wear a jacket and tie' etc., etc. On arrival, each extra was handed a straw hat and an official 1924 programme on the back of which was a number. At the end of filming, there was to be a raffle. Now, this wasn't just any old raffle, it was for a brand-new car – God knows how much sweet-talking had been going on behind the scenes to secure that. The hook was that the raffle would be drawn at the end of each day, thereby cunningly ensuring that no one left early. Of course, what it also meant was that no one had the slightest idea how many people were going to turn up. A couple of hours before filming on the first day, the set was being frantically prepared and there was an air of expectation and excitement, just as if it was all for real. The only thing was, not one single extra was sitting in the stands. One hour to go: still no one. David began to sweat. No extras meant a whole day lost – too disastrous even to think about.

About ten minutes, literally, before filming was due to start, a small trickle of people started to file in. We watched with growing disbelief as thousands and thousands of people took their seats, all immaculately topped off with their straw hats and waving their programmes. It was an absolutely magical moment – another one! It had been bucketing down earlier in the day, but, of course, once it came to filming, the sun came out – and another!

I remember being very scared as the time for my race approached. I had to come in second and, as I crossed the line, I remember screaming with a mixture of joy and agony. That scream can be heard on the soundtrack – they decided to keep it in. My favourite moment of the whole film comes just after Abrahams crosses the line in the hundred yards. The wonderful Ian Holm plays the part of Sam Mussabini, trainer to Harold Abrahams. In those days, it didn't do to be seen to be trying – it was considered 'rather poor form', so hiring a trainer must have been thought of as the height of vulgarity, something which fitted perfectly with the outsider character of Abrahams, and Mussabini, being a prickly old bugger himself, understood what drove him.

On the day of the race, Sam couldn't bring himself to watch in the stadium, and sat in his sparse hotel room nearby, listening through an open window. As Abrahams crosses the line to a colossal roar, the film cuts to Sam sitting on his bed and we see him punch the top straight out of his straw hat as he shouts, 'My son!' His face is just wonderful, conveying oceans of pent-up pride and emotion in one look.

Great excitement – the Royal Ballet were in town! David decided we needed some light relief and took a group of us, together with some of them, out for dinner. Afterwards, we all went back to his gaff, which had a fabulous swimming pool in the basement. I have a rather hazy recollection of some pretty racy stuff going on that night. I particularly remember looking up at one point and seeing Ian on the diving board with Wayne Sleep – now there's a vision to conjure with.

The last day of filming in Liverpool required a photographer to take the official team photo. The night before, the photographer, a chap called Terry, arrived. I felt a bit sorry for him not knowing anyone, not understanding the in-jokes etc., and decided to take him under my wing. 'You OK there, Terry?' I kept asking, thinking he seemed remarkably cool considering how intimidating it must all seem to him, assuming he'd never been on a film before. 'Yeah, fine, Nigel, thanks,' he'd reply. The next day, I discovered my 'rookie' was in fact Terence Donovan – bloody hell, I was so embarrassed. I've still got a copy of that team photo. If you look carefully you can see some members of the Royal Ballet posing in the back row.

It was sad to say goodbye to Liverpool. Ben and I drove back to London in his Jaguar – the same model that Inspector Morse was to have several years later. I hope he had better memories of it than I did. Our journey took seventeen hours, and we broke down what seemed like every twenty minutes. Goddam classic cars – who needs them? Give me a purring brand-new Mercedes any day.

Once back in London, we only had a few interiors to shoot, so with great relief I threw away my running shoes. One day, Hugh came up to me and said, 'Sorry, Nige, I need a close-up of you hurdling.'

'You've got to be kidding!' This was a nightmare. More early mornings pounding the track to get back into the rhythm of things. After another week of torture, I duly arrived to do the shot. It was a wind-up. The entire cast and crew were in on it – fuckers.

Some of the last scenes were filmed at Eton, the stand-in for Cambridge due to the Dean's hissy fit. We had – yet again – the most incredible weather and the evening sun gave the buildings a magical glow. Funnily enough, a few years ago, a DVD was produced to celebrate the film's twenty-fifth anniversary and we went back to Eton – the very same weather: after days of rain, golden sunshine. I'm beginning to believe in the Eric Liddell magic myself now!

When you film on location, especially somewhere like a

central London church, where we filmed the memorial service for Harold Abrahams, the background noise has to be eliminated, and the dialogue re-laid in a studio; the process is called post-syncing. Once the filming of this scene was completed, I found myself in a huge studio at Shepperton, sitting in an audio booth in the dark, re-saying the words of my speech as an old man: 'We can close our eyes and remember those few young men with hope in our hearts and wings on our heels.'

As I approached the last line, I heard a sort of 'ding ding ding' noise in the background. I stared at the screen, alone in that dark studio, nudging midnight, as Vangelis's haunting and unforgettable score burst around my ears, and the 'sandpipers' started their lung-bursting dash along that glistening and deserted stretch of sand. I sat spellbound as something magical started to unfold – one of the most masterful beginnings to a film ever made. I never cease to thank my lucky stars that I was part of it.

One night after filming had finished, David and Patsy had dinner with Caro, me and my mum and dad at home. It was David's idea. When he arrived he was carrying two bottles of Dom Perignon Rosé. Bit over the top for a casual supper at home, I thought, but I wasted no time in opening his generous offering, and the evening got off to a cracking good start. Caro was, and still is, a fabulous cook and an excellent hostess, and we were not short of a willing storyteller so midnight came and went without anyone looking at the clock.

Some time around one-ish I heard David say to Dad, 'You don't happen to know anyone on the Royal Command Film Committee do you?' Suddenly, I realised where the Dom Perignon fitted in.

At last Dad was able to deliver the goods. 'As a matter of fact I do,' he said, 'and what's more, I'm shooting partridge with one of them next week.'

Done deal! *Chariots of Fire* was the Royal Command Premiere of 1981. It was the Queen Mother's turn to attend. I remember standing in line waiting to be presented and feeling nervous. In the event, I needn't have worried. 'Do you have double glazing?' she asked. There was no answer to that.

The film went on general release the following week at the Odeon in London's Haymarket. The first night, it was only half full. The matinee was even worse. Sunday came: no better. The box office was disastrous. And then that old Liddell alchemy kicked in again. On Monday, inexplicably, it was full. The Sold Out sign went up, and there it stayed for months. The music was playing on every radio station, and people were starting to talk – it's called word of mouth and it can knock the socks off any million-dollar publicity machine. The snag is people have to love the film. One person who really did love it was Sandy Lieberson, top man at Goldcrest Productions, the biggest British production company at the time. David Puttnam rang me out of the blue.

'Fancy a spot of lunch at Joe Allen's?'

'Sure, why not?'

Lunch wasn't for two. I sat opposite Sandy and eventually, round about coffee, the point of lunch was revealed.

'How do you feel about selling a bit of your points on the film?' Sandy asked.

'In what way?' was all I could muster.

'Well,' he said, 'how about this for one of your two and a half per cent?'

A cheque was slid across the table. It was made out to me

for ten thousand pounds. Boy, could I do with that money, I thought. Ten thousand pounds! Why was he doing it? 'Why are you doing this?' I asked.

'You could do with the money and I'll take the gamble.'

Bollocks, I thought, and for the first time in my life I made the right decision. 'Thanks, but no thanks, I think I'll take the gamble.'

On to Cannes Film Festival. Our film wasn't included in the competition, it was just being screened for publicity in Europe. We were doing thirty to forty interviews a day – totally exhausting – and I asked myself more than once whether it was worth the hassle. Finally, we dragged on our dinner jackets and sashayed up the red carpet – a rather more jet-set affair than Leicester Square – and suddenly I started to get very excited. David told us that he had no idea how it would be received, so if it went well he'd tell us to stand up to take the applause, and if it didn't he'd signal for us to beat a hasty retreat. 'Stand up,' he hissed as it ended. We were bathed in an enormous spotlight and the place erupted. Now this was more like it!

After a very ritzy dinner given by Twentieth Century Fox, and buoyed up on a wave of euphoria, I said, 'Where to now? Anyone know of a good nightclub?'

Ian said, 'Actually, I already have plans.'

'Great,' I said, 'let's go.'

'I really don't think so, Nige. You wouldn't enjoy it.'

The penny dropped: not the sort of club where I would normally hang out, so I trudged back to my lonely hotel room. I poured myself a large brandy and raised a toast to my old mate Liddell.

* * *

Dirk Bogarde had been in the audience that night and the next day he invited us up to his beautiful house near Grasse for lunch. I sat next to him and was immediately captivated. He made you feel that you'd known him all your life. He and his partner, Anthony Forewood, were charming hosts and sitting up there in his exquisite, lavender-scented garden seemed like heaven. I told him that I had recently bought the rights to *The Vortex*, a play by Noel Coward, which in 1957 had been a personal triumph for both of them in the West End. I thought it was the sort of play that would make a great revival and it had a cracking part in it for me. I'd never bought the rights to anything before, so this was a real risk for me, and having Dirk Bogarde on board would have been something of a coup.

The play centres on a mother–son relationship with dark undertones of incest. The final scene ends up with the pair of them having a punch-up and Dirk told me that on the first night, he struck his mother rather too hard and her wig fell off. The audience gasped because suddenly this over-glamorous Mummy, played by Isabel Jeans, looked her age. At the curtain call, a mortified Dirk could hardly bring himself to hold her hand. She turned to him and whispered, 'Keep it in,' and that wig flew every night thereafter.

'Would you ever consider directing it?' I asked Dirk. Before I could finish the sentence he said, 'Yes.'

Would it have been a triumphant success? We'll never know, because within three months, Forewood had contracted the cancer that would rapidly kill him, and our plans never came to anything. Many years later, a production was staged with Rupert Everett in the title role. Now, Rupert is what could be termed an unpredictable character at the best of times, and on a whim he can decide to be audible or totally inaudible. After one performance, a lady wrote in complaining that she had been unable to hear one word that he said. Rupert replied, 'Dear Mrs Snodgrass, I'm sorry you found me inaudible and I have pleasure in enclosing one of my pubic hairs.'

Nothing in this world compares to the Oscars for a surreal experience. Especially when you're a little-known Brit appearing in a low-budget British production about people no one in America has ever heard of, and you find your film is up against *On Golden Pond* with Henry and Jane Fonda and Warren Beatty's massive epic *Reds*.

'We're only here for the beer,' David said, 'so just enjoy the experience. Have fun and relax, secure in the knowledge that we are definitely not going to win.'

Everyone had said that the early Oscars of the evening are a big pointer as to who will do well. So, first Oscar: Costumes – Milena Canonero for *Chariots of Fire*. Second: Best Original Score – Vangelis for *Chariots of Fire*. Hang on, maybe the beer could be exchanged for some decent wine? Best Original Screenplay – Colin Welland for *Chariots of Fire*. Let's send for the wine list! Best Picture – *Chariots of Fire*. Time to crack open the best champagne in the house! David said later that all he could think at the time was, 'Bugger, I wish I'd had my hair cut,' but he made a characteristically brilliant and generous speech, and insisted that Hugh join him on stage as some consolation for not picking up Best Director. I suppose they probably thought, with that flawed Oscar logic which surfaces from time to time, a first-timer had many more opportunities to come, but it remains a crime that he was overlooked.

'I think we should all stay on for a few days and bask in the glory,' one of our number suggested.

'Sorry, not me,' I said, 'I've got to get back to do an episode of *Jackanory*.'

Sad but true. How many actors would miss the chance of strutting their stuff in LA the day after their film has won Best Picture Oscar in order to come home and sit on a low stool in front of a video camera and say, 'Good morning, children. Once upon a time there was a little cottage in the wood'? Only me.

The following Christmas, all the glitz and glamour was a rather distant memory. There was no noticeable knock-on effect from being in an Oscar-winner; I was still struggling to get work and money was still tight. Sometime after tea on Christmas Eve, the doorbell rang. Bugger, I thought, it's bound to be some enormous hood brandishing knuckledusters, sent round to retrieve one of the many Havers loans outstanding. Ever the hero, I made Caro open the door. Phew! At least it wasn't the bailiffs. It was an unmarked recorded-delivery letter. I put it on the table, thinking it was bound to be a bill and I'd deal with it later – maybe in a fortnight.

'For God's sake open it,' Caro said. 'You never know, it might not be as bad as you think.'

It was a cheque from David for thirty eight thousand, nine hundred pounds.

Oh, Eric Liddell – Merry Christmas, my friend.

Every capital city has its fair share of ghettos and London is no exception. In the late seventies, most of the Aussies living in England crammed themselves into little flats in and around Earl's Court. It was London's Little Sydney and whenever I found myself in a pub in that neck of the woods, I would tap myself on the shoulder to remind me never to go 'down under'. It was the accent, I think – that ghastly drawl with everything ending in 'innie' like 'You fancy a tinnie?' which means 'Would you like a pint?' or 'Where're your sunnies, mate?' for 'Have you got your sunglasses with you?' and worst of all 'Don't forget your swimmies.'

Peter Ustinov told this story. He arrived at the main airport in Hong Kong on a Friday afternoon, and the place was teeming. As he sashayed his way through the huge terminal, no one made any kind of physical contact – and he was a big man. The following week, he arrived at Sydney airport on a Sunday morning. The place was deserted apart from one bloke in shorts and sandals. As Peter made his way across the terminal, the bloke bumped into him. 'Sorry, cobber, didn't see you there.'

That just about summed up what I thought about Australia: basically, they were nothing but a bunch of convicts. Boy, was my attitude about to change.

In those days, the Aussies took all the period drama the BBC could throw at them; they loved it, and just couldn't get enough of it. By the time I had completed both *Nicholas Nickleby* and *A Horseman Riding By*, I was apparently quite well known down under, which explains why I found myself aboard a Qantas first-class flight to Sydney, all expenses paid. We were promoting *Chariots of Fire*, and the main characters were all sent to various far-flung parts of the globe to spread the word. Ben Cross got America – lucky bugger, I thought. Ian got Europe and North Africa and was pleased as punch. I got Oz. Bloody marvellous, I thought, as I opened a tinnie, wearing my sunnies, while packing my swimmies. Bloody, bloody marvellous. When the tickets arrived, I noted that I was in first class. I'd always turned right boarding a plane before, so I was looking forward to turning left for the first time.

Qantas was nicknamed 'Quaint Arse' in those days, on account of its reputation for having a large number of gay stewards – richly deserved, let me tell you. On my flight, the first-class attendants made Graham Norton seem like John Wayne, but they made a great fuss of me and looked after me beautifully. I was seated next to a really interesting guy, who travelled to Australia at least once a month and who gave me some useful tips, such as walking around as much as possible during the stopover in Singapore, to avoid any risk of deep-vein thrombosis, and to drink lots of water. I followed his instructions to the letter. I must have walked ten miles at Changi and was never bored for a second. I had never seen a terminal like it. Apart from being able to buy pretty much anything you wanted, I was mesmerised by the sight of a waterfall that went upwards. Crafty buggers.

What my friend from first class didn't know, though, was that I wear contact lenses, and I'd forgotten to take them out during the interminably drawn-out thirty or so hours in that dry, dehydrating aeroplane air. By the time we arrived in Australia, they were stuck to my eyeballs. To begin with, this didn't seem to be much of a problem. I was met by the publicity team, who were young and seemed like fun, and was immediately whisked off to a bar, where we all started to work our way through the cocktail menu. After the third margarita kicked in, Sydney began to look a little different. Not only was it a beautiful city, but the people were just fabulous! The accent took on a whole new and attractive lilt, so much so that I started to pick it up myself.

'Good on ya, mate!' I said to 'Bruce', my new best friend, when he asked if I was ready for my fifth margarita.

'Cripes, mate, we're in for some bonzer time here,' he said.

I smacked him on the back so hard that he practically shot over the bar. 'Christ, you're too right there, mate.' I was almost fluent.

I was somehow checked into the Sebel Town House Hotel, together with all my new best friends, and while they raided the mini-bar in my palatial suite I hit the sack and instantly passed out. A few hours later, I woke up to find them all littered about the place, out for the count. I later learned this was normal behaviour: no one ever had any desire to go home, they slept where they fell.

My first job that morning was to appear on the Australian equivalent of *Film Night* and the film crew came to set up in my suite while I was in the shower, trying desperately to feel like a human being. Suddenly, as I turned the shower off, I heard a deafening noise. Was it in my head or was it the film crew scraping furniture along the ground to make way for the cameras and lighting? Either way, a crazed and caffeined version of me was soon sitting in a blaze of hostile light, staring into the lens of a camera.

'So, first of all, Nigel, tell me what the film's about.'

I sat there like a rabbit caught in the headlights. Nothing came out of my mouth.

'All right, mate, tell me a little bit about the character you play, then.'

Not only had my brain turned into a cotton-wool mush, rendering me totally incapable of remembering the first thing about the film, but even the name of my character was beyond my reach. I saw the interviewer's expression turn from mild amusement to serious concern.

'Are you feeling all right, mate?'

I couldn't even answer that properly, but it did start me thinking about the state of my eyes. When I'd arrived the day before, I'd realised that my contact lenses were Velcroed to my eyeballs, but the ensuing piss-up had put that little problem on the back burner. Now was the time, I thought, to bring it out into the glaring sunlight and use it as an excuse for my total incompetence.

'Actually' I replied, 'my eyes are killing me.'

I was immediately rushed to the nearest optician, who first of all gave me a shot of valium in order to deaden the rather unpleasant shock of having an anaesthetic administered directly into my eyes in order for them to scrape the lens from each eyeball. The combination of valium, margaritas, anaesthetic and practically no sleep gave me a fantastic high.

It all seemed to be going extremely well until one of my new publicity friends looked at me with a shocked 'Oh my God!' expression when I returned to the hotel. I looked in the mirror and, to my astonishment, a Mekon gazed back at me: the whites of my eyes had turned a fetching shade of lime green. Apparently, this is quite normal, but the optician had failed to mention it, and I hadn't thought to ask. It only lasted a couple of days, but those two days were spent doing back-to-back publicity events, and at each one my eyes looked more and more bizarre as green started turning into the red of extreme tiredness.

I don't remember ever feeling so exhausted. The Australians were all charming and no one mentioned my startlingly odd appearance. I can't claim to remember much about Sydney, except that it was a 'bonzer' place to be, but after two more days of back–to-back press interviews, not to mention two marathon evening drinking sessions, it was with huge relief that I boarded my flight home via Los Angeles.

I don't remember much about that flight, either, except that I was woken up on landing at LAX by another camp steward.

'Christ, mate,' he said, 'we thought you were dead.'

'What are you talking about?'

'Well, you haven't moved a muscle for fourteen hours. Burning the candle at both ends were we, sweetie?'

There was no answer to that.

I was excited to be back in Los Angeles and I was glad I had chosen to go home via America. LA has its knockers, I know, but I love the place: the climate is perfect, the energy is palpable and it makes me laugh. On this occasion, I was staying at the Beverly Wilshire (of *Pretty Woman* fame), smack in the middle of West Hollywood, which has to be one of the prettiest hotels I've ever stayed in. They've played around with it since, but back then it was pretty much as it was when David Niven first went to Hollywood and blagged his first dry martini at the famous Long Bar.

On arriving at the desk to check in I was asked for my credit card.

'But surely this has all been paid for?' I said in alarm.

Of course it had, and it was just the hotel policy. I know that now, but back in those days, the thought of having to pick up the tab at such an expensive joint was enough to induce a severe panic attack. I only had a couple of interviews to do there, so before I could click my fingers to 'Seventy-Seven Sunset Strip' I was on my way back home and I forgot all about Australia – for now anyway.

Chapter 11

A Passage to India

India was obviously going to be a bugger. At least, that's what everyone told me.

'You're going to hate it there; very untidy, not like you at all – nothing but beggars and bhajis.'

'I'm off to India to make a film with that David Lean chap,' I'd say.

'You don't want to do that,' would come the response. 'You'll never come home.'

'Bollocks. Of course I'll come home – one day.'

Having been invited to a farewell dinner with a director chum of mine, Jim Cellan Jones, I found myself sitting next to none other than Rex Harrison. God, he didn't look like Professor Higgins any more – in fact, I thought he needed a jolly good ironing – but the voice was still there, every vowel as crisp as a linen handkerchief. I had been warned he was a grumpy old bugger, so to break the ice I heard myself bragging that I was off to India to make a film for David Lean, with Peggy Ashcroft, Alec Guinness, James Fox, Judy Davis and—'

'What? India?' he said, his eyes glinting dangerously. 'You'll die in India. I bloody nearly did.'

Hindsight, of course, is a wonderful thing, and it's probably only now that I realise that anyone with a heartbeat would sell their mother and throw the kids in for free to be given the chance to work with the main man, David Lean. He was the complete film-maker, a master storyteller, designer and editor. The man was, quite simply, a genius. He directed *Lawrence of Arabia*, for Christ's sake.

Back in 1981, I was short on cash, long on responsibility and grateful to be working. *Chariots of Fire* – with a little extra help from an eye-watering mortgage – had recently provided us with a run-down semi-detached in Wandsworth. An unbelievably long wait for completion, coupled with the months spent doing it up, meant we had to bunk up with Mum and Dad.

That was not as bad as it sounds, thanks to the IRA.

Back in 1975, my father had acted as prosecuting counsel at the notorious Birmingham Six bomb trial. All six were found guilty (and served fifteen years in prison before being acquitted). As part of the inevitable IRA reprisals, my parents' house in Wimbledon (Dad's constituency) was blown to smithereens. Apparently, you could hear the blast in Balham. Mum's fur coat was found wandering dazed and confused on Wimbledon Common. Thankfully, she wasn't in it. In fact, no one was at home, apart from a couple of coppers guarding the front and back of the property. Actually, that's not correct – they were both in the Crooked Billet opposite, having what turned out to be a fairly explosive pint.

The first I heard of it was when I was woken at my flat in

Shepherd's Bush at two in the morning by a hack from the *Daily Telegraph*. 'Are you aware that your parents have just been blown up?'

'No,' I said. 'Not a clue.'

'Do you have any comment?'

'Yes. You can go fuck yourself. Thank you for letting me know and goodnight.'

As it happened, Mum and Dad were in Spain. They should have been at home, but had decided to stay on as the sun was shining. Saved by the weather.

The resulting homelessness – not to mention the severe shock – had a profound and long-lasting effect on them both, but as far as I was concerned, it was not without its advantages.

Dad was still attorney-general, and the Falklands conflict was beginning to simmer, so he needed to be housed somewhere convenient for his late-night confabs with Margaret Thatcher and the rest of the cabinet. He was given the most glorious and enormous apartment at 1 Carlton Gardens, overlooking the Mall and next door to the Queen Mother. It was a hell of a place; a little soulless, perhaps, but very fuck-off grand and a great place to entertain – as befitted the London abode of the foreign secretary. The dining room could seat twenty-eight very comfortably.

We didn't wait for an invitation and swiftly moved in. I had all my stationery reprinted. Kate kept an iron grip on her bicycle in order to perfect her skid turns down the miles of wide corridors. I seem to remember she left the most satisfying skidmarks all over the polished parquet.

At the time, I was rehearsing a big television drama, *The White Guard* by Mikhail Bulgakov, which was to be Play of the Month – those were the great old days when the BBC still did big drama productions. With the parents away, I decided it was a good time to test out Carlton Gardens. We threw a wonderful party for cast and crew. It went on a bit, until two or three a.m., and the next day I overheard one of the duty policemen downstairs whispering to his mate, 'Apparently, they were up till four in the morning.' I gathered from the tone of his voice that this rarely happened when Douglas Hurd was in residence.

As luck would have it, David Lean was watching television the night *The White Guard* was broadcast. The next thing I know, I have my agent ringing and telling me that the great man would like me to have tea with him at the Berkeley Hotel the next day to discuss a part in his next film, *A Passage to India*.

I went along expecting some sort of audition, but was greeted by David and his wife, Sandy, and a most delicious tea. It's always hell for me, tea. I don't really do it (I don't really do lunch, either) and I noticed that neither did David. We drank the stuff, of course, but the sandwiches started curling. He was exquisitely polite and we chatted away about this and that. He got up at one stage to show me a picture of where he intended to shoot the cave sequence. I couldn't help noticing how tall he was and how extraordinarily large his ears were. He was wearing a crisp white shirt and dark-blue trousers. I learned later that that was his uniform.

He said that he found London rather baffling, not a bit like it used to be. 'These days, you can actually eat something worth eating.'

Every so often, he would turn to Sandy and say, 'Wouldn't he be perfect for Ronnie?' or 'Doesn't he sound just like Ronnie?' Once I remembered what a boring arse Ronnie was, this seemed like less of a compliment, but at the time I found it charming, and by the end I seemed to be on board.

Thank God he was British. In America the same scenario

would have meant I definitely hadn't got the job. There, 'You're perfect for this part' means 'I'd rather have Hitler; is he available?' I later discovered that David's rule of thumb when casting was that his main actors had to pass the Dinner Test. He used to say that he'd never cast anyone with whom he couldn't sit through dinner. 'Not a bad actor, but bloody good fun at dinner.' Maybe that's me; maybe that's what I should have on my tombstone. 'OK actor; gives good dinner.'

Anyway, in my euphoria, on leaving the hotel I went straight to Doug Hayward and blew my next month's wages on a new suit. It seemed like a good idea at the time. A new suit always seems like a good idea at the time.

Of course, there was a snag. I'd already agreed to make another movie, *The Shooting Party*, starring Paul Scofield. This had been delayed because Paul was ill, but was now back on track. At the same time, David Puttnam had a movie up and running, *The Killing Fields*, and offered me a meaty part. Typical. You wait all day for a part and then three come along at once. There was no competition, though. I was already in training; I'd been to the Star of India three nights in a row that week. I was going to India.

The Shooting Party wasn't the luckiest of productions. On the first day of filming, Paul Scofield had a scene in a horse-drawn carriage and the horses ran amok, throwing him and three other actors, including Edward Fox, from the carriage. The resulting broken bones led to another lengthy delay, which meant I was free to do *A Passage to India*. It was yet another example of how big a part luck, whether good or bad, plays in any actor's career.

I had studied *A Passage to India* for A-level and fallen in love with it, largely due to an inspiring Indian tutor who had been taught by E. M. Forster himself while up at Cambridge, and whom I'd pestered with endless questions about that literary giant. He eventually took me to meet the great man, who had been elected an honorary fellow of King's College some twenty years earlier, and therefore had free accommodation for life, subject to certain conditions. He was a dirty old queen, basically, and was effectively on probation; if he was ever found under an undergraduate he would be out on his ear.

He turned out to be rather grumpy and unattractive; hardly the erotically charged figure of myth and legend, more a tired old poof with an inquisitive twinkle in his eye. We banged on about the enigmatic conclusion of the book, mostly with his hand on my knee. He seemed curious about how each of us interpreted it. Then he told me, with a pained expression, that he couldn't find a satisfactory way to end it; try as he might, every time he closed the final chapter it seemed somehow both trite and, at the same time, overblown. What did I think?

I thought, bugger all, actually, and would you mind removing your hand from my knee?

Funny how, fifteen years later, David Lean would struggle with his ending too. Maybe there isn't one. God bless the Whirling Dervishes.

Most of the filming was due to take place in southern India, and Caro and Kate were staying behind in London until the New Year. Kate was five and had just started proper school, and Caro was keen to get settled in the new house.

As the start of principal photography approached, I began to get more and more nervous. The best part of filming is always the period before you film. You spend all the money you're going to earn having fun, and tell everyone within earshot that you're doing A Passage to India, working with David

Lean. Mmmm, that's right, A *Passage to India* . . . Yes, with David Lean . . .

Prat, they're probably all thinking.

Then, little by little, D-Day gets nearer and nearer, and you have to go off and . . . actually make the film. At that point, you stop boasting, and start sweating.

However forewarned you are, nothing really prepares you for India. It's like having the skin stripped from every nerve ending, every minute of every day, leaving you on sensory overload. Every experience is more intense than you can possibly imagine: the noises louder, the smells stronger, the colours brighter. The heat is ridiculous, and everything takes for ever.

Trying to complete visa control and exit the airport with an entire film crew seemed to take the best part of ten years; their interrogation techniques were worthy of the KGB. Every camera case, every piece of technical equipment, was examined microscopically by Immigration officers who didn't know one end of a long lens from another and often looked at the operation manuals upside down. Driving into Bombay at six in the morning is an unforgettable experience. The road was lined with bottoms as people went about their morning ablutions.

Ronnie was beginning to feel rather queasy. When the man in the next seat on the following morning's flight down to Bangalore vomited on take off, Ronnie started wishing he'd never left Tunbridge Wells.

I hoped it wasn't an omen, but when we arrived at our hotel (a colonial relic which consisted of miles of corridors linking a mere handful of rooms) we were greeted by a dead body sprawled across the drive. I knew it was a dead body because the driver told me it had been there for a day or two. I thought it best to mention this when I checked in. 'It will be removed' was the cool response. Welcome to the world's largest democracy.

I was shown to my room, a pitch-black hole five miles away from reception. You could get really depressed here, I thought; bloody good place to top yourself. When I opened the door I was greeted by a large monkey helping himself from the fruit bowl. Rather him than me, was my first thought, you don't know where that fruit's been; but it was still my property, not his, so I grabbed my spongebag and chucked it at him, hard – very hard. He caught it, cool as you like, and made off with it. Bugger it, I thought, I'll never get Vidal Sassoon in Bangalore. This was war. I used to lie in wait and pelt him with oranges, machine-gun fashion, every one of which he caught, whatever the angle, however hard I threw them, with the precision of a Godfrey Evans, despite the lack of wicket-keeping gloves.

That first night Richard Wilson and I were invited to dine with Priscilla John, the casting director. No one mentioned wine when we ordered our food. 'I'll do the honours,' I said, and confidently chose a bottle of Hirondelle, the only name I recognised from the almost wholly incomprehensible list. I failed to notice that there were no prices marked until the bill came to be signed after dinner. I checked it over and promptly choked. Hirondelle was the cheapest wine, but still racked up a cool £78 per bottle.

'You could probably buy a motorbike for that,' I said.

'Two, actually,' replied Priscilla with a wry smile, who had known all along there was 600 per cent import duty in southern India.

From that moment on, I never went near anything that came from anywhere other than India. I drank nothing but Kingfisher beer and a rather strange concoction called Paul Scott whisky, both of which had an unmistakable hint of curry about them. Except when I had dinner with David and Sandy. He seemed to be invisibly welded to a leather-bound copy of A Passage to India. Boy, is this man committed, I thought; until he passed it to me under the table. It was a hip flask, specifically designed before we left, which he'd smuggled in with a case of Johnny Walker Black Label. 'I'm not paying two hundred pounds a bottle,' he said.

I returned to my room in a filthy mood, not helped by the fact that I absolutely hated curry. I'd loathed it when I'd eaten it at the Star of India in England, and I loathed it even more here. 'It will taste so much better when you're actually there,' everyone had said. Bollocks. At this rate, I'd go home thinner than Gandhi.

My first scene required me to drive a horse and cart, and a certain amount of rehearsal time had been scheduled. Little did they know that any BBC regular worth his salt had cut his teeth driving these contraptions into the nation's sitting rooms every Sunday night. The production manager had bought a couple of dozen emaciated horses. He was gradually feeding them up, but I wasn't going to leave anything to chance; they benefited from a certain amount of food smuggled out of the hotel dining room by yours truly until my scene had been shot. After filming was over, they were sold back into a life of starvation, plump and confused.

I was assigned a driver called Danny. He was inordinately proud of his old Ambassador, the car of choice in India – in fact, the only car in India. Apart from David's specially imported Mercedes ('Part of the film, dear boy'), I don't recall seeing another model. When David parked in the middle of nowhere the Merc would draw a crowd of at least five thousand people. Was it from Mars? Yes, it certainly was.

As Danny had no stereo or radio and I would be spending considerable time sitting in chaotic traffic jams while driving to and from the various sets, I decided to buy him one as a present. He was thrilled, and I was thrilled that he was thrilled – until I realised that from that moment on I would have to endure Indian music played at full volume for at least eight months. What is it about that music that makes you want to kill somebody?

'Turn it down, Danny!' I would scream.

'What?' he shouted back.

'Turn the fucking thing down!'

'Fucking what?' He loved saying that: 'It makes me sound as if I am from Britain.'

Danny's driving consisted of two speeds: stationary (frustrating) and full-tilt (terrifying). Night driving was particularly hazardous, as we hurtled past cattle, camels, humans or whatever else was occupying the road at high speed without the benefit of any reassuring distance between us and them. Most alarming of all was Danny's misguided dedication to thrift. Should I happen to doze off on the way home when it was dark, I would wake up to find he'd switched the headlights off and a cow's rear end, and sometimes even a bull elephant's gigantic arse, would rear up in front of us like a tsunami.

'Lights, Danny!' I would scream as I dived into the recovery position.

'Oh, don't worry, Mr Nigel,' he would cheerfully reply. 'Saving on battery.'

'Turn the bloody lights on, Danny.'

As I dozed off again, I would hear the telltale click as he resumed driving Blunkett-style. 'Turn the fucking lights on, you Indian cunt.'

Maybe Rex Harrison had a point after all.

The part of Mrs Moore was to be played by Peggy Ashcroft, who by this time was in her seventies. The first couple of weeks in Bangalore were spent rehearsing and getting to know one another. Everyone was being extremely charming to everyone else, primarily because we were all so nervous. I had worked with James Fox before and he is a delicious man, quiet, unassuming, not in any way an 'Actor' at all. Peggy was very urbane, just as I had imagined. Fiercely intelligent and with a dry sense of humour, she kept herself pretty much to herself. As for Victor Banerjee, I think he was clinically insane. Mad as a box of monkeys. He would come up and pinch you from behind, cry on demand or scream with laughter – never a dull moment.

Quite early on, David took me to one side and asked me very politely what rehearsals were actually for.

'Um, er, well . . . rehearsing, really . . .'

'Don't be ridiculous. I know that, but do they actually help you?'

'Yes,' I said, 'believe it nor not it always helps, however many times you do it.'

So there we were on a Wednesday afternoon, rehearsing my first scene with Peggy and Judy Davis. 'If you could all just walk in and say the lines,' David said.

Peggy turned to me with a confused look. 'What did he say?'

'What did she say?' David said.

'She said, "What did you say?",' I said.

'What?' said David.

Oh, Jesus, they're both over seventy and deaf as posts; we'll be here for ever. I'll be buried here and they still won't have finished the film. OK, Rex, you win. No, this will not happen . . .

I turned out to be one of the best interpreters for deaf people in the whole of India. Whatever came out of David's mouth, I immediately made sure Peggy understood, and vice versa. We were going to finish this film if it killed me, which at that moment seemed highly likely.

I soon abandoned all pretence of liking curry and settled into a diet of boiled eggs, cashew nuts, bananas and *lassi*, a delicious yoghurt drink common in India which comes in two varieties, salted or sweet, both of which, beguilingly, taste exactly the same. This concoction was meant to keep you off the potty long enough to complete a scene or drive to a location, and it pretty much lived up to its reputation.

I continued to report any alarming observations to the enigmatic receptionist. One day, I was horrified to see an electrician tinkering with wires while standing in the swimming pool. Actually 'swimming pool' is a bit rich; it was a hole in the ground full of murky green water and enough animal life to keep David Attenborough happy for weeks. If anyone behaved badly they were threatened with being thrown into it. But as there was a rather large wedding coming up in the hotel grounds, something was being done to smarten the place up a bit.

'What happens if he electrocutes himself?' I asked.

'He will be replaced.'

'What do you mean, "replaced"?'

'He is an untouchable,' I was told, with a definite hint of 'Do please stop bothering me with your trivial observations.'

Since the pool was off limits, keeping fit became something of a challenge. Running wasn't an option, either – if the traffic didn't kill you, the smog certainly would.

Richard Wilson and I stumbled on a badminton court tucked away behind the laundry outbuildings. It was in a bit of a state, and lit by old car headlamps, but we decided it was the perfect place to let off a bit of steam after spending the day acting repressed Brits in the Colonies, so we took to playing regularly.

One evening we burst on to the court to find – shock, horror – it was being used by a couple of the hotel staff. I marched smartly off to reception. 'Excuse me, but I think you will find some of your staff playing on our badminton court.'

'Indeed, sir,' was the reply. 'It is their court.'

We returned rather sheepishly to sit it out until they'd finished. They, equally sheepishly, asked if we'd like to join them. Now, Richard and I had been playing rather a lot recently, and fancied ourselves to be, if not championship standard, at least pretty bloody good.

Gratifyingly, we whipped their arses in the first set.

As we changed ends, Richard whispered, 'They're not even sweating.'

'Do you think they're trying?' I said, wringing out my T-shirt. We started the next set. 'Please feel free to play your own game,' I said, rather idiotically.

We never saw the shuttlecock again. Boy, could those guys play. We became great friends, and they became great instructors. By the end of our stay we even managed to take the odd point off them.

Finally, the first day of filming was upon us. I didn't sleep a wink the night before; I even telephoned Richard Wilson at three a.m. to ask for a sleeping pill.

'What time's your call?'

'Five thirty,' I said.

'Forget it,' he said.

And so I arrived on the set looking rather sick and feeling

like death. David came up to me and asked if I was OK. 'Fine,'
I said. 'Just didn't sleep a wink.'

'Is that all?' he replied. 'Neither did I, old boy.'

I realised that for all his brilliance and experience, the great
David Lean was probably as nervous as I was. This was his first
film for fifteen years, and yet again he was putting his reputation
on the line. Could he still cut it? Of course, the answer to that
was a triumphant 'Yes', but he was not to know it then.

No producer at the time really trusted him; he was made to
sign an undertaking that he would complete every scene in the
time allotted. By lunch the first afternoon, we were three days
ahead. The clever old bugger had managed to persuade the
suits that the first scene would be more difficult to shoot than
the storming of Aqaba. By the end of the first week, they couldn't
believe their luck. We were ahead of schedule and it looked
beautiful; you could smell India in every frame. Perhaps this
would be the first time the real India was caught on film.

The part of Adela was played by Judy Davis, a wonderful,
feisty Australian actress, who had just received rave reviews for
her performance in *My Brilliant Career*. Judy and David did not
get on. I think one of the main reasons was that Judy was a
creature of her time and wanted to go for realism at any cost
– including little or no make-up and, I couldn't help noticing,
dirty hands. This made perfect sense in scenes like the one in
which she rides her bicycle out to a remote and overgrown
temple, but David was old-school and liked his women to look
perfect. The most he would allow was the merest hint of a glow.
This cut no ice with Miss Davis, and they had some spectacular
rows, one of which ended in a Mexican stand-off. It also sealed
my fate: I was not only in the first shot to be filmed in India,
but also in the last.

Ronnie comes home to find his wife, Adela, sitting by the garden pond, dangling her feet in the cool water. That would have been fine for Ronnie, except for one small but explosive problem: Godbole, the Indian mystic professor, was also dangling. You did not dangle with an Indian.

'What are you doing?' Ronnie says in that tight-arsed, British way that comes alarmingly naturally to me.

Judy turned round to reply and David suddenly shouted, 'Cut!' Then, 'Judy, darling, could you shift your body further round to face Nigel? I don't want to see the creases in your neck.'

'Jesus Christ,' I heard Judy mutter. Her eyes flashed. I knew we were in for the big one. 'I want them to see the creases in my neck,' she said.

'Allow me to know better,' David replied.

This was greeted with 'What decent film have you ever fucking directed?'

There followed what we in the business call a freeze-frame. Everything stood frozen for what seemed like hours. Then the cast and crew started to melt away, until David shouted, 'Nigel!'

I sidled up to him. For once, his hearing hadn't let him down. 'Did she just say, "What decent film have you ever fucking directed?"'

I took a deep breath. 'That was pretty much the gist of it.'

'Right, she's off the film.'

Now that didn't suit me at all. For a start, they'd have to re-cast her – that's at least a month. Then we'd have to re-shoot all the scenes already shot – that's another two months. No, this wasn't going to happen. 'She's a fantastic actress,' I said.

'Yes, you're right,' he said, and she stayed. Actually, I don't think he ever really meant to replace her; she's far too talented and was a vital part of the film.

One of the crew helpfully offered to get her a copy of *Brief Encounter*, thinking it might ease the situation. The offer was roundly refused, with a few choice antipodean adjectives.

I stuck up for her, more to get home than to get her an Oscar nomination – which she did – but it did me no good. The dangling scene remained resolutely on the call sheet until our last day in India – Scene 28, Day Exterior, Fielding's Garden, Standby To Be Completed.

I waited over three and a half weeks, doing fuck all, just waiting to complete that scene – David's punishment to Judy, and I got wrapped up in it. That's filming for you.

Early on during filming, Peggy asked for a complete read-through.

'I've never really seen the point of a read-through, have you?' David asked over dinner, tilting *A Passage to India* in my direction.

'Well . . . er, I, um,' I said.

He gave it some thought. 'I mean why would anyone want to do it?'

Most of the cast and crew felt the same way, but beneath the 'favourite granny' exterior, Peggy had a core of pure tungsten. The upshot was . . . we had a read-through.

We had been filming for nearly three weeks and ninety per cent of the cast were fully on board, so on that Sunday roughly a hundred rather bad-tempered people squeezed themselves into a small and very steamy room.

David kicked off the proceedings by giving a brief introduction. 'I'm David Lean, the director.' He got a big laugh, which rather startled him. 'I'm making a film called *A Passage to India*.' Another big laugh. He was beginning to enjoy this.

Before every scene was read, he introduced it, telling us exactly how it was going to be shot and where the cuts were. He had the film, complete in every detail, filed away in his head. The rest of us had to struggle to catch up with his total understanding of plot and characterisation. It was like watching a conductor conducting a Beethoven symphony from memory. I could see every scene in the film; in fact, I could see the film. It was very beautiful and moving, some scenes making me cry, others laugh. I suddenly didn't mind how long I was going to spend in India; I just knew that I would never work with a better director. Whatever happened to me during this film would be worth it.

He only ever filmed on specially constructed sets. He chose the location for my house because of the proximity of a beautiful avenue of mahogany trees. The market, which ran for nearly a mile, was entirely built for the production. When we started filming it, he decided it was the wrong way round. 'The light's in the wrong place, darling.' Another day off.

At some point during that afternoon, Peggy asked a question about Mrs Moore. David replied that it was much easier when one understood that she was always three feet off the ground.

'What on earth are you talking about?' she said. 'How can anyone be three feet off the ground?'

But when the cameras started to roll she found the key quite effortlessly – and walked away with an Oscar. (Characteristically, she refused to go to Hollywood to collect it, and when woken at four a.m. to be told it was hers, snapped, 'Do you realise what time this is?')

Staying in a hotel for a long time is always a strange experience. In India, it's surreal. You never know what's round the corner, or even in the next room. I was woken at four one morning by the most unholy racket; it sounded like someone strangling a cat. As my call was for five thirty, I was well pissed off. I shot out of bed and banged on the wall.

It turned out to be a holy racket: early-morning prayers.

'Excuse me,' I yelled nevertheless. 'Would it be at all possible to internalise?' In other words, just shut the fuck up.

It seemed to have the desired effect – until four the following morning.

More wailing.

'What happened?' I cried.

'I'm so sorry,' came the reply. 'It is quite impossible to internalise.'

Thankfully, my neighbour only stayed a few more nights. I bumped into him at reception as he was checking out.

'I prayed to God that you might leave,' I told him.

'Your prayers have been answered,' he said.

I felt rather guilty later, when I discovered that he had left me a charming note, apologising.

On my way to work that morning, I happened upon 'the wrapping of the glasses'. I watched in awe as staff with the dirtiest hands this side of Calcutta swathed fresh glasses for the rooms in paper which boasted, 'This glass has been hygienically wrapped for your convenience.'

I made a mental note to drink straight from the bottle from that moment on. I'd grown to like India rather a lot – but I still didn't want to die there.

One day, David took me to one side and told me that Alec Guinness would be arriving at the weekend. He asked if I wouldn't mind looking after the great man, indeed taking him to dinner his first night.

As David and I mostly ate together, I wondered what he meant. It all boiled down to a fearsome row they'd had a million years ago during *The Bridge Over the River Kwai*. Appropriately enough, the row took place on the bridge itself. David had decided to film a significant moment towards the end of the film between Alec and the Japanese camp commander at sundown, smack in the middle of the thing. A scene like this takes a couple of hours at least to capture, but as he wanted it to be shot at 'magic hour' – film jargon for that extraordinary light you get immediately before the sun sets – it was going to take three or four nights to complete.

'I want you to drop your stick, by mistake, into the river, Alec,' David said on night one.

'No,' came the reply.

'Why the hell not?'

'Nicholson just wouldn't do it,' Alec said.

This went on and on, until it was dark.

David won in the end, of course, but he lost Alec as a close friend for years. David always did have a reputation for taking his time, but that's an epic tiff by any standard. They never really forgave each other.

I think one of the reasons David liked me was that I would drop my stick for anyone.

'I just need a close-up of you saying that word, Nigel.'

'Fine, no problem.'

'You don't need to do the whole speech, then?'

'No, why would I?'

He liked to get on, really, and that suited me down to the ground. I had some serious badminton to play.

I was still chuckling about all this when the phone went in my room and I heard that famous voice. 'Hello, Nigel, I've arrived. Shall I meet you in the bar?' And what a voice! Undertones of *The Lavender Hill Mob* with a hint of Obi-wan

Kenobi, a definite twist of *Bridge Over the River Kwai* and just a sniff of *Lawrence of Arabia*.

It was one hell of a moment for me; you see, out of that whole generation of heavyweight actors, Alec Guinness was always my favourite.

Poor Alec had only just arrived in India and was looking a bit shell-shocked. I was fine by now; I'd been there for three months, for heaven's sake. He'd been there for five seconds, his cream linen suit looked as though it had been slept in for three days, the panama hat was on at a jaunty angle and he looked rather like startled mongoose.

He was dying for a cocktail. 'What do you drink around here?' he gasped.

'Well, er, there's Paul Scott whisky, or Paul Scott vodka,' I said.

'I'll have one of each.'

I watched and waited. 'Which do you prefer?'

'They both taste exactly the same,' he said, 'with a slight undertone of curry.'

Five Bloody Marys later, we staggered off to bed. It was a hell of a night, with some wonderful stories, from *Oliver Twist* to *Lawrence of Arabia*. He told me how much he'd loved playing Pip in *Great Expectations*, and afterwards, when he found out that David Lean was going to direct *Oliver Twist*, how he yearned to play Fagin. 'Don't be ridiculous,' David had said to him. The following week he turned up at the auditions dressed and made up to look like Fagin. He did the screen test. David didn't know it was him – the job was his.

'No, no, Colonel. Young men are passionate, and they must say their say . . .' I heard myself quoting the line from *Lawrence of Arabia* with him. At the time, it was pure bliss, but I wonder now if it wasn't a bit sad. I know every line from the film – what an anorak.

On my way out the next day, reception handed me a crisp envelope. It was a thank-you letter from Alec, who wasn't called on set that day, and an apology for keeping me up so late. Would I please ignore everything he had said, and promise not to repeat anything I remembered? He needn't have worried; I wouldn't have spilled any beans. The fact that he ended up wondering what on earth he was doing in Bangalore at three in the morning, about to play a part he didn't want to play and being directed by a man he didn't want to be directed by, playing the part of an Indian when he thought it should be played by an Indian, was neither here nor there.

The first scene Alec was to film was the moment when Mrs Moore is leaving India by train. It was a night shoot and the railway station was overflowing with extras and lookers-on. The train was straining at the leash, with steam escaping from every orifice. It gave the scene a terrific feeling of urgency and expectation, like a greyhound in the slips. As the train slipped away into the night, out of the shadows appeared Godbole, Alec's character, beautifully calm and serene. Suddenly, totally unrehearsed, he raised his arms aloft with a dramatic flourish. Everyone held their breath, expecting David to shout, 'What the hell are you doing?' Instead, he simply said, 'Clever old bugger. That was wonderful – print it.' It was a spine-tingling moment of pure theatre.

The inevitable onset of Delhi belly led to the occasional outburst of bizarre behaviour. During our famous read-through, David had made it plain there was to be no embarrassment if any of us were caught short, 'even in the middle of shooting'. One particularly dramatic scene between Peggy and me took an absolute age to complete. 'Ronnie,' she would say imperiously, 'I really cannot under—' and she was gone, her matronly rear disappearing purposefully back into the building.

We'd kick our heels for a bit and be ready for take two. 'Ronnie, I really ca—'

We didn't finish it that day, and I didn't see Peggy for at least a week.

Caro and Kate had joined me by this stage and quickly succumbed. They were laid very low, and I had to get the film unit doctor in. Doctor Death, he was known as; I've no idea why, because he carried around a huge briefcase full of every imaginable drug. His job was really to make sure the actors made it on set at all costs. I got rather hooked on his vitamin B12 injections. Apparently, it does you absolutely no good at all, but I felt happy as a cricket. After ten days or so, Caro and Kate emerged from our hotel room. In fact, Kate couldn't wait to get better as Doctor Death scared the hell out of her. He could have been straight out of a Hammer horror movie – all dark and sinister. On the other hand, I think Caro took rather a shine to him – she always did like the darker look; Elvis Presley was her pin-up, for Christ's sake.

When Peggy eventually recovered, she mentioned how much she missed good old English Sunday lunch. I had a little time on my hands and decided, after negotiating with the kitchen staff, that I would cook the Real McCoy the following weekend.

I told the chef I'd be cooking for at least fifteen, whereupon he produced two anorexic chickens. 'You're joking,' I said. 'I'll need at least twenty of those.' I sourced some potatoes, carrots, Brussels sprouts (would you believe?), and even managed to filch a couple of white loaves off the catering truck while filming one afternoon. That was the most important ingredient of all.

The making of the bread sauce was conducted with a bit of a ceremonial flourish, as far as I was concerned. The kitchen staff, on the other hand, were perplexed, deeply perplexed.

I offered it up for their approval.

'I'm sorry, Mr Nigel,' was the response. 'But this is having no taste, none at all.'

I smiled quietly but triumphantly. That was exactly what I wanted. But to tell the truth, just like the Paul Scott, everything had an underscore of curry. Despite that, Peggy loved it and was polite enough to say that it was just like being back at home.

When the time came to shoot in the hills, the entire cast and crew were transported through Mysore and up on to the cool plains of Ootacamund. Danny drove with the inevitable Indian music full blast, but it was a fascinating journey. We passed elephants being washed in rivers and a cattle market which stretched for ten miles along the road. We stopped at the tea-picking area for a cuppa – very hot, very sweet and very black, with a mild aftertaste of, you guessed it, curry.

Some of us were lucky enough to stay at the Ooty Club, famous for being the spot where snooker was invented, and it gave me a hell of a kick to be able to use the very same baize.

The three weeks we had up there above the tea line was a glorious throwback to the golden days of colonialism. We had fires in our bedrooms, because the temperature plummeted at night, and the menu had remained unchanged since Partition. There was mulligatawny soup with bread and butter for lunch, consommé with Melba toast (no butter) for dinner, roast lamb, Brussels sprouts, even strawberries, all grown at the same time, side by side.

The only problem was that Kate was having quite a bit of difficulty sleeping, and no difficulty at all screaming, so we had to take her down to dinner with us. One night, Caro and I finished our meal and left, and it was only when we were about to get into bed that we realised we had left her fast asleep under the table. Nowadays, she would have been whisked straight into care.

To my great delight, looking through the library one day, I found the father of one of my school friends, Johnny Ampthill, was mentioned in the shooting book which kept meticulous record of all the animals killed during the club's colonial heyday. Johnny's father was pictured sitting cross-legged in front of a huge tiger. Shooting tigers stopped years ago, thank God. The last tiger sighting in the area was at least two years before. As I flicked on through the book, I suddenly realised that those old colonial buggers would stop at nothing in order to recreate old Blighty. They imported foxes from England in order to hunt, they grew strawberries on the slopes in front of the club house, they even had Yorkshire pudding with their Christmas dinner. God knows what the stirrup cup tasted like – Pimm's with a hint of curry?

We were above the clouds here, looking down into the green, rich valleys below us. Driving to work every day was a truly magical experience, and at night you felt you could almost touch the stars, they were so close. This was the first time I really enjoyed being in India. I told David I was beginning to get the hang of the place, to really understand it.

'You never will,' he replied. 'Just as you think you've got a grip on it, you'll turn a corner and there will be something else that takes your breath away.' Of course, David knew more about India than anybody, and he loved it. I had the feeling that for the first time in his career he was actually enjoying making a film. He seemed relaxed when off duty and genuinely concerned

avid Lean and a well-decorated elephant show each other mutual respect.
Painting them was a relatively pain-free experience since each elephant
had a bottle of rum in their morning feed

How India fell in love with
David Lean: the beginning of
Passage to India. Left: First day
of filming. With Judy Davis still
in make-up, director David Lean
stood in for her... My expression
of concentration was for real –
the director and Dame Peggy
were in my nervous hands

Kate in India – looking none the
worse for her diet of cashew nuts

David Lean, famous for giving his actors dramatic, beautifully set up entrances, talks about my own

Dame Peggy and me getting on like a house on fire

'Have you ever thought of doing it this way?' Showing off to a true legend, Alec Guinness

On the set of *Burke and Wills*: 600 miles from anywhere, but surrounded by lorries, sand machines – and exhaustion. I'm the one asleep in the middle

The lettuce leaf in my right hand was all I was allowed to eat…

It might not look much but the Riviera of Cooper's Creek was St Tropez to us. I lived in that hut on the right for three months

With Sidney Nolan, the legendary painter – he made me smile for the first time

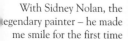

''Ello my son.' Me and my screen Dad from *The Whistleblower*

On the set of *The Whistleblower* with the lead actress Felicity Dean

and with the director, Simon Langton

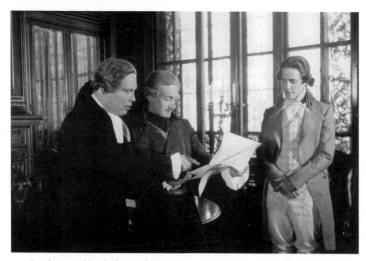

On the set of *Lord Elgin and Some Stones of No Value* with playwright and thespian Julian Fellowes and a young tea boy with a promising career ahead of him – Hugh Grant

he Charmer wedding. From left: Alan Gibson (director), Philip Hinchcliffe (series producer) and Nick Elliott (ITV producer)

'I've got them over a barrel.' A stellar sherry signing at Gonzales Byass. Christian Bale and Leslie Phillips are in the audience and on the barrel

Pretending to be mean and moody on set of *Empire of the Sun*. Or maybe I was just bored…

A continuity photograph for the night I busted my ribs

Nigel Havers conquers LA… not!
A press shot for *Farewell to the King*

Can you imagine being rescued by Nick Nolte?
110°F, 100% humidity – another routine day
filming *Farewell to the King* in Borneo

James Fox and I manage
a slightly weak and
weary smile for the
camera. The last week
of filming and I was
ready to come home

On set in
Sarawak

With Polly

about other people's problems. One member of the cast discovered she had breast cancer when she returned to England having completed her scenes. David got to know about it and paid for all her treatments at a top clinic in London. He was that sort of man. He never spoke about these things, but he was generous through and through.

One of the last scenes to be filmed in the hills, the one in which I bring my mother, Peggy Ashcroft, back from the Malabar Caves, involved a couple of thousand extras. In England, that would present a huge logistical problem: not only would it cost a fortune, but there's always a worry that half of them wouldn't bother to turn up. You also have to feed and water them to such an extent that it's quite often worth writing those sorts of scenes out of the script. In India, it's easy. For every thousand extras you hire, there will be another thousand watching.

On the first day, as Peggy and I rehearsed in front of the railway station, David suddenly went into a panic. 'My God! Peggy's hair!'

'What's the matter with it?' I asked.

'Look! It's exactly the same shade as the station walls!'

I did as I was told, and he wasn't wrong. The stucco boasted a greyish-purple tinge which bore a passing resemblance to Peggy's rinse.

David paused for a second. 'Repaint the station, and make it darker . . .'

We all stood down for two days. The entire station was repainted black, even though we didn't use half of it.

'Right . . . Nigel, I want you and Peggy to get off the train, push your way through the crowd and exit through the main station gates.' David yelled all this from forty feet up on a crane.

217

'What?' Peggy predictably replied.

On 'Action!' she kept veering out of shot, despite David screaming directions from on high. Eventually, he ran out of patience, climbed down and whispered in my ear, 'For God's sake, grab her by the arse and keep her in shot!'

I think Peggy rather enjoyed being grabbed by the arse. I just hope she didn't think I was making a pass at her. By all accounts she was quite a girl, in her time.

It was a shock getting back to steamy Bangalore after the coolness of Ooty, but time was running out and David had to wrap things up.

The last major part of the film takes place in and around a court room. The exterior of the court was chosen by David because of the enormous and wonderfully impressive mango tree outside its main entrance. He wanted extras hanging off every branch, like inquisitive crows, squawking their disapproval of Adela as she arrives. Madras grass was the name of the local brand of marijuana. It cost nothing, and was widely used by locals. When filming started, everything looked perfect, but as the day progressed we began to hear the odd thud. These thuds became more and more frequent, until we had to break filming and investigate.

The Madras grass was a particularly strong brew that day and had stoned the crows. They were dropping out of the tree like rotten apples – except that they were giggling as they hit the ground, and immediately being replaced.

David kept asking, 'What's that funny smell?'

'Someone must have lit a bonfire,' I said, taking a deep breath and almost choking on the fumes.

The extras hadn't completely lost their marbles, though. Our second assistant director couldn't work out why their wages were twice the allocated amount – until somebody spotted them pocketing their pay packets and nipping smartly round the back to rejoin the queue.

We adopted various waifs and strays along the way – film crews always do. One particular guy became the company mascot. He had no legs, so the crew built him an extraordinary contraption, like a go-cart with no sides; it turned him into the fastest Indian in history. We set up a charity for him, and a year later I was sent a photograph of Mr Patel grinning from ear to ear, showing off a brand-new pair of legs.

The final few weeks of filming took place at Shepperton.

I watched David arriving on the first day. Immaculately dressed in his habitual uniform – crisp white shirt, dark blue trousers, black shoes – he sailed magnificently through the gates in a beautiful Bentley Continental just like my father's.

Funnily enough, Dad told me that during a lull in matters of state he had been chatting to Mrs Thatcher about the film, and David in particular.

'Is he still alive?' she asked in amazement. 'Then why on earth haven't we knighted him?'

I invited Sir David, Lady Sandy and a few other mates to the Garrick to celebrate his elevation. After dinner, I spent some time showing Sandy round the club.

'Come up and see my etchings,' I said, with startling originality. I was nevertheless rewarded with a very enjoyable fumble in the library, among the finest collection of theatre memorabilia in existence – very enjoyable, that is, until we were rather rudely interrupted by David. He didn't seem to mind. She was very pretty and a bit of a flirt, so I guess these things happened.

The film was chosen for the Royal Command Performance that year. Funny thing, filming. When you get the job it's fantastic, you celebrate. Then you go and make the thing; it's ghastly, people shouting at each other. Then you meet again at the premiere and it's 'Wonderful, dahling, didn't we have such a fabulous time?' It's all bollocks, really.

Caro and I scrubbed up and went to meet the Queen Mother and have dinner at the Savoy. I was sitting at David's table. During dinner, a man came up to him, whispered in his ear, turned on his heel and disappeared.

David turned to me. 'Do you know who that was?'

I raised my eyebrows. 'Of course I do. Steven Spielberg. What did he say?'

'He said he wants to produce my next film; whatever I want, wherever I want.'

'Blimey!' I said. 'What's it going to be?'

For an instant he looked crestfallen, and then slowly his face broke into the most wonderful smile.

'*Empire of the Sun.*'

Pause.

'Is there a part in it for me?'

Chapter 12

Australia

After my first visit to Australia, I didn't give the place a thought for months and months, especially as *A Passage to India* took most of the following year. Australia might as well have been on Mars as far as I was concerned. Until, that is, the phone rang. My agent, to tell me that a director called Graeme Clifford was staying at Blake's Hotel in South Kensington and wondered if I would like to have tea that coming Sunday. (What is it about directors and tea?) He was making a film about Burke and Wills, and wanted to talk to me about it. I had never heard of either Burke or Wills, and the thought of having to up sticks and go off to Australia so soon after finishing in India was less than appealing. Kate was well into schooling by now, and had passed the age when we could reasonably take her out for any longer than the odd week or so, which meant that Caro wouldn't be able to come with me, and filming can be a lonely old business on your own, among a load of strangers – very nice they normally are, but strangers nonetheless.

Sunday came and we went out for lunch with some friends. We were enjoying ourselves, so when four o'clock approached, the last thing I wanted to do was bugger off to Blake's. I nearly flipped a coin for it, but then decided I had better do as I was told, and off I went, in a fairly foul mood. Needless to say, Graeme turned out to be absolutely charming. I liked him immediately. He was a very dapper man, ten or so years older than me, and had just had a big success with a film called *Francis* starring Jessica Lange, who had been nominated for an Oscar. He had started life as an editor, and in that capacity had worked on one of my favourite films, *Don't Look Now*. There was obviously not much this man didn't know about film. He had a very easy manner, and a rather beguiling American/Australian accent. I thought there and then he was someone I could get along with.

In his beautiful hotel suite, while he played mum with the tea, he told me that he wanted me for the part of William Wills, one of the two main characters of the story. As he spoke, I glanced at a huge table covered with photographs of Burke and Wills, together with maps, proposed locations and loads of stuff covering the story and the history involved. I picked up the first book lying on the table and read the opening paragraph. It took all of ten seconds for me to become completely hooked.

On August 20th, 1860 Robert O'Hara Burke and William John Wills set off with their cavalcade from Melbourne's Royal Park, with twenty extra men, twenty-eight horses, twenty-seven camels, six wagons and twenty-one tons of equipment and supplies to 'conquer the country', to explore the last great uncharted land on the planet. It was like an abyss, a black hole; it could have been filled with gold, diamonds, grasslands or a shimmering inland sea. But as far as most people were concerned, that vast empty expanse in the centre of Australia could have been on another planet, an alien world where death waited. As it did for some of the men on that great Victorian exploring expedition in 1860, their names now forgotten and swept away with the dessert winds. Incredibly, they did it. They 'wrote the map', as Burke would often say. They crossed the mystic land through elemental storms, survived the white heat of the brooding, prehistoric desert and finally forced passage across the swamplands, where crocodiles and leeches waited. They covered three thousand seven hundred miles. Most of it on foot. They were the first to cross the country, but by this time the four men, who had left their comrades and most of their supplies in Cooper's Creek so that they could move more swiftly, had been virtually forgotten by their backers in Melbourne. The five hundred pounds needed to get relief supplies hadn't been dispatched. From that moment on, the story assumed all the ingredients of a Greek tragedy. By the time the money was finally sent, it was too little too late. William Brahe, the man left in charge of Cooper's Creek base camp, had decided it was time to leave. Their supplies were almost finished, and one of his men was dying. He left the famous stark message 'Dig' carved into a coolibah tree. Burke and Wills had told him to wait for three months. He stayed four, but could no longer wait. Only hours after Brahe left, the three living skeletons staggered in, Burke, Wills and King. Gray had died in the desert and they had spent a day digging his grave. A lost day that would have got them back to Cooper's Creek before Brahe left. As they dug under that tree, they unearthed a tin box. In it they learned their fate. Their systems ravaged by beri-beri and malnutrition, their minds slowly fragmenting, they waited pitifully at Coopers Creek for rescue. However, Wills was on the edge of death and Burke, for once, just a step behind him. Only King the young Irishman, sensitive to the ways of the tribal people, and therefore able to come to terms with them, survived. He returned to tell their story.

I sat in silence for a while; a shiver went up my spine. I knew then that I'd be seeing Australia for a second time.

I spent the journey home working out how to tell Caro. I didn't exactly tell her the truth at first, I sort of drip-fed bits of information.

'How did the audition go?' she asked.

'What audition?'

'You know, that Australian thing.'

'Oh, that,' I replied. 'Haven't heard a word.'

A few days later, I had Graeme Clifford on the phone.

'Why's he ringing you?' she asked.

'For a chat,' I replied.

'Bollocks, you're going to do that bloody film and disappear for another year. You don't give a bugger about Kate and me, all you want to do is film, film, film. Why can't you find something to do at home?' She went on and on, but after a day or two she realised that it was a great opportunity and would never have stood in my way. She was brilliant about things like that, always encouraging and selfless. Anyway, my career was still not secure enough to say no to something as big as this.

Luckily for us, I had to be out there six weeks before filming to prepare, which coincided with the school holidays, so all three of us took off for Sydney. I knew how long a journey it was, but poor Caro and Kate had never flown anything like as far as this before. As it turned out, they both loved the journey, and I had difficulty getting them off the plane when we landed at six in the morning.

'But, Daddy, this is my new home,' Kate said. She had been thoroughly spoiled by a couple of 'quaint arses'.

Instead of putting us into a hotel, the producers decided that a serviced apartment in the middle of town would be much more fun, and they were right. It was just like having our own flat in the middle of London, except that the temperature was perfect, the sky blue, and the sea just round the corner. It was fabulous, a really glamorous place to be, and we loved it. Sydney was just beginning to exert its ultra-cool vibes, and cutting-edge chefs were starting up classy places all over town. Paddington became one of the hippest places on the planet, and the rest of the world sat up and began to take notice. Of course, it wasn't all about fashion and food. For Kate, the outdoor life was a glorious change from grey old London, and to have beaches five minutes away was a dream come true. She wanted to be Australian and stay for ever – who wouldn't? As for Caro, she was a colonial girl, born in Ceylon. Being abroad and living in a hot climate didn't worry her one jot; in fact, she took to Australia like a duck-billed platypus to water.

I had to start work straight away and immediately began to realise the immensity of what we were taking on. It had the feel of an Australian *Lawrence of Arabia* epic about it. I had so much to learn. First up, I had to learn to ride a camel. Now this, in itself, is not too daunting, but try putting forty camels together with fifty horses, and things get a lot more difficult. Camels are a pretty unfazed bunch by nature, but they are also very grumpy. They moan all the time, not to mention spitting gobs of disgusting snot on to the unwary, and they have the most potent breath this side of a rotting crocodile. Horses, on the other hand, are scared of practically everything, especially camels, and if they find themselves in close proximity to anything with a hump they get very skittish and try to scamper off – fast. As a result, the first few days were spent in a chaotic skirmish of flailing hooves, bellowing – oh and farting: I forgot to mention that other endearing camel trait. All these animals were watered, fed and generally looked after by an extraordinary bunch of Australian cowboys – wranglers, they were known as, and they were mostly girls, great big butch girls.

'Nigel,' one would scream in a low baritone, 'for fuck's sake ride the fucking thing!' All very dainty.

I was assigned a camel named Simon, so called because there was a famous director called Simon Wincer who became known as Simon Whinger. My camel was a grumpy old whinger – voilà! I decided a bit of bonding was in order, so every morning I took him a goodie or two, apples and other titbits. Simon soon decided that I was the main man, or at least a source of breakfast, and we developed a strong bond.

Having mastered the basics of camel riding, I had to learn how to walk. Now, I like walking, and I had just done a couple of charity walks of thirty-odd miles each, and also a half-marathon, *Chariots of Fire*-style, but these guys walked nearly four thousand miles – a slightly different proposition – and a trainer had to be hired to make us walk as if we'd been walking thousands of miles already. No easy task.

Amy O'Rourke was a really interesting woman who specialised in training long-distance trekkers across vast expanses of Australia. She was also a tightrope walker, not that that helped us much. The production team hired a huge hall, and day after day Jack, I and some other poor buggers walked round and round this arena like demented show ponies. She did eventually succeed in making us look as though we had walked for ever. It didn't require much acting, actually; I felt as if I'd walked to the moon.

Of course, the various costumes, wigs and beards had to become increasingly battered as the film progressed. The wardrobe department would have to assemble many different costumes, starting off relatively clean and crisp, ending up in shreds. I would therefore have at least eight costumes for each change, and required many different fittings. I thought the look of the film was outstanding.

Camels, horses, wranglers, costumes and tired limbs notwithstanding, the main issue was our weight: we had to get very thin indeed. We were all introduced to our personal dietician. By God, she was scary. She looked like an Australian version of Rosa Klebb.

'This is what you'll be eating for the next five months,' and with that she handed us each a small packet of powdered food. 'This is what they eat when they go to the moon, and if it's good enough for them, it's good enough for you.'

What a bitch, I thought, as I caught my co-star, Jack Thompson, glancing at me out of the corner of his eye. 'Let's go for a tinnie, mate. She never mentioned anything about the grog.'

'Too bloody right, mate,' I said in my finest Australian. And that's pretty much what we did. I seem to remember my father going on what he called the Drinking Man's Diet. It worked a treat, and I ended up weighing a frighteningly gaunt eight and a half stone – not a pretty sight on a five foot ten inch frame. Still it did the trick and I ended up pissed, but thin.

Jack Thompson was playing the part of Robert O'Hara Burke. I had already seen him in *Breaker Morant* and *Merry Christmas Mr Lawrence* and was thrilled to be working with him. He was not particularly tall, but not the sort of bloke you'd want to meet in a dark alley, either. He was thick-set, blond, the blue-eyed epitome of an Aussie sheep-shearer. The sort of bloke you could trust with your life but not with your wife.

The few weeks we spent in preparation prior to filming gave us a chance to get to know one another. He was quite a guy, and became a great friend. He was huge in every sense of the word, and found it a struggle to get skinny. He was open, friendly and generous, and I couldn't think of a better partner with whom to tackle the daunting task we had ahead. He could get a bit scary when he was pissed, as he was so bloody loud – Kate found him very alarming – but on the whole he was a diamond.

The first day of shooting got nearer and nearer. It's rather like the first night of a play; you just wish it could stay in the future, but things don't work out like that. Suddenly it was upon us, and off we went north to Darwin for the first few days' filming, before going to our main location out in the bush.

Caro and Kate came up to Darwin with me and stayed in the hotel for a couple of nights before flying home. By an extraordinary coincidence, the hotel turned out to be owned by a friend of my brother, Phil, but he wasn't there at the time, which, looking back, is probably for the best, as I was getting very nervy and jumpy as filming got nearer. The only thing I remember about staying there was learning to do 'tequila slammers' on an empty stomach in a blur of salt and lemon. The rest of the time I spent in a haze of nerves, trying not to be too miserable with the girls, who were about to leave.

On our last evening, Kate and I decided to go for a swim before she went to bed. She was eight years old going on eighteen, amazingly quick-witted and with a wicked sense of humour. God, I was going to miss my girls.

'Are we expecting to see any sharks, Daddy?'

'Don't be ridiculous, sweetheart, this is the safest sea in Australia. Look, we're only up to our ankles.'

The tide was quite far out so we had a bit of a walk, and when we eventually waded out far enough to swim we noticed people waving at us from the beach. We waved back happily and carried on with our swim. As we walked back up the beach, we were accosted by a group of worried locals who had been trying to attract our attention and get us out of the water. Apparently, it was box jellyfish season. These little charmers have tentacles which can grow to thirty metres long and possess one of the most toxic venoms on the planet. One lash of a tentacle can kill a grown man in a matter of minutes. This information did little to calm my nerves (actually, I think I was in such a state already that I just assumed that the hand of doom was poised above my head, ready to strike when I took my eye off the ball). A few years later, the son of some friends of mine got wrapped up in those toxic tentacles off the coast of Borneo. He was in a coma for a week, but by some miracle survived. I often think of him and our lucky escape when I nearly killed my daughter as I waved happily to the crowd on the beach.

The next morning, I kissed Caro and Kate goodbye. I was in for at least three months on my own – it was going to feel more like three years.

As I was leaving the bedroom, I heard a scream from Kate in the bathroom: 'Daddy, Daddy, come quickly!' I flew into the bathroom to find an enormous green frog staring at her from the basin. 'Can I take it home?' she said. 'I'm afraid not,' I replied, and I popped it in my pocket. On the way into the bush to start filming, I made the car stop and released my little green friend.

As is usual in this topsy turvy world we work in, the first scene we shot actually takes place quite late on in the film. Of course, you've got to start somewhere, and it would be impossible to shoot the film in the right order because we'd be darting backwards and forwards from one location to another. I'd give anyone a million pounds if they could spot the first scene shot on any film.

In our first scene, Jack and I had to walk through a leech-filled swamp, trying not to be eaten by a crocodile. I remember hearing a hell of a noise, and looking up I spotted a group of galahs in a nearby gumtree. Apparently, these most Australian of birds can live up to a hundred years. As I pondered whether the parents of this particular gang might have looked down on the real Burke and Wills, I saw a jumbo jet climbing up over Darwin and wheel off into the distance – my girls going home. How I was going to miss them. I didn't know exactly when I'd see them again, and all sorts of unknown challenges lay ahead. I felt tears prickle in my eyes, and wanted to shout up at them to come back and wait for me. But instead, I made myself listen to the guy who was telling us what to do if a real crocodile appeared – *What?* Are you kidding me? What the bloody hell was I thinking when I agreed to do this? Did I really agree to it, or is this a nightmare?

We only had a short time filming up near Darwin. The bulk of the film was to be made in Nowheresville, slap bang in the middle of the bush, six hundred miles from a telephone (no such things as mobiles in those days), a thousand miles from any place you could call a town and at least two thousand miles from a decent shower. This sure as hell wasn't going to be a picnic, everyone kept telling me. We were to have a couple of days in Alice Springs beforehand, so the night before we left Darwin I agreed to meet Jack in the hotel lobby at eight the following morning to take a taxi to the airport. One thing I had learned about Jack was that he was never on time, so when I was still sitting there at twenty past eight I began to get a bit hacked off. I went for a wander round, and noticed that the gambling room was still open from the night before. In I popped. Dad enjoyed a flutter at the roulette wheel occasionally, and one of his plans was always to bet on number sixteen. I bought myself a few chips and placed them on and all around sixteen, red. I was about to walk away when I heard the croupier say, 'Sixteen, red.' That was a nice surprise, and quite a lot of chips were pushed my way. The croupier then went to clear the table.

'Wait,' I said. 'Leave it there.' I suddenly knew beyond a doubt that it was going to come up again. I doubled the bet. Bingo! Up it came. Time was running out, so I had to leave. After my two big wins, the croupier growled as I walked towards the door. Oh, the tip, I thought, and I tossed a fifty-dollar chip in his direction. I grabbed my stash and was amazed to find that I had won just over two thousand dollars. I cashed them in and ran, pockets bulging, back to the lobby. To my astonishment, as I arrived, Jack got out of the lift with a girl on each arm.

'Hey, Nigel, you're leaking dollars, mate.' Open-mouthed at his luck, I muttered something about having a bit of success at the tables. 'The drinks are on you, mate!' he shouted, and we left for Alice Springs.

My hotel room in Alice Springs was the one that Charles and Diana had stayed in when they visited Australia soon after their marriage. It much amused me to find that it was a pretty poky, basic little affair with a kettle in a corner. I had visions of Charles hunting around for the powdered milk and asking Diana whether she wanted one lump or two.

There wasn't much to Alice Springs, but it was nice and relaxed, and I made a new discovery. I had already come across drive-in cinemas in America, but here they had something called a 'drive-in offie', basically, a huge booze warehouse. You drive in, wind down the window, get handed a cold tinnie while you place your order. By the time you're ready to toss the empty can into the bin, they have loaded your order into the boot of your car. Later, I found that these places had fags and even oysters by the crate in some towns. I suppose it's now the norm in towns like Calais, but back then I thought it was all impossibly glamorous!

On our second morning, Sidney Nolan arrived. Probably Australia's best-known artist, Sidney was most famous for his series of paintings of the notorious outlaw Ned Kelly, which he painted in 1946. But soon afterwards he also did an 'explorer' series of paintings, based on the travels of Burke and Wills, so he was keen to join us on set to do another series of sketches and paintings which he had nicknamed 'living history'. I immediately fell under his spell: he was the most wonderful man, charming to all and utterly fascinating company. He was quite tall, with iron-grey hair and glasses the size of Eric Morcambe's. There was a marvellous twinkle in his eye, which went hand in hand with a killer sense of humour. He carried a tiny sketchbook and a pencil with him at all times, as well as a Polaroid camera, the latest model. He took photographs all day, mostly of silly things that made him giggle. When he was serious, he'd whip out that little sketchbook and make extraordinarily accurate drawings of something he'd seen. His knowledge of Australian history was second to none, and I could listen to him all day – and did. He invited me to go with him to Ayers Rock. I needed no persuading, and flung myself into the tiny plane he had chartered for the brief hop to Uluru. We arrived at teatime. I hadn't known until then that the rock changes colour in tune with the light throughout the day. I stood open-mouthed as Sidney talked of the ancient history of this huge mound, and the brownish-grey stone gradually changed to the most vibrant, flaming red in the clear evening light. It took us a hell of a long time to climb to the top, but, my God, it was worth it. I gazed about in awe at the vastness of the landscape. I felt my character, William Wills, take shape inside my head as Australia began to weave its magic and inspire me.

The next day, we departed for base camp. It felt as if we were off to the moon, all very scary stuff. We were herded into a flotilla of small planes, taking only the basics, and off we set, into the unknown. So unknown, in fact, that the pilot couldn't find the bloody runway. It turned out that it had been built by our crew and was lit by tilly lamps – not exactly Heathrow central. Still, we made it in one piece, for which I was truly grateful. It was dark by the time I found my accommodation, Hut B43, which consisted of a bed, a shelf and a small cupboard.

These sorts of huts are apparently used by miners, and aren't the sort of rabbit hutch you want to spend much time in. The temperature in the desert climbs to well over a hundred degrees in the day and drops to freezing point at night. It was impossible to keep the hut a sand-free zone. Every time I opened the door, a blast of red-hot sandpaper hit me between the eyes. The ceiling became an adventure playground for every conceivable insect, but there was one that ruled the roost – a huge tarantula-like spider.

'Whatever you do, mate, don't mess with the big one,' my next-door neighbour told me. 'He'll eat up all the nasty stingers, but won't eat you.'

So I lived with Sammy the Spider in perfect harmony. The only alarming habit he had was dropping off the ceiling on to my bed in the middle of the night. I, of course, like Sean Connery in *Thunderball*, remained icy calm.

The communal showers were about fifty metres further on. God, they were depressing. In Alice Springs, one of the props guys had presented me with a rather beautiful home-made book which he'd backed with an piece of antique binding, to use as a diary – such a thoughtful gesture. I dutifully filled it in for two nights, but after that I gave up as waves of depression continued to wash over me.

Still, there we all were, in the same dismal boat, at dinner on that first night. Speeches were made by the producer and by Graeme Clifford, the director. They both reminded us of the scale of the task that lay ahead. They banged on about how hot and tiring it was all going to be – basically, how ghastly – and said that we should all stick together as a team. It was going to be a life-changing experience. (Oh, Christ, I thought, please can I change my life right now? I want to be back home in Ramsden Road with my darling wife and sweetheart of a daughter. Will I ever see them again?) They droned on and on, warning us about dangerous snakes and man-eating insects. Almost everything out here was going to try to bite yer arse and probably kill you in the process. (Jesus, I thought, what's this 'brown snake' all about? How can something with such an ordinary name kill you in five seconds? Better keep my eyes open for one of those little bastards.)

We all decided we'd better get howling pissed, and fast. In fact, we drank the place dry, which turned out to be a huge mistake as the supply plane only came in twice a week and we had to wait another three days for a cold tinnie.

I lurched my way back to bed that night in a fine old state and immediately passed out fully clothed on the hard little bed. I was woken what felt like almost immediately by loud banging on the door. Head pounding, I found myself face to face with one of the lady wranglers – built like a submarine, with a moustache.

'Fancy a fuck, my old darling?' she asked in a brisk, no-nonsense fashion.

'Really kind, but not tonight, thanks,' I stammered. It was the moustache that did it.

I slept like a baby for the rest of the night, but awoke to a scene of utter devastation. Two crew members had set their trailers on fire, thanks to a discarded cigarette stub in one and overturned candles in another. The two sand buggies that had been shipped in specially had been taken on a formula one race and had crashed into a tree. Maybe the fact that no more booze was available for three days had its good points after all.

Some time during the previous evening, I had been invited by the owner of the land to look round his ranch. Loaded up with enough tinnies to sink a ship, I soon found myself agreeing to his invitation. That accounted for the banging on my hut at six fifteen the following morning.

'Christ, you look like death,' he said. 'You better come with me.' His property, I soon found out, was something the size of Wiltshire. I spent the entire day bumping around in the blazing sun, enthusing over a variety of animals, all of which seemed to have horns, although I couldn't see clearly out of my bloodshot eyes, and my head was pounding so violently I had to ask to stop twice to be sick – he seemed to think this was entirely normal and carried on talking, paying no attention to the constant gurgling and belching going on beside him. He banged on about this and that, none of which I could understand, or wanted to. I just wanted to get back to my hut, lie down and go to sleep.

We finally got back to 'base' at dusk to find all hell had broken loose. We obviously had to travel with a resident medic as part of the crew. An encounter with any of the local wild life was potentially fatal, and a thousand-mile truck journey to see a doctor was less than helpful. Our doctor was not only a doctor, she was also a surgeon. When I was introduced to her she looked utterly incompetent, but what do I know about doctors? On my way to Hut B43, I spotted a queue snaking for miles from the door of her 'surgery' – more of a hut than a hospital, but better than nothing. I joined the queue.

'What's going on?' I asked one of the sparks standing in front of me.

'We've all got to get a jab,' he said, winking at me.

What's with the winking? I wondered. 'Oh right,' I said, winking back.

A lot of sniggering was going on in front of me, which made no sense at all. My head was thumping fit to burst by the time I stood in front of Matron.

'Drop your pants,' she said.

'Christ,' I said, 'you're worse than the wranglers.'

'Well, that's why you're here, matey,' she said, loading a huge syringe.

'What the hell's going on here?' I asked, backing towards the door.

'Seeing as none of you could keep your dicks in your trousers, we've got a clap epidemic on our hands.'

The penicillin hit me like an express train. I couldn't admit that I wasn't one of the lads and hey, who cares?

'Bloody good shag, though,' Steve the carpenter told me. 'Damn well worth it, don't you think, mate?'

'Couldn't put it better myself,' I replied. Now I truly was one of the lads.

By the end of the following week, any whiff of female wrangler had been exchanged for some very serious cowboys.

I soon settled into a reasonably pleasant routine. One huge bonus was that I really liked my character. As I had plenty of time on my hands, I started to read everything I could find about him, and the others, and became totally fascinated with the research. I'm often asked about my research into a part, and what I do to get in character. I'm not very good at explaining it, probably because I don't know how to. I certainly don't go in for any Method style, or remain in character after filming as some actors do, but there are times when you do feel that you've got to the heart of someone, and know exactly what makes him tick. Actually, when I think about it, however many times I've told people that I can walk away from a part and not think about it again, that isn't strictly true. I get involved far more deeply with each character than I care to tell people. I felt this very strongly about Wills, and as soon as I put on his battered old clothes I really felt as if I was him and I almost didn't have to learn my lines – they were instinctive to me.

Another bonus was that I made some really good friends. One of them, Ralph Cotterill, had appeared in Peter Brook's famous production of A *Midsummer Night's Dream* for the Royal Shakespeare Company. The production went on tour all over the world and ended up in Australia – and so did Ralph. When the Company packed their bags to go home, he unpacked his to stay in Sydney. He hasn't stopped working for the last twenty-five years – an eccentric, rather wizened character with a great sense of humour.

Our living huts were next door to each other. We nicknamed the space between our huts 'the Riviera'. We cleaned and raked the sand, put out a couple of chairs, a table and even an umbrella. We were short on Ambre Solaire, but Ralph had Matron whip up a concoction which stopped us burning and gave us a nice all-over tan. There's a tradition in Australia that at the end of every day's filming each member of the cast and crew is handed an ice-cold tinnie of beer – there would be a mutiny if this tradition failed for a single evening. Ralph and I used to sit on the Riviera after filming, sharing our beer, and feel a fleeting hint of faraway civilisation, wondering what our loved ones were doing and generally bitching about the frustrations of the day. I used to hallucinate about that evening beer from the moment breakfast was over. Of course, we had to have one day off a week, even though there was nowhere to go and nothing to do.

'I'll meet you in St Tropez, Ralph,' I'd say after breakfast. On occasional Sundays I could even hear the sea.

*   *   *

Pretty soon, even the simple pleasure of a beer after filming was denied me. I had to lose more weight and was put on an even stricter regime. Breakfast was a pint of water and a banana. Lunch was a small salad which seemed to consist of not much more than a couple of limp lettuce leaves, and my evening beer went out of the window. Each Saturday night, there was a crew piss-up when the supply plane bought in the booze, but, oh no, not for poor old me, and not for Jack, either – water was the only allowed tipple. Life was hell.

The lack of food and sleep were beginning to turn me stark staring bonkers, added to which, looking back, I think I truly began to believe that I was William Wills – for the one and only time in my life, a part began to inhabit my being and I started behaving very oddly. One day, as I was putting on my filthy old costume and having the make-up done, I noticed that the shot required us to be practically crawling on the ground. It was to be filmed by a sodding great long lens and Graeme and the crew were sitting miles away, waiting for us to get into position.

'I'm not going anywhere until that bastard director comes over to say good morning,' I said.

Shock registered on the face of the third assistant – this normally mild-mannered and quite cheerful actor throwing a hissy fit? Or 'spitting the dummy' as they call it over there.

He quickly walked over to Graeme. 'Nigel says he's not doing anything until you come and say good morning.'

Pause.

'Has he lost his fucking mind?'

'Well, er, I think he means it.'

I screwed up my eyes and watched Graeme, dressed in his habitual white linen, walk the hundred yards or so to where I was standing.

'Good morning,' he said, and he turned on his heel and walked back.

I knew they thought I was being a tosser, but I didn't care. The outback can do strange things to a person.

One scene took place in a duststorm, and we had to have aeroplane propellers chucking dust in our faces for three whole days – unimaginably foul for us, piece of cake for Simon and the rest of the camels. Those guys can survive anything. We also had to contend with the flies. I know everyone talks about those Aussie flies, but until you experience them at first hand, you can have no idea how hellish they make your life. I wore a hat with a net whenever I wasn't actually on camera, but on one close-up a fly actually walked across my eye – right across the middle. I'm quite proud of the fact that I didn't flinch, but the secret fact is that because I wear contact lenses I was just about able to bear it.

Another time, we were filming on some salt flats. You could see at least a hundred miles in every direction, everything dancing in that torrid heat. The crew were about half a mile away, filming with the longest lens in existence. There is only one of those lenses in the entire world because it is so expensive to produce. Directors have to put themselves on a list and queue to use it, all of which adds to the pressures of filming, as there is absolutely no margin for error.

Jack and I were acting up a storm, half crazed with thirst and exhaustion. One of us glanced over at the crew, and found that they had broken for lunch and forgotten to send the runner to tell us.

'Fucking bastards, I'll kill them!' I yelled. Jack was able to find this quite amusing, but, madman that I had become, I sulked for days.

Of course, it wasn't all bad. Quite a lot of the time it was rather amazing. I got myself a pet. A baby galah (a kind of parrot) which was needed for filming became known as Nigel and used to sit contentedly on my shoulder for hours. I loved him and didn't feel right unless he was there. When filming finished, I took him back to Sydney with me – I wonder where he is now? Probably run over by a truck. They are without doubt the stupidest birds in the world, hence the expression 'Don't be such a galah.'

One scene we did was a dusk-into-night shot which was astonishingly beautiful. A group of Aborigines were walking in the distance and the moon was the size of a building. Everything shimmered with a silver haze and I remember a feeling of sloughing off civilisation, rather like a snakeskin, as I listened to Jack telling me wonderful stories of Aborigine history, tied in with the geological landscape. It was truly magical – a moment of heaven.

Although 'civilisation' was hundreds of miles away, we did have two lifelines relatively close by: a pub and a general store. They were truly in the middle of nowhere and were run by two blokes who had had a row twelve years ago and hadn't spoken since! One night, we got back to base to find the pub owner there with one of his mares, which was in season. He had seen our horses and fancied one of them as a pretty desirable sire. Our horses were in fabulous condition. Not only were they well fed, but the desert is a very clean place, so their coats gleamed like velvet once they had had a good roll in the sand. The mare was put in with the lads, and the pub owner stayed the night. In the morning, he left with her – history doesn't relate whether she got lucky or not, but it seemed to be normal behaviour in those parts.

The bloke from the store was more sociable, and often came

over for a beer in the evenings, even though he had to set off after lunch. It was only forty miles, but it took that long to get to us. He originally came from Newcastle, but had had to leave in rather a hurry; I thought it best not to ask why. We got on like a house on fire. He offered to teach me to fly, and I jumped at the chance. The following Sunday, I borrowed a truck and set off for the store. After a couple of tinnies, I helped him push his single-engine Cessna out of the garage and we took off down the road directly outside his store and flew over the creeks, nearly touching the trees as we passed – it was fabulously exciting.

One day, he spotted a 'road train', one huge lorry pulling over a hundred containers behind it. These giants criss-cross Australia all the time, and we immediately flew down to 'buzz' the driver. This entailed flying ten feet off the ground and timing a fly-past inches from his windscreen. This was good sport for us, but must have pissed him off somewhat as a) it was a hell of a shock, and b) those road trains take about five miles to stop, so slamming the brakes on is not an option. I'm surprised he didn't take a pot shot at us as we yelled with laughter and wheeled away.

Kevin, the store keeper and Concorde pilot manqué, did eventually teach me the rudiments of flying. I learned how to take off and land on the road by his store, and felt I'd done pretty well. When I got home, I decided to have a lesson at Biggin Hill and confidently took the controls. After about ten minutes, my instructor, white-faced, took back the controls and promptly landed the plane. He said I was a complete cowboy and unfit to fly until I had unlearned everything I'd been taught – thereby at a stroke removing all the fun and excitement from my newly acquired hobby. I have never flown again.

One Sunday, our producer, John Sexton, told us that he'd been out on a recce and found some strange markings on the ground which he'd learned were mining 'shot lines', used by geologists to trace the rock formations in their search for oil. This meant that there was, inevitably, a camp where these guys lived. Apparently, this one was called Mambuba, which is Aborigine for 'arsehole' – something that amused us greatly. It was about a six-hour drive away and not of the remotest interest to us except for one thing: it had a telephone. Jack Thompson, John and I decided to go the following Sunday, our day off, and I could hardly sleep for excitement. We were on our way before it was light and got there without any difficulty. The camp was incredibly luxurious, full of the latest mod cons. It seemed ridiculously sophisticated after months spent in our Spartan outpost. As we had mail delivered once a fortnight by the supply plane, I knew from Caro's latest letter that she was spending that weekend with friends in Devon. Jack had phoned his girls and was all dewy-eyed as he handed the receiver to me. It was my turn. I put my hand in my pocket to get the number. Wrong pocket. I felt the other one – no piece of paper. Feeling slightly sick, I frantically searched in my shirt pockets, back pockets – everywhere. I had left the number behind. I couldn't believe I could be so stupid. I could see where I'd left it: on the bed so I wouldn't forget it. I tried to remember the number . . . 0122 . . . no, 01123 . . . Bugger, this is hopeless.

'Is there an operator here?' I asked a bloke sitting nearby. 'I'm looking for some directory enquiries for a village in Devon.'

'Devon? Where the hell's that? Is it anywhere near Adelaide?'

'Not exactly,' I said, choking back tears. I can't possibly let them see me cry. Please God, don't let me cry. I promptly broke down and cried like a baby. I couldn't help it. I hadn't spoken to my girls for over two months; it was driving me mad as I missed them so much. Now I'd blown the only opportunity I'd have to speak to them for another two months. The drive home was hell, especially as I got such stick from the rest of the crew for being such an idiot. I didn't care about that, I just missed my girls.

The last scene to be filmed in the outback involved Jack dying. I found it impossibly emotional and had great difficulty in getting through it. At one point, I looked up and saw that the crew were in tears; even Graeme could hardly bear the pain. We had all been touched by the experience of making this film and leaving the bubble was going to be extremely hard.

But suddenly there I was one day, sitting on the bank of Cooper's Creek, saying goodbye to the outback with Jack sitting beside me.

'Tell me, Nige,' he said, 'was it hell?'

'No, Jack, it was heaven, truly heaven.' The funny thing was, I meant it. Truthfully, hand on my heart.

An hour later, I was sitting in the little twin-engine supply plane, ready for take-off. Despite longing to see Caro and Kate again, I was terribly depressed about leaving, so much so that I was almost in tears – again. I remember asking the pilot if I could take a turn at the controls, and he let me, which made leaving a bit more bearable, as it gave me a hell of kick to be able to fly a rather bigger beast than I was used to. We eventually arrived in Adelaide, where we had a few days off before some more shooting just outside the city.

It was terrifying. Suddenly I found myself on my own in the middle of an enormous city and I couldn't deal with the culture shock. By the time I got to my hotel room, I was a bundle of nerves and I didn't leave the room for two days. I rang home to speak to Caro and give my love to Kate before I passed out. I just slept, ate room-service food and generally got my head together. The rest of the cast were doing exactly the same thing; we were all completely drained and exhausted. Eventually, I felt brave enough to venture out, and found that Adelaide was quite lovely. It reminded me of Brighton in a strange way. Pretty houses, all with front gardens, wide streets and an unhurried atmosphere. The people of Adelaide are very proud of the fact that their ancestors were free settlers. I began to feel like myself again, and to enjoy what the place had to offer. I went to watch a game of cricket at what turned out to be the prettiest ground I have ever clapped eyes on. Halfway through the afternoon innings, I felt a tap on my shoulder. It was a friend of Dad and fellow member of the Garrick Club. He invited me into the members' enclosure, despite my rather raggedy appearance, and generally spoiled me rotten. Amazingly, he remembered Dad telling him about me breaking my wrist while making *Chariots of Fire*. When I showed him the misshapen joint, he became very excited. It so happened that he was a consultant orthopaedic surgeon, and he was in Australia to give a series of lectures on varying bone conditions. He asked if I would mind if he borrowed my wrist the following day for a session of X-rays and photographs. I was delighted to agree, especially as he took me out for a delicious lunch afterwards. Apparently, my wrist was to have a starring role in the lectures – it probably had more exposure to an Australian audience than the rest of me put together.

The break in filming was to allow us to rest and gain a bit of weight before shooting some of the earlier scenes in the story. It was as though we were making a completely different film, and strange from an acting point of view. As Wills, I'd not only walked across Australia, but died as well, and here I was playing the same man and having to pretend not to know his fate. It gave it all an unreal quality which, I must say, I rather enjoyed. And sleeping in a real bed at night had its advantages. There is nothing in this world like a good kip.

One important scene involved getting our entire caravanserai across a fast-flowing river. We had one advantage over Burke and Wills. We knew that camels can't swim, they very stupidly just keep on walking until they sink. Apparently, Burke and Wills lost several on the real crossing, but luckily ours all lived to tell the tale – well done, Simon!

The highlight of our brief time in Adelaide was the arrival of the gorgeous Greta Scacchi, who played Burke's girlfriend. The camera operator immediately fell head over heels in love, as did the rest of us – who could resist such a gorgeous creature, especially after months of looking at nothing but sweaty, smelly maleness? She seemed like a creature from another world – with great tits. Unfortunately, she was only there for a week, and I didn't really get to know her.

We returned to Sydney for the last couple of weeks, and with perfect timing Caro came out to join me again – sadly, without Kate, who stayed behind with some friends as it was still term time. At the airport, Caro walked straight past me – she didn't recognise the gaunt creature standing in the crowd, which made us both very emotional. We talked all night, she about Kate and life in London, and me trying to explain the journey I'd just taken and the effect it had had on me. She said she found me changed by it in some way – something which I think still remains true. Every image of that time remains burned into the negative of my brain – the sky, the smells, even the iridescent flashes of green as a flock of budgerigars spun from side to side as they took off from the trees. I'd come a long way from that pub in Earl's Court a few years before.

'Don't forget us,' Jack told me as we left for the airport. 'I know we're a long way away, but we'll be friends for life.'

How true that was. Years later, I bumped into him in a bar in Los Angeles. He squeezed me for hours, hugged me with tears streaming down his face. We *are* friends for life.

We left Australia just before Christmas. I boarded the plane walking rather like Douglas Bader. I was suffering from a bruised scrotum as a result of an incident involving a camel and the Sydney traffic. Almost the very last scene involved me riding a camel in the suburbs, and Simon got a bit blown away by the experience, and took off.

Needless to say, the doctor had pissed himself. The last thing I remember hearing was, 'Hey, guys, come and take at look at Nigel's balls – we could throw a party with these red balloons.'

I'd been away for six months, so it was difficult not to feel a bit displaced on my return. Of course, it was wonderful to get home and see Kate again, but there's no denying that I found it hard to pick up where I'd left off. I felt as if I'd lost a limb. Luckily, fate intervened and made the process rather more gradual. Graeme had come over and managed to raise enough money to shoot the beginning scenes of the film at Hever Castle. Hever has a famous maze, and the film starts with the Wills family playing in it and getting hopelessly lost in the high-hedged pathways. We shot it a couple of months after we returned, so I didn't have to go completely cold turkey on the story. I also had to do a bit of post-syncing on some scenes, as the background noise of the birds and general wildlife proved too noisy on the original film. One of those scenes was the difficult one of Jack's death. I was really reluctant to do it, as the original had been so draining, but it had to be done. Watching the film in the studio was almost unbearable and I could hardly get the words out, but it worked and Graeme was thrilled. I let out all the emotions that I had been trying to suppress over the previous couple of months and we got a scene as good as, if not better than, the original. It was a cathartic experience. I felt reborn and ready to carry on with my life.

I invited David Lean to one of the pre-release screenings. To my delight he loved it, but the editor in him wanted twenty minutes cut. I thought about it and decided he was probably right, so I mentioned it to Graeme and they compromised on ten!

Despite all our best efforts, the film never took off, which is one of the great disappointments of my career. It transpired that, because of a contractual argument with the producers and the distributors, the film was never properly released. The people who saw it in America loved it, but it wasn't shown over here. Disastrously, it coincided with the release of *Star Wars*, and a more unfortunate piece of timing is hard to imagine. It was a huge disappointment after such a life-changing experience, but it remains one of the films I am proudest of. Even now, I think it stands as a fine testament to two remarkable men.

Chapter 13

Life on the Box: II

Christopher Miles is a good man. Not a bad director, either – *The Virgin and the Gypsy* is one of my favourite films. He's the brother of Sarah Miles, that wonderful, eccentric actress. Christopher has a little bit of that, too. I can say all this because I spent a lovely couple of months in Greece making a television film about Lord Elgin.

It was the spring of 1986 and my letterbox didn't have to do much work to let this script in – it was that slim: *Lord Elgin and Some Stones of No Value*. Was someone taking the piss? I wondered: those marbles must be worth a fortune. Actually, it was one of those titles that are meant to grab the attention, rather like Alfred Hitchcock's *The Birds* – when the film came out, the posters read 'The Birds is coming.' Same sort of thing.

The script took all of ten minutes to read, but something about it fired my imagination. I didn't know anything about Lord Elgin before, but now I was riveted by him and what he did.

During the first decade of the nineteenth century, Lord Thomas Elgin was the British ambassador to Constantinople. He hired agents to remove whole boatloads of ancient sculpture from Greece's capital city of Athens. The pride of this collection was a large amount of fifth-century BC sculpture, taken from the Parthenon, the temple to the goddess Athena that stood on the Acropolis Hill in the centre of the city. The Parthenon sculptures included about half (some seventy-five metres) of the sculptured frieze that once ran all round the building, plus seventeen life-size marble figures from its gable ends and fifteen of the ninety-two metopes (sculpted panels) originally displayed high above its columns.

I was getting hooked. I couldn't imagine how the workmen got those things off the building. With only ropes and ladders and a hell of a lot of muscle power, they prised hundreds of tons of incredible stonework from a building that was already crumbling. Lord Elgin paid for them, hauled them into various boats, including one of Lord Nelson's frigates, and shipped them back to London.

In London, the Elgin Marbles started a new chapter of their history – as museum objects. Acquiring the sculptures had bankrupted Elgin, and he was keen to sell them to the government. In 1860, a parliamentary select committee looked into the whole affair (examining everything from the quality of the sculpture as works of art to the legality of their acquisition) and recommended purchase, though for much less money than Elgin had hoped. From that point on, the sculptures have been lodged in the British Museum.

There was only one thing for it: I had to go and see them for myself. Rather cheekily, I rang the British Museum and spoke to the main man. 'Sorry to bother you, but I'm making a film about Lord Elgin.' I went on to explain exactly what we were planning to do.

'We would be delighted to show you round,' he said. 'Would seven o'clock tonight be any good?' I had no idea if he knew who the hell I was, but his invitation seemed to be genuine.

We met at the main entrance. Mr British Museum reminded me of a headmaster at a rather academic school. 'This way,' he said, and we strode past two thousand years of history. I suddenly realised that we were the only people in the building. 'We're actually closed,' said Mr BM, 'but I thought it might be nice for you to see them on your own.' We came to an abrupt stop. 'Let me tell you something amusing,' he said. 'Last month, we had the cultural ambassador for Greece here, Melina Mercouri – you may have heard of her?' Indeed I had. She was a famous actress who had turned into a political animal, passionate in her quest to bring the marbles back to Greece. She banged on endlessly about how they didn't belong to the British people, and their rightful home was back in the Parthenon.

'Quite a piece of work, Miss Mercouri. When we reached the point where we're standing now, she threw up her arms and cried, "At last! My marbles!" I had to point out to her, in the most sensitive way I could, that these were Roman marbles carved a thousand years later.'

We strode on. At the end of the walkway I found myself in a huge annexe lit from above by natural light, with walls of the palest sandstone colour, the floor almost translucent.

And then you see them, displayed at eye level. The most glorious things I think I've ever seen. The sheer energy and passion of the carving . . . it quite literally took my breath away.

Mr BM smiled. 'Are they what you expected?' I didn't reply. I couldn't. I was Lord Elgin. These marbles will never leave this building, I thought. Over my dead body. I'd just got a job I knew I was going to enjoy.

So off we went to Athens. It was all Greek to me. Lovely cast – Clare Byam-Shaw playing my wife, Julian Fellowes playing some reverend or other and a nice young chap with floppy hair called Hugh Grant.

'Be an angel would you, Hugh, and fetch me a cuppa.'

'Of course, your lordship,' he would reply. A very personable young chap – should do well.

After the first day of filming, I realised that Christopher didn't have a great deal of money sloshing around. 'You wouldn't look after your own costumes, would you?' he said.

'I'm sorry, I don't know what you mean.'

'Well, we haven't got anywhere to store them you see, so if you could go home in them after work, and then turn up in the morning wearing them, it would solve a whole lot of problems.'

The following morning, I walked through the hotel reception as Lord Elgin, in full military regalia – rather dashing, I thought. As I passed the newspaper stand on my way to the Parthenon, I saw my picture on the front page of the *Athens Herald*. It was quite a big picture, and the headline above it read: 'Lord Elgin returns'. Lord Elgin returns? It was a picture of me, for Christ's sake. It struck me forcibly that I was dressed up as Lord Elgin, the most hated man in Greece, and I scuttled off to the set. The wig was a slight give-away, but I kept my head down, and my dark glasses made me totally anonymous, of course.

One of the key bits of kit on any film set is the Motorola. All the crew are connected by it – that's how they communicate. It's a sort of two-way radio multiplied by a hundred. It means you can be a mile away from the camera with some poor unsuspecting third assistant director hiding in a bush, shouting, 'Action!' – a command he/she has just received from the director. Actors find the Motorola bloody irritating, always crackling and hissing and generally pissing you off. Just about to solve eight down in your second crossword of the day, and crackle . . . crackle, 'They're ready for you, Mr Havers' explodes over the airwaves. It may be hard to imagine making a film without the Motorola, but we did – not enough money in the budget. So there I'd be, sitting on my donkey, the wife behind me, miles from camera, looking out for a white handkerchief on the end of a stick waving from the horizon.

'Is that waving, Clare?'

'Hang on a minute . . . No, it's stationary.'

'No, it's waving, surely?'

This sort of thing would go on for hours. Eventually, Christopher would arrive, out of breath and slightly pissed off.

'We've been waving frantically, you sods, and wasting miles of film. Now get it together. When you see the white flag . . .' And it went on. Fucking drove me mad.

It happened that part of my contract stipulated that I had to return to London to complete three days of filming on *Burke and Wills*. This was fine with Christopher and co. but a bit of a slog for me. I nipped back to London and put in three long days. Hard work, but great fun to see all my Aussie friends again. While I was wrapping up the last day, about to take the plane back to Athens, I asked the first assistant director, an old friend, if I could borrow four Motorolas.

'No worries, mate,' he said. 'Just make sure you bring them back in one piece.'

And he gave me the box of tricks. Rather like a camera case, it contained four walkie-talkies and two chargers. Perfect, I thought, and took off into the night air. With only carry-on luggage, I was first through customs, and just slipping out into the terminal when a hand was laid on my right shoulder.

'What you carry in there? We want see now.'

No problem, I thought.

They hauled me back into a smoke-filled office. The case clipped open and I was in big trouble. In fact, I was a terrorist spy as far as they were concerned. I spoke no Greek, and they spoke no English, but I knew I was in deep shit. Eventually, I managed to get them to ring Christopher at the hotel in the middle of town. By this time, it was two thirty in the morning. He was hauled out of bed, and made to come to the airport to vouch for me. They confiscated the Motorolas, and I only got them back when I left the country.

'What the hell did you think you were doing?' Christopher asked.

'I was just trying to be helpful – thought it might be a nice surprise.'

Well, we live in the world we live in. What utter bollocks. No good deed goes unpunished.

My agent, Michael Whitehall, rang one night to tell me that he'd got a new girlfriend. 'I thought I might bring her out and have a few days' holiday with you guys. What's the hotel like?'

'Absolutely fantastic,' I lied. We had moved from Athens all the way down to the southernmost tip of the country, to film near a place called Methone. I was staying at the Methone Beach Hotel, which had sounded gorgeous until I discovered it was the only hotel in Methone. In fact, the hotel made up most of Methone. There was a beach in front of it with a bit of sea, and that was that.

'Terrific,' Michael said. 'See you Friday.'

'Hang on a minute, what time does your flight come in?'

'Seven thirty.'

'I'll be there to meet you,' and I duly rented a car.

It was a fun drive and took twice as long as I thought. The airport was bloody miles away, so thank God their flight was a couple of hours late. After a lot of hugging and kissing, Michael introduced me to Hilary and we set off into the night. Now, I knew how bad the Methone Beach Hotel really was, and any minute now I was about to be found out. It's stupid to say something is good when it's not. A bit of dinner before reaching home might soften the blow, I thought, especially if I throw in a couple of gallons of wine. To be honest, we only drank the wine because the food in the restaurant was filthy. It was midnight when we reached the 'prettiest little seaside village in southern mainland Greece'. I thought I'd approach the hotel from the beach, as that was the only angle from which it looked halfway decent. I checked that the tide was out, swerved off the road and glided majestically towards the front of the hotel. A lot of giggling and screaming from the car encouraged me to drive further out towards the sea.

'This is Methone at its very best,' I said.

'Can't see a bloody thing,' Michael said from the back of the car.

Actually, neither could I. A mist seemed to envelop us all of a sudden. No, it wasn't mist, it was a bloody great wave. We were out to sea and heading for Albania. I'd slightly misjudged the tide. Completely misjudged it. The car spluttered to a halt and the engine died. Silence.

'Right,' Hilary said, 'we'd better get out and try to get this car back on dry land.'

We opened the doors and water poured in. It was going to be a long night.

Michael was pissing himself as he opened up a bottle of duty-free. 'Anyone care for a Cointreau?' he said.

Eventually, we managed to ground the car, but that was as far as we got. She was stuck fast.

I noticed, way up on the beach, a large camper-van. 'You two hang on here,' I said, and off I went in search of help.

After I'd banged on the camper-van door for a couple of minutes, a huge man appeared. 'Vat ees it you vant?'

'I'm so sorry to trouble you, but I seem to have got my car stuck out in the bay there. Any chance of you towing me out?'

'I vil try,' and with that he started up and reversed towards the sea. 'Take ze rope and tie it to your car.'

'Yes, mein herr,' I felt like saying, and off I waded towards my car. Michael and Hilary were polishing off the Cointreau as I struggled to tie the rope round the front bumper. A lot of thumbs-up and waving, followed by the sound of an engine straining. With horror, I saw the camper-van's back wheels slowly disappearing into the sand. I ran back to find our German friend in a real frenzy.

'Now I am stuck, and I have ze children in ze back – vot am I going to do?'

This was turning into a nightmare. I looked back at Michael and Hilary. They seemed to be doing some sort of a dance in the sea. I took another glance at my German friend. 'Stay here. I'll go and get some help.'

It's OK, I thought, I can deal with this. I can walk into a village at three in the morning, not speak a word of Greek and find someone to help me. That's what happens in life. You just have to, you just have to – Good God! There's a man on a tractor!

All of a sudden, I seemed to be getting one of those lucky breaks that happen once in a blue moon. I jumped up and down and waved my arms in front of him. He realised I needed help and I leaped up next to him and off we went. Minutes later, he attached himself to the camper-van, which was attached to my car. Tremendous amounts of engine revving and swearing in Greek, followed by tying of more ropes and more swearing in Greek. It went on for what seemed like hours and then suddenly we were all moving majestically out of the sea as dawn broke over the Methone Beach Hotel.

'One of the besht nigsh of my life,' Michael said as he wandered off towards Reception, Hilary in one hand, empty bottle of Cointreau in the other. I left my car out of harm's way behind the hotel dustbins. I gave the tractor driver every penny I had in Greek money, and told my German friend that I'd take him to dinner at the Garrick next time he was in London.

And so ends the longest and most boring story I have ever told.

Lord Elgin and Some Stones of No Value came and went on television. I know I watched it, and so did Caro and Kate and my mother and father. That makes an audience of five certain viewers. In retrospect, the things that happened off camera were far more interesting than the things that happened in front of it. That's probably true of most films.

I never really enjoy answering the telephone. I don't know why, but I don't. I suppose it's quite often the bearer of bad tidings. Your agent rings to tell you that you haven't got the part, or to tell you that you did get the part but the film's been cancelled. I picked up the receiver very reluctantly.

'I'm sorry to bother you at home.'

'No, no, not at all,' I said.

'Well, my name is Harold Snoad, and I'm the producer/director of a new comedy series we're doing called *Don't Wait Up*, and I wondered if we might meet.'

That brief phone call pretty much put me on the television map. For the next eight years I had the best time of my life doing what I loved most: comedy. Good, old-fashioned, classic situation comedy. Harold Snoad turned out to be one of the good guys. We had a very nice meeting and he ran through the casting. I was to play Tony Britton's son, Dinah Sheridan was to be my mother. Can't go wrong there, I thought, and within what seemed like seconds I was sitting round a table at the read-through of episode one, series one – a very scary moment.

Sitcom is a very different kettle of fish from anything else one's ever asked to do as an actor. It's a sort of hybrid, and by that I mean a cross between film, television and theatre. Let's take the film bit. On average, a third of each episode will be shot on film, on location. The other two-thirds will be recorded on videotape in a studio in front of an audience of five hundred or so people – not nerve-racking at all.

It goes like this. On Monday, you sit round a table and read the sitcom through. Costume and make-up discuss what's needed for the episode, then they all bugger off, leaving the actors and director to rehearse for four days in a room with all the sets marked out by different-coloured sticky tape. On Friday, all the production side and the camera crew turn up to have a look. We 'perform' for them. On Saturday morning, we have notes and do a final run-through. On Sunday, we go to the BBC TV studios and camera rehearse all day. At five o'clock, we do a dress rehearsal. At eight o'clock, with an audience watching us, we perform for them and the cameras. Was I scared? You betcha. Did I enjoy the first episode? More than life itself.

'You took to it like a duck to water,' Harold said as he gave me a hug. 'How do you feel about doing sitcom now?'

After a while, you get the hang of it and can play comfortably to the audience as well as the camera, which is the key. Tony and I even did our own version of a warm-up before the show started. 'Warm-down' was what Harold used to call it, but what did he know? He was just the director.

I'd tell the most appalling jokes and get huge laughs. 'God, they're a great crowd,' I'd say to Tony. 'They just laugh at anything I say.'

'Well,' Tony said, 'they're not paying to be here. In fact, I think we're paying them.'

'Right,' I said. 'Not quite like the theatre, then.'

I watched Tony Britton like a hawk. He taught me everything I know about sitcom acting. He was always incredibly funny but, at the same time, totally real. He never missed a line, or indeed a trick. I studied him very carefully. We spent six months of the year in each other's pockets for eight years. We never had one cross moment. He was, and still is, my second father.

In one early episode, we were living together in my little flat, both divorced and generally getting on each other's nerves. Some chaps living upstairs had invited us to a drinks party and off we went to it.

After a couple of minutes, Dad looked round and asked me, 'Have you noticed anything strange?'

'Er, no.'

'There don't seem to be any women arou—'

At that moment, someone tapped Tony on the shoulder. He turned to camera, his face a picture.

'Care for a dance, sweetie?'

It was a gay party, and our friends upstairs thought we were two of a kind. It was Tony's look for that split second that sold it. The audience laughed for five minutes. That's comic genius.

We did our filming inserts in Bournemouth, of all places. Harold decided that London was far too expensive and difficult to film in, and anyway, no one would spot the difference. He was wrong, of course: it didn't look anything like London – but it was much easier to film in. People are much friendlier as soon as you leave London, so if you're filming a driving scene and you need to stop the traffic, the people of Bournemouth are more than happy to oblige. Apart from one.

One sunny afternoon, I was being filmed backing out of my drive and zooming off in a terrible state. It had to match the weather from the day before, which meant having rain machines put up. The rain machines were started, and the runner went to stop the traffic.

'I'm sorry, sir, we're doing some filming here. Would you mind waiting for just a couple of minutes?'

Our boy racer in his open-topped Mazda told him to shove it and roared on. Whoops! An early shower. That was the only dissent ever shown in Bournemouth.

The first episode was transmitted on a Monday night on BBC 1. There was probably sod-all on BBC 2, and *This Week*, an arse-paralysingly boring political programme, was on ITV. We got sixteen million viewers, and we had a loyal audience from that night on for the next eight years.

One phone call did all that.

Entr'acte

LA Stories

Over the years I've often been to LA. Most people complain about the place, but I think it's because they don't really know it and let the place use them. I've always had a Hollywood dream – show me an actor who hasn't – but I've never stayed long enough to do any good. I have found agents who do ring me back, but that's not enough there. You also have to have a lawyer and a manager, someone to wipe your arse and, most important of all, a publicist.

Eventually, I did find an agent, a great guy. Actually, he's a great guy first; second, he's a bit of an agent, a bit of a manager and a lot of a hustler all in one. Didn't get me many jobs, but he's a hell of a good friend. Russell Lyster and his wife Pam became my home from home whenever I went 'visiting' as they called it. When a casting sheet (the information sheet telling agents what parts are coming up in what film, with a short description of the character) hit Russ's desk, he'd scan it with a magnifying glass. Anything within the age range twenty-six to fifty-seven was fine by him. Obviously, anything English, whatever age, was even finer.

One night, I got an urgent call in the small hours, and soon afterwards found myself flying over to LA. When I got there, Russ showed me the breakdown.

'Russ, this guy's a twenty-seven-year-old rancher from Montana.'

'You can do the accent.'

'Bollocks.'

I ended up in a hideous office, sitting in a row with all the other hopefuls. I turned to Billy Connolly. 'What part are you up for?'

'Logan.'

'Great, so am I.'

Oh, and there was Robbie Coltrane. He'd obviously been told he was 'just perfect' for – Logan. In the end, I think Denzel Washington got it.

I was once flown over to LA by Dreamworks for an audition for a comedy pilot. I was filming a TV serial for the BBC at the time, but just managed to spare forty-eight hours to flip over. I learned the part, quite an effort as the script was pretty awful, and the audition went OK. Then I noticed the next guy they were looking at – Ian McNeice, who is sixteen stone and has a false eye. Neither of us got the gig. In fact, no one did because it never got made.

It all boils down to the 'Ridiculous Audition'. You have to get to grips with their *abc* of double talk. 'My God, you're perfect for the part' means you couldn't be further from what they're looking for. 'Tell me a bit more about yourself' means you might make it into round two. 'We'll let you know, but it doesn't look good' – you're in with a chance. And if they don't speak, just stare – you never know, you might just have struck gold.

Of course, proper grown-up actors don't need to go through the 'Ridiculous Audition'. If you've been at it for the last thirty-five years there are a few films and TV credits for a director and producer to look at. Maybe they can judge from that.

The first time I flew first class to LA was when I went there to meet Steven Spielberg to talk about *Empire of the Sun*. I noticed that you get a much prettier stewardess up the sharp end of the aircraft, and I made a slight fool of myself over one of them. She asked what I was going to be up to in LA. Well, I must have waved the script around and one thing led to another . . . I found myself asking her out for lunch, dinner, tea – can't remember which. She agreed to meet the following day at a new restaurant in Rodeo Drive, a caviar bistro, if you can believe it.

When we met, I was hung over and pretty jet-lagged as well – that eight-hour time difference affects the body in all sorts of ways. Still, I was celebrating, and caviar and vodka were the order of the day – we both got rat-arsed. Off I went for a pee. I took a look in the mirror as I passed the bar. White linen jacket, white trousers, sea-blue shirt and Oliver Peoples shades – very LA cool, I thought. Having the pee of my life, I decided to complete my total happiness by letting one go. Total disaster: I followed through. Oh, God! White trousers. Somehow, I managed to salvage them, but my boxers were a write-off.

After a few visits, I got fed up with staying at Russ's place. For a start, it was in Venice, miles from Beverly Hills where most of the meetings took place. So, I discovered the Belage Hotel on Sunset and San Vincente. It looked like a prison, but on a hundred and twenty dollars – the actor's rate – it was a godsend. The Belage's dark little bar turned out to be a legend in its own right. Stars flocked to it to see Nicolai, the head barman. Sean Penn, Brad Pitt, Raul Julia – they all came in, and I was introduced. It was always so dark I'm sure they had no idea what I looked like or even what I did, but it was super fun for me. I'd go off for the 'Ridiculous Audition' and then get on with my day in LA. Up early, no way do I spend a penny actually in the hotel, so it's off to Duck Soup, legendary newsagents, to buy the LA Times and whatever else they have, a breakfast at Le Petit Blanc on Sunset Plaza, and then cruise into Oliver Peoples emporium – well, you have to look your coolest in LA. Then off to another 'Ridiculous Audition'. I came very close at one of them not long ago. For a joke and a bit of a wind-up, I went along to audition for the part of the new captain in Star Trek. After Patrick Stewart left, they cast a female captain, but she hated doing it so the part was up for grabs again. Russ was convinced I'd fit the bill, the dollar signs were nearly blinding him, and so I found myself reading the captain's speech to a load of po-faced executives at Paramount. It seemed to work and they offered me the job. One small hitch: I'd have to sign for five years.

Five years? 'Shall I just do a year and see how it goes?'

I was shown the door so fast my eyes watered. I was mightily relieved. To sell my soul to the devil is one thing, but to the starship *Enterprise*?

Russ was devastated. 'How could you do this to me?' he wailed.

So it was back down to Venice and dinner at Russ's. We stopped off at the biggest supermarket in the world, bought enough to feed an army, made a few calls – Trevor Eve, Pierce Brosnan, whoever was around – and celebrated another day wasted on RAs. I refused to stay the night – I couldn't stand the combined breath of two basset hounds waking me up and the hard-as-nails concrete bed – so I headed back to the Belage Hotel, a little the worse for wear.

Ten minutes down Olympic at two in the morning, I was the only car for five miles – the only car, that is, apart from the police car that suddenly sprang to life, all sirens and flashing lights. 'Jesus,' I thought, 'this is going to be really interesting.' If you're ever stopped in the USA, remember to stay in your car. He comes to you. This time he took what seemed like an hour.

I wound the window down.

'Do you know what speed you were doing?' the cop asked.

'I, er, well . . . Around thirty?'

'Eighteen miles an hour. Are you OK?'

'I'm fine,' I said, trying not to open my mouth wide enough for any fumes to escape and so sounding like a ventriloquist's dummy.

'Do you have any ID?'

By an enormous stroke of luck, I had remembered to put my passport in the glove compartment. He flicked through it. 'The Honourable Nigel Havers?' he said.

'That's right.'

'Are you the son of a lord?'

'I most certainly am.'

He snapped to attention, saluted me and said, 'Drive carefully, sir, and enjoy your stay in the USA.'

Some of the RA's did pay off. I managed to get myself into *Farewell to the King*, directed by John Milius and produced by the legendary Al Ruddy. Al was a terrific chap with a voice like gravel that came from sixty Camel Lites a day and a bottle of Jack Daniel's a night. He was always known as Ruddy, I suppose, because of his facial resemblance to a red cabbage. I got the part after one meeting and both Ruddy and John became great friends. I noticed Ruddy kept a huge bottle of what appeared to be oxygen in his office.

'Christ, yes,' he said. 'I take a gulp of the pure stuff first up in the morning – makes me feel like a million dollars.' He jammed the mask over his face and sucked in a lungful. 'Come on, give it a try,' he wheezed.

My God, I was blown apart. I practically imploded.

'See what I mean?'

'Fantastic,' I squeaked.

I suppose the most enjoyable role that came out of an RA was Michael Wilding in *Liz: The Elizabeth Taylor Story*. The first scene I had to do was, typically, a love scene with Sherilyn Fenn, who was playing Taylor. Now, in all love scenes you have to be careful; a quick introduction at 6.20 a.m. isn't a great start to a whole day filming making love. I have a ruse I nicked off Roger Moore. I always apologise to the girl if I get a hard-on and, of course, if I don't. To be honest, I don't think Miss Fenn was too impressed with that approach, but never mind. As the day dragged on, I looked into my leading lady's eyes and thought, 'My God, I'm fucking Elizabeth Taylor!' Hollywood has an uncanny knack of producing lookalikes at the drop of a hat and she really was the living spit.

Whatever anyone says, filming in Los Angeles is bloody good fun. They never seem to get everything right, especially period drama, but you do get a spooky feeling of filming where it all began. My hair wasn't cut short enough, the clothes weren't quite right and the props were all wrong, but I felt special.

LA really is a city of dreams, and I have fabulous memories of it. There's the bar at the Four Seasons Hotel. Two martinis are just about OK, but sometimes, with the help of an old mate, you slide down the slippery slope and hit three. Once, while shopping on Rodeo Drive, I was asked to leave the store. 'What the hell for?' I asked. 'Because Madonna is on her way in.' Having Sunday lunch at the Bel Air Hotel with Maggie Smith, who told me who could act and who couldn't. Picking up Robbie Coltrane for dinner in my little Mustang convertible – he didn't fit into the seat so stood up for the entire journey, hair blowing in the wind, like an enormous dashboard gnome. Being invited to a dinner party by the guys who wrote songs for Elvis Presley, or having dinner in a famous restaurant when Tom Jones got up and sang us a song or five.

LA is full of surprises. I always leave wanting to stay.

Chapter 14

The Whistle Blower

In the spring of 1985, I had met a film producer called Geoff Reeve. He was one of the last of a dying breed of independent producers who actually made films because they loved making films. They were the sort of guys who read a book on holiday, thought it would make a good movie, bought the rights, found the money, sourced the writer and director with absolute taste and then cast it and shot it like it was a stroll in the park. Fantastic. Where the hell are those guys now?

Anyway, Geoff had asked me to be in *The Shooting Party*, an adaptation of Isobel Colegate's wonderful novel about Edwardian England in the lead-up to World War One. We were all getting geared up to start work when, as I explained earlier, first Paul Scofield, one of the major stars in the film, was taken ill, and then there was a further delay when Paul and three others were injured when some horses bolted.

That sort of situation is a film producer's nightmare, as the entire cast and crew are no longer under contract, and often take other jobs, sometimes resulting in the project going belly up. Geoff made it perfectly clear that the cast were no longer under any obligation, but he said he'd be grateful if we could all stick around.

Now, there is nothing an actor likes more than being asked to stick around, secure in the knowledge that there is guaranteed filming just round the corner.

'I think it's time for a little holiday. What do you think?' I asked Caro.

'Perfect,' she said.

At that moment the phone rang. It was the call that led to my playing Ronnie in *A Passage to India*. Geoff was totally charming and understanding, and said under no circumstances should I turn it down. He even paid me for the two weeks' preparation I had put in before Paul was taken ill. I'd felt guilty ever since about letting him down.

A couple of years later, I was relieved of my guilt when Geoff offered me a part in his next film. I grabbed it with both hands, even though it was for slightly less cash than I would have liked – hell, I owed him one.

'You've obviously been on holiday again,' I said.

'What do you mean?' he asked.

'Well, you've found another book.'

'You're right,' he said. 'Barbados it was, the perfect place to read a thriller about the Cold War.'

The Whistleblower was based on a gripping novel by a much under-appreciated writer called John Hale. Michael Caine was in place to play the lead, Frank Jones, and Geoff wanted me to play his son, Robert. Interesting, I thought, very interesting. I suppose you could say this casting was a leap of faith by anyone's standards, despite the script notes describing Michael as a single parent who had spent every cent he had sending me to a private school. Michael ran a publishing company in London while I worked as a linguist at GCHQ at Cheltenham. GCHQ means spies, listening in to other peoples' conversations and general James Bond-type behaviour. Not only that, but I was to get thrown off a roof and meet a grisly death. I couldn't wait to get started.

Before filming began, Michael invited me for lunch at Langan's Bistro, a famous brasserie at that time, co-owned by him and his friend and fabled hell-raiser Peter Langan. It was the first proper brasserie to open in London, and with a first-rate chef in the kitchen and Michael and Peter front of house, it was an instant success. Every famous actor and actress who passed through London (and quite a few of the Great Train Robbers!) had dinner there at one time or another. It was a thesp magnet, and I went there as often as I could afford.

Before the doors were opened for the first time, Michael and Peter decided to buy an eclectic collection of modern paintings by the yard. It cost them a pretty penny, but thirty years later the paintings were worth twenty times more than they had paid for them. Michael Caine was not to be underestimated. Peter, on the other hand, was a drunk. He was brilliant at it, and people came from all over the world to watch him get pissed.

When the producers of *Burke and Wills* came to London to cut a deal with an English distributor (complete waste of time), I took them to dinner at Langan's. There were ten of us and ordering our food took a bit of time. The patient head waiter explained the menu to my Australian friends.

One of them slipped away to the gents, and when he returned

he interrupted the explanation: "Scuse me, mate, but there's a bloke asleep under the urinals.'

'Yes, sir, that'll be the owner.'

My Aussie mates were incredibly impressed. 'Christ, to take a nap under the urinals, that takes a bit of drinking.'

Michael was sitting at his table. This was a table that belonged to Michael. It could seat between four and twelve and was always at his disposal. Today it sat two. It didn't take him long to order my food (his choice), the wine (his choice) and the speciality of the day – anchovy soufflé (definitely his choice).

'You know what, Nige, you're my new new best friend.' And another bottle of wine arrived.

'Michael,' I said, 'there's a little question I've got to ask you. Am I going to have to talk like you or are you going to posh up?'

Michael pissed himself. 'You're never going to be able to talk like me, so I'm going to have to posh up.'

And that was that. On the first day of filming, the first lines we spoke on the film went like this: 'Hello, Dad.' "Ello, Son.' Poshing up at its best.

I was already in awe of him as a huge star, but from that moment on I fell completely under his spell. Michael is an incredibly generous actor, who always seems to have the right quip to hand. In make-up on the first morning, he sat down and said to the make-up girls, 'I'd like twenty minutes on the left eye and half an hour on the right.'

Later that day, as we completed the third take of a rather complicated scene, Michael suddenly turned to me and said, 'God, I love my job.' This took me by surprise. He'd been at it for years and I rather assumed that the shine must have gone off by now, but not with Michael. He relished every take, every aspect of the filming process. It was incredibly infectious, and all of us were amazed by his enthusiasm, and found it very inspiring. We fed off it, making it one of the happiest experiences I can remember.

The director was Simon Langton, whom I'd known for years, and who I was to work with again later. Simon ran both a tight and a contented ship and, uniquely in my experience, we made the entire film on schedule, on budget and minus tantrums. He was also very canny. Halfway through the film I get pushed off a roof. It's murder, but only the audience know. Everyone else thinks I've thrown myself off. Simon wanted a close-up of my face as I hit the deck. We tried several ways of doing it, including the prop department dropping me from a couple of feet on to the pavement and into shot, but nothing seemed to work.

'I'll end up with a broken nose and no teeth if we go on like this,' I said.

Simon came up with a brilliant idea. I was placed in a harness attached to a wire, and on 'Action!' four burly men whisked me up out of shot. When the film was reversed it looked as if I'd fallen like a stone. It worked perfectly, and is a trick I am keeping up my sleeve for if and when I start directing more stuff of my own.

During the first week or so of filming, things were pretty quiet, with everyone eating in the hotel and going to bed early, but with Michael around that was never going to last for long. He's passionate about his food, refusing to eat or drink anything but the best, and soon he was ready to hit the top restaurants in and around Cheltenham.

'Nige, where's your copy of *The Good Food Guide*?'

'In the back of my car,' I said, and off I went to do some research.

We took it in turns to choose the restaurant. It became quite a responsibility. If I chose somewhere a little below par, I'd be ribbed for the next week. Of course, being such a big star, he had his own driver, so sometimes we drove as much as sixty miles for dinner. We formed a sort of dining club, the core members being Michael and I, James Fox, Barry Foster, Ken Colley and Gordon Jackson. Others sometimes joined us, one of whom was Felicity Dean. She played my girlfriend in the film, and very nice she was. Michael was quite taken with her, too.

'Bloody hell, she's got an enormous pair of tits,' he said regularly. In the make-up caravan one morning, he greeted her with, 'Morning Felicititittitiy.' The whole place broke up. She didn't seem to notice, and if she did she was far too charming and flattered to let it worry her. I quietly pissed myself and encouraged Michael to greet her that way for the rest of the movie. It guaranteed that we would start each day with a smile. It killed me every time.

On my days off, I would nip back to London for the night. The journey took me past the door of Simon Williams, whom I had first met in *Upstairs, Downstairs* and later worked with in *Don't Wait Up*. Sam, as he's known, rang me one day to suggest that, instead of slogging all the way back to London, why didn't I call in there and stay the night?

'Henley's only an hour and a half away,' he said. 'It'll break your journey and we can catch up.'

We had a fantastic dinner, far too much to drink, and rolled into bed far too late. At breakfast the next morning, head splitting, eyes like piss holes in the snow, I spied Sam from the corner of my eye.

'Any chance of a couple of Alka Seltzers?'

'I'll get them.'

'You said that without moving your lips,' I told him.

He hadn't said a word, the voice came from behind me. I turned round and there she was, this beautiful blonde girl with a wry smile, red cashmere sweater and brown corduroy trousers.

'Thank you so much' I said. She didn't move, and neither did I.

'Let me introduce you to my sister Polly,' said Sam. I'd known him for ten years and he'd never mentioned a sister. What a terrible shame, I thought; she was definitely worth mentioning.

It was time to set off home and Sam walked me to my car. Parked right alongside me was a car identical to mine.

'Who the hell does that belong to?' I said.

'Polly,' Sam said, fixing me with rather scary look. 'Let me give you a bit of advice. She's off limits – and I mean off limits.'

'I don't know what you're talking about,' I said.

As I slipped into the driving seat, Polly appeared behind Sam's shoulder. With her fingers she tic-tacked her phone number, like a bookie signals the odds. Simultaneously, Sam's finger wagged a different message. In that single moment, I realised that life was about to get complicated.

One of the most moving scenes in the film took place in a mortuary. Michael had to identify the body of his son, and naturally was crying his eyes out. It turned out that we filmed in a real mortuary and it made my blood run cold.

'This won't take a minute,' Simon said to me. 'Just pop yourself into this drawer and we'll be out of here in no time.'

I lay down, was covered in a sheet and pushed into the darkness. It dawned on me that I was lying there surrounded by real dead bodies. My blood was beginning to freeze. I lay there for what seemed like an age. Suddenly, the drawer was jerked open and there I was, lying on the slab, trying not to breathe as the sheet was pulled back. I heard Michael sobbing, and then I felt him kissing me on the forehead, his tears falling on my cheeks. He seemed to be getting closer to me all the time. I heard him whisper, 'It's your turn tonight, Nige, so where are we having dinner?' And with that, a huge sob erupted and I heard him fumbling for something. A handkerchief. As I was pushed back into my drawer, he blew his nose and it sounded like the *QE II* leaving harbour. What an actor. Me, I'm talking about. I hadn't breathed for five minutes.

The final scene, involving Michael and John Gielgud, who plays the villain of the piece, was of the Remembrance Day parade, with the war veterans all filing past the Cenotaph. Of course, the easiest way of doing this was to film during the actual parade. As I was long dead by this time, and as I wanted to watch Simon pull off this scene, I became part of the crew for the day and was able to watch spellbound as those courageous old timers made our last scene almost unbearably poignant. It was a one-take necessity, which not only worked out brilliantly, but provided a memorable ending to a film that we were all very proud of.

For some reason, it was difficult to find a distributor for the film and it never took off. However, as time went by, its popularity grew by word of mouth and it became a minor cult film, especially once the Cold War came to an end. For me, it was memorable for lots of reasons, but one of the best was that it allowed me to work with Michael, and to this day, when we see each other, he always says, ''Ello, Son,' and I reply, 'How're you doing, Dad?'

The Whistle Blower was also memorable for one other reason. I had met Polly.

Chapter 15

The Charmer

One spring morning in 1987, the clattering of my letterbox went on for rather longer than usual. Six TV episodes, under the umbrella title of *The Charmer*.

Caro peered over my shoulder. 'Who's playing the Charmer, then?'

'Have a guess.' I said.

'Adolf Hitler?'

'No, not quite. Have another guess.'

'I know – it's obvious, Anthony Andrews.'

'Anthony who?' I said irritably.

'You know, that really good-looking guy who—'

'Oh, bugger off.'

I piled it neatly on my desk. I'll read it later, I said to myself. At about eleven o'clock that night, I settled down, large Scotch in left hand, episode one in the right. The first few pages of any new script are always torture for me. I so desperately want it to be good, I will it to be good, I almost make love to it, hoping that it's going to be the best script I've ever had. Nine times out of ten it isn't.

I put the last episode down at dawn. She must have been good, she lasted all night. She was good, she was the best thriller I'd ever read.

Philip Hinchcliffe, the producer, rang me the following morning.

'Does the character have a single redeeming quality?' I asked him.

'Not one,' he replied.

Blimey, I thought, much as I love it, is this a wise move? After several years of my being Mr Nice Guy in TV series such as *Don't Wait Up*, *Hold the Dream* and *The Little Princess*, what will the viewers think? The character I was thinking of playing was a complete bastard. Hang on a minute, what's going on here? It's completely the wrong thing to worry about. It's exactly what I should be doing. Anyway, if people don't like it, what can I do about it? It was just too good to refuse.

In 1952, Patrick Hamilton wrote a novel called *The West Pier*, and invented a character called Ralph Ernest Gorse, a really nasty piece of work. He followed it with another book called *Mr Stimpson and Mr Gorse*, and it's that second novel that *The Charmer* is based on. With those two books and the script shoved into my hold-all, I disappeared to the South of France to do a bit of heavy-duty reading.

I booked myself into a rather fancy hotel in Cap Ferrat for two reasons. First of all, I'd never been there before so would know no one. Secondly, my mother and father were staying with friends a mile or so away, so I could see them for the odd free dinner. There's nothing I like more than lying in the sun and reading a book, occasionally clocking the odd beautiful pair of tanned tits – but back to work.

The novels were sensational and I decided that if one is going to play a complete shit, it's best to really go for it full-on. The strength of the story is that the audience knows more than the characters. It's almost like a pantomime. I felt like shouting, 'He's behind you!' all the way through as I read the scripts. 'Don't do that,' I wanted to shout, 'because if you do, he'll kill you.' I knew it was going to be a scorcher.

I checked out of the hotel and paid my bill.

'J'ai acheté l'hôtel, monsieur,' I said. The receptionist's face remained impassive. Bloody French, I thought – they fleece you without even smiling.

As I stomped down the hotel steps towards my taxi, I was tapped on the shoulder. 'Sorry to bother you, but do you mind a photo?' I looked up to find the inevitable English family staring at me.

'No problem,' I said, adjusting my T-shirt and jacket and striking a pose.

He handed me the camera. 'Ah, thank you,' I said. 'Say cheese.'

The first shot on the first day of filming involved me driving my open-topped MG down a country lane towards Folkestone. After the first take, I stopped near the camera while they adjusted hair and make-up. Somehow, a bee lodged itself under my shirt, and as I drove off it stung the shit out of my left tit. Christ, is this an omen? I thought.

I needn't have worried. Alan Gibson, the director, never put a foot wrong. The whole series was shot on videotape with a single camera and in the same style as film. That was a decision taken by London Weekend Television in order to save money. Film is more expensive than tape and takes twice as long to shoot because of the complications of lighting and developing your film stock. There was nothing I could do about that – I would have much preferred to have been shot on film, but the choice was shoot on video or no shoot at all.

After three weeks of shooting in and around Folkestone, we started rehearsing in the LWT studios. We were to split our time between there and locations for the next three months. We had the luxury of a week's rehearsal to sort out all the opening interiors. Alan set a style and pace that suited the period. At the end of the week, quite late on Friday night, he called us all together. 'This isn't working and it's entirely my fault. What we've shot on location is fabulous, fast-paced and bags of energy from all of you. I've got this interior bit wrong. We've got to push the envelope even more, rack it up almost into melodrama.'

Boy, I thought, this could be dangerous.

'I know tomorrow is meant to be a day off, but I'd love you all to come in to see if we can fix it.'

And that's what happened. We all 'racked it up' and the show took on a different tone. I realised that we could be doing something special. I can't say it was a barrel of laughs to do, primarily because I couldn't take my eye off the ball. Being shot totally out of sequence, I had to bury myself in the script. Carrying around six hour-long episodes under one's arm is as good as going to the gym. I had to keep the chronology in my head, something I'm not very good at, as many people know. Whereas usually I can lark about between takes, this time I couldn't afford that luxury. Alan and the rest of the cast and crew kept their distance and I became a bit of a loner on the set for the first time in my life.

We worked flat out, six days a week, over nearly fourteen weeks. On my one day off, I used to sleep mostly, so it wasn't much fun for Caro and Kate. Alan was on a very tight schedule as the first episode was due to be broadcast only a few days after we finished shooting. Of course, he delivered it on time. He died shortly afterwards from cancer, a real loss. Apparently, he knew how ill he was all the way through shooting, but never mentioned it to anybody. I have a feeling that we would have made a great team for years to come. As it is, his legacy to me was not only one of the most important highlights of my career, but he also lumbered me for life with my signature nickname 'the Charmer'.

Chapter 16

Empire of the Sun

In the summer of 1984, we went to spend a couple of weeks with Andrew Brudenell-Bruce in his house in the South of France. It was a wonderful family holiday – all the children mucking in together, giving the oldies plenty of time to sit about soaking up the sun. These are my favourite sort of holidays. I can remember lying by a pool reading a book I had plucked at random on my way through Heathrow. It was called *Empire of the Sun*, by J. G. Ballard. I knew who the author was, of course, but I had no idea what the book was about. It turned out to be the story of a small boy living a comfortable life in Shanghai in the early days of the war. I was engrossed in a normal pick up, put down sort of way, until I came to the part where the boy loses his parents in the crush to get out of Shanghai before the Japanese arrive.

It sent a shiver up my spine, and as I turned the light out to go to sleep I could picture the whole scene in my head. I could almost smell the boy's panic. I had terrible nightmares that night and woke up the following morning in a cold sweat. What does this say about me? I thought. I'd had a really happy and fulfilled childhood; perhaps subconsciously I didn't want to lose it. Lying by the pool again the following morning, I cautiously started the next chapter. My feelings of insecurity got worse. So much so that I tossed the book across the pool. I wanted to be as far away from it as possible.

'That bloody nearly hit me,' Andrew said.

'Sorry,' I said. 'That book's put me in a terrible state.'

Andrew was curious to see what had upset me so much, so he read it himself. The following day, he announced that it was the best book he'd ever read. 'You'd be mad not to read it, Nige.'

So I tried again. I read the entire book, utterly engrossed, and finished it quite exhausted, but from that moment I was a lifelong fan of J. G. Ballard. The following year, when I heard that Steven Spielberg was making it into a film, I was prepared to kill to be in it.

I didn't have to audition, for once. I was finishing a series of *Don't Wait Up* when I got a call from Hollywood – as one does! Would I be interested in playing the doctor in *Empire of the Sun*? It took less than a heartbeat for me to say I most certainly would.

Would I mind flying out to LA to have dinner and meet Steven? He'd never cast anyone without actually meeting them – not the first time I felt the shadow of Mr Lean watching over the proceedings. Quite right, I thought. So there I was, off (in first class, I might add) to the City of Angels. A marked script was handed to me at the airport and I was told it would be removed from me as I arrived. It was like working for MI5.

Once I was off the plane, the script was indeed whisked away. I looked around for the car, and there was Mr Spielberg himself, rather proud of the fact that he had driven out personally. He was utterly charming and chatty.

'Amy might be annoyed,' he said, 'because we're going to be late. I want to take you to the office first and show you some stuff about the movie.'

The office turned out to be a hacienda-style construction, built to his own specifications on the Universal lot. It had everything in it – screening rooms, production offices and a fabulous kitchen and dining room. The whole operation seemed friendly and happy. 'Nice to have you on board,' they all chirruped in unison. The story board for the film looked amazing. I'd never seen anything like it before. (In the finished film, the scene on the rooftop, planes screaming past while the doctor tries to tell the boy to forget about his past, looks exactly like the drawings.)

'Tell Amy that the plane was late and it's all your fault,' he said as we drove home.

'No problem,' I said.

He went on to give me a serious bit of advice. 'If you're ever late home for one reason or another,' he winked, 'keep a small bottle of gasoline in the trunk of the car. Just before you go up the drive, splash a little on your hands – the car broke down. It always works.'

Their home was pretty much as I expected, super-comfortable Californian with a dash of Mexican/Spanish thrown in.

'Amy, I'm so sorry we're late – bad weather in London,' I stuttered.

'Steven,' she said, 'why did you ever think Nigel would be good in this film? He can't act at all – you've been at the office, I can tell.'

Dinner was fun. Richard Dreyfuss was there with Barbra Streisand. I was slightly thrown by this, the more so because Richard decided to speak entirely with an English accent to make me feel at home. It was a superb accent. In fact, he spoke to everyone as me – rather embarrassing. I spotted the delicious wine and tucked in. Halfway through dinner, I noticed that I was the only one drinking; the others were either alcoholics or just plain Californian. Still, I was warming up and having fun. So much so that I abruptly announced that all the pictures in the dining room were hung too high.

'If you've got a Picasso and a Cézanne, for Christ's sake hang them at eye level,' I drawled. Thank God, Steven thought it was a good idea – he told me later they'd had to redecorate the dining room completely in order to do it.

There was some luggage attached to this film and the story goes like this. Steven Spielberg wanted to produce a film – any film – directed by David Lean, and David had the idea of doing *Empire of the Sun*. Steven set about buying the rights. It was owned by a major Hollywood studio, which initially refused to sell. Steven kept raising the ante and eventually money talked.

The second he owned the rights, he rang David in England. 'I got 'em!' he screamed.

'Got what?'

'The rights to *Empire of the Sun*.'

'I've gone off that idea, old boy. You see, I've already directed a film about the Japanese, *Bridge over the River Whatsit*, and I've also directed a film with a young boy as the lead, *Oliver Twist*. So I have an idea: why don't you direct it? I'm sure you'll do a terrific job.'

This was greeted by total silence. Steven hadn't tackled a film like this before.

'OK,' he said eventually, 'but I'll need your help.'

'I'll give you all the help you need, dear boy.' And he did.

On my first morning back from Los Angeles, I had a professional dietician at my door. As most of my scenes were to take place in a concentration camp, obviously I had to look severely malnourished. 'Here we go again,' I thought.

'You look in pretty good shape,' she said. 'I can soon put a stop to that.'

I was given a diet sheet and told to stick to it. I did. By the time we started filming, I weighed around nine stone. I looked like a garden stake with eyes. I worked out that the simplest way to lose weight was to stop eating. It works every time. On the telly in America one morning, one of those terrible daytime chat shows had the most alarming-looking woman telling us all how to lose weight. 'Eat naked' was her philosophy. 'If you eat naked, you'll see how fat you are. That'll put you right off food.' Not a bad idea; but Caro disagreed, and so did Kate.

The first few weeks' filming was done in London, which meant we all got to know each other on my home turf which made it a lot easier. Christian Bale played the part of the boy, Jim. He had a slightly sad, intense little face – perfect for the part – and was totally professional throughout. It was obvious that he was going to be a big star. His concentration was awesome, and he was very single-minded. His performance is quite astonishing for one so young. Of course, Steven is known for coaxing magical performances out of children – just think of E.T. for a start, and he certainly brought the best out of Christian. Jim's final scene is where his parents come after the end of the war to the holding camp for children who had been interned. It is heart-rending enough to see the parents and Jim failing to recognise each other, but there is a moment when he and his mother finally know each other and hug. Steven told Christian to close his eyes for that second, and you suddenly realise it's the first time you've seen the child relax. It kills me every time I see it. That tough little kid finally becomes the child that he was before the war started and you can feel the tension drain out of him – magical stuff.

John Malkovich was a hell of an interesting guy. By no stretch of the imagination does he have typical movie star looks, but he has something much more important in my mind: charisma. He engages on a one-to-one basis with everyone he talks to, you feel as if you've known him all your life after only a few minutes. He prefers theatre work, but for someone who professes not to like films, boy, has he made some good ones. He's incredibly intelligent, and spent most of his spare time playing chess or cards. For the majority of his early scenes, he decided to wear a baseball cap way down low on his face, which meant the audience couldn't see his eyes. It was a brave thing to do. If you don't allow the audience to see your eyes when they first get to know you, it's hard to build up a relationship with them. Your eyes are indeed the windows to your soul, and film really picks that up. John didn't want the audience to know how he ticked in this film, and those first few scenes, baseball cap jammed across his face, barely any expression visible, is a lasting image for his character throughout the film. In other words, he is an enigma. Brilliantly thought out, and he pulled it off perfectly.

Miranda Richardson, who played Mrs Victor, one of the other characters in the camp, was quite a girl. I think she saw herself as one of the blokes. She enjoyed a beer and a fag and seemed utterly unaware of her understated glamour.

She also had a touch of completely barking madness, something a lot of actresses seem to have – that's what makes them interesting.

Steven was totally prepared and professional, but managed to be easygoing for the most part. He kept himself to himself, but was charming and friendly to all. This is going to be fun, I thought.

After ten gruelling days filming in Shanghai, Steven and the entire cast and crew moved to south-west Spain. A totally authentic Japanese prisoner-of-war camp had been built forty miles south of Jerez, and that's where we were going to be filming for the next two and a half months. I had to fly from Nice – I'd been promoting *The Charmer* at the Cannes festival – to Jerez to join the party.

This was easier said than done. I was picked up in Málaga by a charming driver in a clapped-out Seat and driven, via Ronda, across the Sierra Bermeja. Beautiful scenery, couldn't see a thing – pitch black. I stopped for a pee in a little village at around midnight. It was a truly Spanish moment. All the bars were still humming. I had a beer, a few tapas and a fag, enjoyed my pee and returned to the car – all very civilised and unlike any roadside café experience in this country. I finally arrived at the Hotel Jerez at about three in the morning. It was charming and very comfortable. I fell into bed, totally exhausted, only to be woken up at the crack of dawn by the production office to say that I wouldn't be required for the next ten days. That's filming for you – the rush to wait.

To say things had got complicated at home would be an understatement. I had been seeing a great deal of Polly and by this time had fallen deeply in love with her, but at the same time I was desperate not to hurt Caro and, of course, Kate. Of course, ultimately, that's exactly what happened, but in those early days I was frantically trying to sort it all out in the best possible way. I had no idea how to deal with the situation. I'd never been in this predicament before and, as my relationship with Polly was a secret, I had no one to turn to for advice. Whether right or wrong, I decided to invite Polly out during that break so that we could spend some time together away from prying eyes, and get to know each other properly.

She flew out to Seville and I met her at the airport one hot evening in May. She came through customs and we stood looking at each other, not quite knowing what to say. She was wearing white jeans, a dark-blue blazer, sunglasses. She looked like a movie star and I sort of knew then that there was no turning back. I had booked us into the wonderful Hotel Alfonso XIII. This was the setting for some of the most memorable scenes in *Lawrence of Arabia*, so for me it was a double thrill, both to see the surroundings that I already felt I knew so well, and also to have Polly there to share something with for the first time. We had a fabulous few days there, and then decided to drive down the coast to stay at the Reina Cristina in Algeciras. It was all completely magical and, of course, totally unreal. By the time Polly left for London, I was more in love than ever and, as a result, more depressed about the inevitable hurt that I was about to cause. I decided to throw myself into filming and try not to think about it for the time being – there was nothing I could do from a distance.

I had to take every day as it came; it was the only way I could survive. One minute, I couldn't believe I could ever leave Caro; the next, I couldn't believe I could ever live without Polly. I could see myself ending up split in two. Good for neither of them, and a nightmare to everyone else. But back to the job.

The private part of my life was so fragmented and confused that the only thing that kept me sane was to work obsessively on all the tiny details of my character.

I had my first costume fitting. I was determined to wear the simplest of costumes: a doctor's white coat, which I felt was the right look. After the costume fitting, I had to take an AIDS test as I had to do some mouth-to-mouth during one of the scenes. This didn't worry me at all – in fact, I thought it was quite sensible, and anyway it was standard in those days. Steven had had to have one in order to be able to rent a house in Spain – he was American, and the Spanish perception was that all Americans must have AIDS.

Our huge set was incredibly realistic and awe-inspiring. Steven liked to work very fast and sometimes started shooting even before the director of photography had finished lighting. It was as if he was in a terrific hurry to get the film made. He had already shot the entire film in his head, and was keener to get the story down than he was on the mechanics involved. In fact, I sometimes wondered whether he wouldn't have preferred to have directed the whole thing via video link-up from his office in LA! David Lean was similar in that he also had the whole thing planned in his head, but he used to take an equal interest in the lighting and the general look of the film. However, they both remain unsurpassed in their ability to tell a simple story on an enormous scale.

I had several quite harrowing scenes. The first was a fight scene with the camp Commandant, outside my hospital. The Commandant was a Japanese actor who spoke no English at all, so in between filming other scenes, we slowly rehearsed each move of the fight, everything having to be translated into Japanese as we did so. We got quicker and better at it each time, and at last it was time to put the fight on camera. It was a night shoot, and we started to rehearse in front of Steven at around two in the morning.

'Fantastic,' he said, 'let's go for a take.'

As I was getting myself together, the head stuntman whispered in my ear, 'A word of warning, Nigel: sometimes this guy tends to get a bit carried away, so just watch yourself.' The Commandant was a big, tall guy, not the sort of chap you'd want to meet on a dark night in a narrow alleyway, so I took the warning to heart.

The scene started fine, but then the Japanese actor lost it. And boy, did he lose it. He was back in 1945, Commandant of a Japanese prisoner-of-war camp – for real. I couldn't move by the end, and it transpired that he had broken two of my ribs; they took six weeks to mend. I gave him a very wide berth from then on.

By this time, most of the Yanks had moved out of our hotel and rented rather posh villas, but Frank Marshall and Kathy Kennedy, the producers, had stayed. They had a wonderful suite which had a gym, and they gave me a key so that I was able to do some gentle exercises to keep fit while I was nursing my battered and bruised body. The hotel had a lovely bar and pool area which was a popular watering-hole. Tom Stoppard used to come and go all the time. He was, in theory, writing the screenplay, but was constantly fired, re-hired and fired again. Nothing unusual about that; it happens all the time during the making of a film. There he'd be one day, and I'd say, 'Glass of fino?' 'Fantastic. Thanks.' 'Hired or fired?' And he'd reply, 'Hired – I think,' with a shrug of the shoulders and a swig of his chilled aperitif.

It was a very social company, and we all got on well. Steven, on the whole, kept himself to himself, but occasionally he joined us for a drink. One evening, the cry went up, 'Your round, Steven.' He didn't have a clue what that meant and anyway, rather like a member of the royal family, he didn't carry any cash on him, so I coughed up for him. He still owes me twenty-three pounds.

One of the most dramatic moments in the film is when the camp is bombed. The main reason for the siting of the set was that it was quite close to Jerez airport so that the planes could take off from there and within minutes be overhead. The only problem was that we arrived to find that the airport had been closed to do runway repairs, so the bomber planes had to come from Seville, nearly an hour away. Filling the fuel tanks to brimming allowed the planes just one go at the scene before having to turn round and return to Seville to refuel – not only time-consuming, but very expensive. This meant that we had only one shot at the enormous scene in which the hospital and other parts of the camp get blown to smithereens. A lot of the action had the planes overhead, and all the explosions had to be carefully choreographed.

The first assistant said, 'Planes taking off,' and fifteen minutes later reported, 'Ten minutes away.'

Our hearts in our mouths, we watched them approach, knowing that it was now or never.

'Nigel,' Steven said, 'don't fuck up.'

'Stop worrying,' I replied, sweat trickling down my back.

There must have been about five hundred extras, and with all the noise and chaos it felt like the real thing. It was terrifying. On 'Action!' I flew across the prison-camp courtyard and practically spun into the people coming in the opposite direction. 'What the fuck? You're going the wrong way!' one of them yelled. 'Hang on, shouldn't you be . . . ?' We couldn't hear each other from then on. What with the sound of the planes, the smell of explosives and fuel, the dust and general choreographed chaos, we might as well have been in the front line during World War I – with one big difference, of course: the bombs weren't real. It felt real though. All in all, I got rather a kick out of it. I just hope it's the nearest I'll ever get to the real thing.

After that, it was good to have a day off, and we were invited to a barrel-signing ceremony at Gonzales Byass, the famous sherry producers in Jerez. Apparently, to be invited to one of these events is a very big deal, and to be asked to sign a sherry cask containing thousands of litres of booze is a rare honour indeed. It was a wonderful trip and we all relished the comfortingly damp dark cellars after the burning heat on set. We met the main man, Carlos Gonzales Rivero, and his wife, Sol, who couldn't have been more charming.

After tasting many different varieties of sherry, we were invited to meet the mice.

'Er . . . sorry? Did you say mice, Carlos?'

'Of course.'

They put out a glass of sherry with a tiny ladder propped up against it. Suddenly, a group of miniature mice appeared and took it in turns to climb the ladder and have a sip of fino – rather refined tastes, I thought. Apparently, these mice have been there for generations, gently pickling themselves as they perform their party trick daily for astonished punters.

There was a pivotal scene that I was particularly nervous about. It takes place up on the hospital roof where the boy, Jim, has raced up to salute what he thinks are American planes flying over. They turn out to be enemy bombers and it is a very intense, intimate scene between the two of us, with all manner of hell breaking loose overhead and in the background.

Several large hangars had to go up in flames immediately behind us, one after the other, and the whole scene required three separate film crews to make sure that each shot was covered. We obviously only had one crack at it. It was carefully choreographed, actors and crew having to work in total harmony, right down to the scene ending with a pilot parachuting slap bang through the middle of the shot. We rehearsed and rehearsed till we were blue in the face.

Finally, it was time to do it for real. 'The planes are in the air' . . . 'The planes are five minutes from target' . . . 'The planes are . . .' We didn't need that last one, we could hear the bloody things. We did the scene, and Christian and I nailed it perfectly.

As the chaos started to die down, over the walkie-talkie I heard Steven ask the first camera crew, 'Did you get the first hangar explosion?'

'Er, no. Sorry, Steven, Christian's head was in the way.'

He asked the second crew cameraman, 'Did you get your explosion?'

'No. Sorry, Steven, Nigel's head moved into shot just at that moment.'

Same question to the third crew; same response.

It was the only time I ever saw Steven lose his cool. The entire set had to be re-built and re-filmed some six weeks later when it could be fitted into the schedule. This is a director's worst nightmare as it buggers up both the budget and the timetable, but when we reshot, it worked absolutely perfectly, and everyone agreed that if anything it was slightly better than the first time. It became one of the iconic scenes of the film.

As we approached the final stages of filming, we had two of the famous 'magic hour' shots that always lift cinematography on to another level. The first became known as the 'Welcome to Hell' shot, as it is the moment when the trucks first arrive at the camp. Steven wanted a crane shot, to give an overall view of the camp. He also had a causeway built below ground level so that, as the trucks arrived, Jim jumped from his truck and ran up the slope, taking the camera with him. Our set was next door to a chalk mine, and Steven had had the entire set covered in chalk dust, so that from high up on the crane the scene looked almost entirely white. There must have been five thousand extras, and it was to be filmed in the twenty-minute window of sunset – the magic hour. We rehearsed it over and over. We would complete other scenes, and then do a bit more rehearsing for this one, as Steven wanted it to be perfect.

At last, one night at seven thirty, we assembled for the shot – too much cloud. The second night – same thing. Finally, on the third night, the sunset was spectacular, and the chalk dust created an eerie atmosphere. As usual, the 'magic hour' came up trumps and the scene was perfect. Everyone did their bit on cue like a well-drilled machine. The Japanese soldiers didn't break any ribs, the actors delivered their lines and the crane rose majestically into the sky without a wobble. It looked like something out of *Dr Zhivago*, everyone covered in a thin film of chalk dust that resembled snow.

The other 'magic hour' moment was at the other end of the day. We had to be called at one thirty in the morning to be on set for three o'clock. We had to shoot a rather surreal scene of a field full of antiques – the lost possessions of thousands of prisoners and dead. The light at this time of the morning, when the sun has just come up, is crystal clear, and it added to the strange atmosphere of the scene.

Sadly, the film never quite lived up to expectations at the box office. It came up against Bertolucci's *The Last Emperor*, which was a little too similar in genre, the words 'empire' and 'emperor' became somehow confusing, and Bertolucci's film seemed to catch the moment better with audiences, mostly due to its sheer spectacle. Personally, I feel that ours is an infinitely superior film – most people I know feel that way, too – but surprisingly it was panned by the critics. I think the title led a lot of Steven's fans to expect an Indiana Jones-type adventure; it could easily have been *Indiana Jones – Empire of the Sun*. If anyone went to see the film expecting the hat and the whip, they must have been sadly disappointed. Nowadays, it's shown regularly on television, and the very critics who panned it originally are quick to say it's 'brilliant'. Anyway, none of that matters now.

Chapter 17

Farewell

During the seventies, a creative gang got together in Hollywood and seemed to dominate film-making for a good ten years. The foremost of them were George Lucas, Steven Spielberg and Francis Ford Coppola, but almost equally important was the director of my next film, John Milius.

Out of the blue, he sent me the script of *Farewell to the King* and offered me the part sight unseen. He had spoken to Spielberg who had recommended me and that was enough for him. I was extremely excited because I had wanted to work with him ever since, in the late seventies, I had seen a cult surfing movie called *Big Wednesday*, an astonishing film which has stayed in my mind ever since. He was also involved in the writing of *Apocalypse Now* and *Jaws*.

'I need a scene on the boat at night before the shark attacks the three of them,' Spielberg told John. 'It needs to be character-driven, and fine if you want to make it amusing.'

John penned that wonderful scene in which they compare scars as the boat rocks from side to side in the middle of the night. Pure genius. In fact, he became known as something of a script doctor for those other giants of the film-making world, and gained cult status as one of the big guns in Hollywood.

Farewell to the King was a pretty strange tale, which was to be filmed in Borneo. Now, this suited me on several levels. First of all, it seemed like a good challenge, filming in the Borneo jungle with Nick Nolte, legendary wild man and rebel rouser, and secondly, I was keen to get away and hide.

When I got back from Spain, I knew things had come to a head and it was time to tell Caro about Polly. She was understandably distraught and managed to demolish most of the kitchen that night. The recriminations went on for hours, and at one stage, out of the corner of my eye, I saw Kate sitting at the top of the stairs.

'What's the matter, Daddy?'

'Everything's all right – just go back to bed,' I lied.

It was about the lowest moment of my life. I felt totally crushed by the guilt of causing such sadness, but Polly was a powerful drug and I just couldn't give her up. I escaped for a couple of days with her to the Colombe d'Or in the South of France. It was meant to be a moment to try to recharge our batteries to face the days ahead, but who should I find on the plane flying down with us but Roger Moore and Michael Caine. That was the end of our secret.

I lay beside the stylish dark-green pool at the hotel and tried to concentrate on my lines. Nothing would sink in. All I could think of was the mess my life was in. I felt like a total monster for hurting Caro and Kate, but everything about my life to that point suddenly felt unfulfilled and mundane compared with the excitement I felt every minute I spent with Polly. I know that's a colossal cliché, but that's the way it was. Looking back, I suppose I knew that I had already jumped aboard the runaway train.

In the middle of these thoughts, I became aware of a group sitting next to me trying to engage me in conversation. I was as polite to them as I could be under the circumstances. I seem to remember even buying them a drink to keep them at bay, but to be quite honest I couldn't tell you to this day what they looked like

The next day, I had to fly to LA to meet with John Milius. As I checked into the Four Seasons Hotel, I bumped into Simon Langton, my old friend from *The Whistle Blower*. We had dinner that night and I told him all about the mess I had made of my life – it was a relief to get the whole thing off my chest. What I couldn't know was that immediately after dinner, Simon telephoned his wife back in England, and she promptly rang Caro. Of course, none of it was news to Caro, and Simon did absolutely nothing wrong, but it didn't really help an already dreadful situation.

I hid in LA for two days longer than was strictly necessary, and then there was nothing for it but to fly home. I hailed a cab at Heathrow and the driver handed me a copy of the *Sun*. 'TV Charmer dumps missus' was splashed all over the front page, with a photo of me with Polly in the South of France. The jolly group by the pool turned out to be the sort of guests who sell stories to newspapers, and they nailed me good and proper. They'd even taken a sly photograph, the one that ended up on the front page. Serves me right, I suppose.

I rented a small flat in Evelyn Gardens in South Kensington and tried to keep a low profile. It was a totally miserable time, especially as Kate sometimes called in after school, and one look at her pinched, confused little face used to reduce me to tears for hours.

Finally the call came for me to get myself to Kuching, the capital of Sarawak in southern Borneo. With enormous relief, I packed a very small bag, which contained not much more than my script, and made my way to Heathrow, hiding behind my dark glasses. Most of my things had already been sent into storage, so I felt curiously displaced. I remember asking for a double whisky once we had taken off, and I looked out of the window wondering what the hell I was doing with my life.

Kuching . . . what can I say? It steams like a Chinese wrestler's jockstrap. The moment you climb off the plane, your clothes wrap themselves to your body like damp bandages, and the humidity never drops, day or night. It takes some getting used to; even getting a lungful of air becomes a monumental effort. It's a bustling river town with considerable but very foreign charm – all of which went straight over the top of my head as I sat on my hotel bed feeling mighty depressed, and that was before I read the filming schedule – a nightmare. Four months with no days off – they've got to be kidding. Tomorrow morning, eight thirty pick-up for weaponry practice. Bloody hell, this was going to be hard. I went to bed trying not to think of my girls back home.

After a night spent sweating despite the air conditioning, I was up at about seven, and the first person I met when I emerged into the lobby was Nick Nolte. He looked like a rather shambolic six-foot-six unmade bed.

'Hi, how're you doing?' he said.

'I'm doing fine, just fine,' I replied.

We stood there sizing each other up.

Nick looked around. 'Hey, where are your people?' he growled.

'Er, sorry?'

'Where are your people?' he repeated.

'I, um, well, I don't have any people.'

'You gotta be kidding,' he said. 'Take one of mine.' He had fourteen, apparently, so he wasn't going to miss one.

I was quite happy wiping my own arse, though, so I gratefully declined.

John Milius loves guns – think *Apocalypse Now* and you begin to get the picture. Guns are macho; guns mean you're a real man. He asked me if I owned a gun. I said I had a pair of Purdys, which was a lie but seemed to impress him. As the day progressed, I began to enjoy myself. It was all a bit barking mad, the perfect antidote to my problems back home. I was handed a Bren gun, a fucking heavy machine-gun, and some live ammo. I totally destroyed an enormous boulder. Nick was nursing his habitual hangover and finding it difficult to remain upright. When he was handed his gun, he fired off a salvo straight from the hip, gunslinger-style. 'That'll do,' and he staggered off. All in all, it was an entertaining day, boys playing with their toys, which was a real shot in the arm for me and I decided to take things, as they say, 'one day at a time'.

Our set was roughly an hour out of Kuching. It consisted of a tribal village complete with longhouses, the incredible buildings that the local tribespeople live in. These rather beautiful structures are referred to by the number of doors that each longhouse possesses, as each family has its own sleeping space, separated from the communal living quarters, and some of the buildings have as many as twenty-five to thirty doors. It was very important to keep the local dignitaries happy while we were filming. This involved much eating and drinking. One sip of their homemade rice wine is enough to turn one cross-eyed, so everyone apart from Nick treated it with caution. I managed most of the food, but I did draw the line at turtles' eggs. I declared myself the president of my local Save the Turtle Foundation back home in Blighty, which not only got me out of eating them, but raised my standing somewhat in the local community.

To begin with, the humidity was incredibly energy-sapping, but I slowly began to get used to it, and eventually grew to love the life out there. Each night, we returned to our hotel for a much-needed shower and a cold beer. We would then walk across the road to the hawker stalls and have ourselves a feast of local shellfish, curry and wonderfully fragrant rice. One night, we found ourselves in Kuching's most hip and happening nightclub. It featured a group of tiny little local girls belting out Beatles songs – sounding exactly like them. To begin with, I thought they were miming, but, oh no, they'd learned it exactly. Alarming and rather disturbing at the same time.

Nick was not required for the first week of filming, which was a bit nerve-racking, but I kept telling myself how much better it was to be involved in every scene, and got on with parachuting into the jungle, getting caught in a tree, arriving in shot upside-down, being cut down and plummeting head first into the rainforest. Normal day-to-day stuff. For extras, we used the real thing, Iban tribesmen from neighbouring villages. They were great, if a little disconcerting. One day, as I was waiting to be cut out of my parachute, a tribesman's arm shot past my nose and grabbed something crawling up the tree trunk which he promptly popped into his mouth. It was an ant the size of a hamster.

Filming was progressing smoothly; however, there was something that I was mighty concerned about. John Milius really was a 'fly by the seat of your pants' sort of guy who still thought of himself as a gung-ho Vietnam vet. His team behaved like a renegade army unit, spouting macho bullshit at all times. When we were filming scenes that required explosions, despite the careful choreography, we had to contend with cloudbursts of dust which made it very difficult for both me and the director of photography, Dean Semler, who had to run with a hand-held camera, to see where we were going, especially as we both wore contact lenses. I asked the armourer – he's the guy who looks after all the explosive devices on set – what would happen if I stood on one of the explosives.

'You won't,' he said.

'But what if I do?'

'Look, Nigel, I'm going to tell you right now exactly where they are and you're going to remember exactly where they are, so there won't be a problem. OK?'

'But what if I make a mistake?' I persisted.

'Well, you'd probably lose a leg.'

In the event, I retained both lower limbs, but Dean and I shared a drink afterwards and I decided to give him a week to see if things got a little more organised – luckily for all of us, they did, most of the time. There were still one or two hairy moments, though. I had a scene where I came face to face with a marauding Jap in the jungle. John told me to point and shoot – straight between the eyes. Now, I knew that our guns contained blanks, but, even so, a blank fired at that range would blind him at the very least, more likely kill him. We had a bit of a row about it, until John grabbed the gun and shot at the nearest camera reflector. The blank tore an enormous hole straight through the damn thing.

Nobody spoke for a few moments.

'I'll just aim a bit to his left, then, shall I?' I said.

On location, we had tents to rest in rather than Winnebagos, as those were hard to come by in the jungles of Borneo. Nick's tent was an American-A-list-star size, crammed full of his 'people'. Mine was a sort of Millett's affair, housing – well – just me. One day, there was a huge scream and the sound of large numbers of people fleeing one of the tents. Now, there had been a lot of talk among the macho males about something called the 'ring of fire'. Apparently, if you make a small circle of flames and drop a scorpion into the middle of it, the scorpion, unable to escape through the flames, whips its tail up over its back and commits suicide by stuffing itself full of its own venom. For some reason, this struck a cord with the musclebound heavies we were surrounded by – until an unimpressive-looking smallish scorpion decided to wander into one of their tents. They all fled, and refused to return until the whole area had been declared scorpion-free – so much for macho men. I was on the scorpion's side. Being born on 6 November might have something to do with it.

Working with Nick Nolte was a revelation. I had no idea how much punishment one body could take until those weeks that we spent together. On our return to the hotel, while the rest of us were standing under a cold shower, Nick would make straight for the bar, and there he'd stay – often all night. He had his make-up done lying down every day. Not just to avoid the sun in his eyes, but also because he found it an effort to stand up. His stamina was beyond belief. At weekends, he drank for two days straight. Very late one Saturday night, while sitting at the bar with him, I spied a half-empty bottle of Pimms on the top shelf; probably been there for years.

'Good God,' I drooled at the barman. 'Give me a Pimms.'

'Give me one, too,' said Nick. No sooner had the barman poured a decent slug into a glass than it was down the back of Nick's throat. 'Jesus,' he gasped, 'fucking thing tastes like cough medicine. Gimme another.'

God, how I like this guy, I thought.

At one point during filming, Caro decided to bring Kate out for part of the school holidays. She was still desperate to try to make things work between us, and I was in such a lonely and confused state that I agreed. I suppose at the time I felt that, if we kept seeing each other, somehow it would all be OK and we could remain friends, despite knowing in my heart of hearts that I was unable to give Polly up and being determined that ultimately she and I would be together. Of course, it was all very strained and pretty miserable. Kate was subdued, picking up on our unhappy vibes in the intuitive way that children do. The energy-sapping climate didn't help, either, as they only had a couple of weeks and then it was time to go home. Everything was still a mess, nothing had been resolved and I was more miserable than ever.

Caro said she would come back at the end of filming and travel home with me. She could see I was nearly at breaking point, and, being the incredibly generous person that she always was and always will be, she decided to look after me, putting her own unhappiness to one side. She arrived a week before we finished filming, by which time I was totally exhausted. She was kind and calm, and made a point of keeping our conversation to easy topics. We both knew we had a reached a crossroads, but Borneo wasn't the place to talk about it rationally. It was time to pack my bags, go home and sort it all out once and for all. I didn't deserve such kindness from Caro and I certainly didn't repay it with any kindness of my own.

Filming finished on time and all the cast and crew were incredibly upbeat, but as we flew home I spiralled into a deep depression. I had no idea what to do. I didn't want to leave Caro and Kate, but I couldn't live without Polly – the immovable up against the unstoppable. I couldn't sleep properly, I lost my appetite and the only peaceful time I had was when I went for a run every morning. As I pulled on my running shoes, I thought to myself, I can sort this out now, but by the end of the run nothing had changed and I was left with the same predicament.

I don't know how, but I ended up talking to a psychiatrist. At the end of an hour's session, he told me to come back to the hospital the following day with an overnight bag. 'You're totally exhausted and need some therapeutic help,' he told me.

So there I was, having cocktails of tranquilising drugs pumped into my system, and a couple of therapists visiting me daily to try to talk through the problem. None of it helped. I just felt more weighed down than ever. Early on Saturday morning, the *Sun* newspaper was delivered to me for some extraordinary reason. The front-page headline read: 'Charmer

Has Nervous Breakdown and is Rushed to Hospital'. It was time to do a runner. I'd hated every moment of being in this loony bin and this was a bloody good excuse to escape.

'Who leaked the story? Who told them I was here?' I asked belligerently. 'I can't possibly stay here, surely you can see that.'

'Well, where are you going?' one of the shrinks said.

'That's absolutely none of your business,' I replied. I telephoned my friend and agent, Michael Whitehall, who told me to drive straight to his house in Kent. At last, I felt I had found somewhere peaceful and totally private – a sanctuary. Michael was married to Hilary, without doubt one of those angels put on earth. She greeted me with open arms and a hug and a squeeze, and neither of them asked any questions, they just absorbed me into their family. It was one of those balmy summers that I had dreamed about while I was dripping in the jungle, and I began to feel some of the tension seep out of my body.

On Sunday morning, Michael asked me if I would mind cutting the grass. As I sat on his mower, ploughing up and down the lawn, I found myself staring at the straight green lines, saying to myself: If I finish on an up line, I'll leave Caro – a down line, I'll give up Polly. Up Caro, down Polly, up, down, up, down . . . I suddenly realised that all I could see ahead was the road to madness. I needed some time to myself. I stopped abruptly and turned the mower off.

Epilogue

I obviously had to move out of the family home. I did so with little more than a toothbrush and a pair of jeans. I had to be alone for a while, to try and let the dust settle.

I rented the first flat I saw, just off the Fulham Road. I couldn't work up much enthusiasm for the whole process; all I wanted was somewhere to lay my head and hang up my jeans. It was a dismal, dingy little hole, but I felt I didn't deserve any better. Caro refused to accept that I wasn't going back, and Polly couldn't understand why I hadn't moved in with her. Not for the first time, I found myself waiting for something to rescue me.

And out of the blue summer sky, something did.

Naked Under Capricorn is a classic Australian novel by a chap called Olaf Ruhen. At a moment of emotional crisis, David Marriner ditches his life in England, sells all his possessions and sets sail to start afresh in Australia. Within twenty-four hours of arriving he is mugged and abandoned in the outback, naked as a jaybird. I knew just how he felt. The part could have been written for me.

As luck would have it, an Aboriginal tribe rescue him. He spends the next five years of his life with these wonderful people until a gorgeous female rancher discovers him and returns him to civilisation. Our hero wanders off into the sunset with her and ends up a millionaire with his own cattle business. These things never happened in real life, of course, but losing myself in David Marriner's dream world for a few months seemed just the ticket. And right now, Australia suddenly seemed like the best place in the world to be.

'I'm not running away,' I told myself, but of course I was lying. That's exactly what I was doing – as far and as fast as possible. I was still in shock about the mayhem I had caused. Twelve thousand miles' distance and four months' work might get my head back into some sort of order.

I was met at Sydney airport at six in the morning by Ray Alchin, a vigorous, stocky producer with a ready smile and a warm handshake. As we swung out of the terminal he handed me several hundredweight of script. Jesus! There were over three hundred pages here. *Naked Under Capricorn* was going to be a four-hour mini-series – two two-hour episodes, shot back to back.

'That'll keep you out of mischief, Nige,' Ray said with a chuckle. 'You're in every scene.'

The whole thing was to be filmed in and around Alice Springs. It wasn't the liveliest place on the planet, but I was soon surrounded by some of the nicest people I've ever met. I was probably wearing my heart rather too visibly on my sleeve but, for whatever reason, they couldn't have been kinder or more understanding.

It was hot as hell and relentlessly demanding, but I relished every minute of it. I threw myself wholeheartedly into David Marriner's life, and managed to keep the real world at bay for long enough to recover my balance.

Then, one day, a few weeks from the end of the shoot, I found myself wrangling a few hundred head of cattle across an endless stretch of bush for the benefit of Ray's cameras. As the dust settled, I caught sight of a distant figure perched on a boundary fence. The sun glinted on her hair – the only blonde thing in the desert.

I wheeled my horse and cantered towards her.

'Good morning,' Polly said, arching an eyebrow.

''Strewth, mate,' I replied. 'What kept you?'

Alice Springs airport was not much more than a couple of tin-roofed huts, but it did have a bar large enough to lose yourself in quite happily – and that is precisely what Henry Jones-Davies had succeeded in doing, with the help of a Bloody Mary or two, when he'd gone to pick Polly up a good few hours before. She'd waited half an hour or so, then grabbed a cab to the set, only stopping long enough at our hotel to dump her luggage.

I realised I was grinning like an idiot. There *was* a light at the end of the tunnel. I knew things were never going to be easy, but there was just a chance that, together, we could get life back on track. With post-production schedules in Sydney, we weren't due back in London for a couple of months. Whatever the future held, I'd be able to take a break from playing with fire.

Picture Credits

Credits are listed according to the order the pictures appear on each page, left to right, top to bottom. 'NH' denotes photographs belonging to Nigel Havers or his family.

Section 1
Page 1: Barratts Photographers; A.V. Swaebe Press Agency; NH
Page 2: Barratts Photographers; The Ramsey & Muspratt Archive, Cambridgeshire Collection; NH
Page 3: NH; NH; NH; NH
Page 4: Hilary Whitehall; Southey Ltd
Page 5: Sophie Baker; Catherine Ashmore; unknown
Page 6: Goldcrest Films/Ronald Grant Archive; Goldcrest films/Ronald Grant Archive; Goldcrest Films/Ronald Grant Archive; Goldcrest Films/Ronald Grant Archive
Page 7: Terence Donovan; Pic Photos
Page 8: NH

Section 2
Page 1: Ken Bray; Frank Connor/MGM; Carolyn Lockhart
Page 2: Frank Connor/MGM; NH; NH
Page 3: NH; NH; NH; David Parker
Page 4: MGM; NH; NH
Page 5: Christopher Miles; LWT
Page 6: NH; NH; NH
Page 7: Bel Age; NH; NH; NH
Page 8: NH

Now you can buy any of these other bestselling
non-fiction titles from your bookshop
or *direct from the publisher*.

FREE P&P AND UK DELIVERY
(Overseas and Ireland £3.50 per book)

By Myself and Then Some   *Lauren Bacall*   £8.99
A remarkable story of the life of the iconic, award-winning American
actress whose career has spanned over six decades.

Living History   *Hillary Clinton*   £8.99
America's former First Lady reveals what really happened during
her eight years in the White House.

All Of Me   *Barbara Windsor*   £7.99
Barbara Windsor, the legendary star of the *Carry On* films and
EastEnders tells her story in this no-holds-barred showbiz memoir.

Treasure Islands   *Pamela Stephenson*   £7.99
The wife of Billy Connolly and author of the bestselling *Billy* follows
in the intrepid footsteps of Fanny Stevenson, wife of Robert Louis.

Following the Drum   *Annabel Venning*   £8.99
The extraordinary stories of the wives, daughters and mistresses of
British soldiers who have followed their men to some of the most
treacherous places in the world.

TO ORDER SIMPLY CALL THIS NUMBER

01235 400 414

or visit our website: www.madaboutbooks.com

Prices and availability subject to change without notice.